NOTIONS OF NATIONALISM

Edited by
SUKUMAR PERIWAL

CENTRAL EUROPEAN UNIVERSITY PRESS
BUDAPEST · LONDON · NEW YORK

First published in 1995 by
Central European University Press
1051 Budapest
Nádor utca 9

Distributed by
Oxford University Press, Walton Street, Oxford OX2 6DP
Oxford New York Athens Auckland Bangkok Bombay Toronto
Calcutta Cape Town Dar es Salaam Delhi Florence Hong Kong
Istanbul Karachi Kuala Lumpur Madras Madrid Melbourne
Mexico City Nairobi Paris Singapore Taipei Tokyo Toronto
and associated companies in Berlin Ibadan
Distributed in the United States
by Oxford University Press Inc., New York

This volume and Chapter 12 © Sukumar Periwal 1995

Chapter 1 © Ernest Gellner 1995. Chapter 2 © John A. Hall 1995.
Chapter 3 © John Armstrong 1995. Chapter 4 © Michael Mann 1995.
Chapter 5 © Miroslav Hroch 1995. Chapter 6 © Nicholas Stargardt 1995.
Chapter 7 © Chris Hann 1995. Chapter 8 © Hudson Meadwell 1995.
Chapter 9 © Hans van Amersfoort 1995. Chapter 10 © John Keane 1995.
Chapter 11 © Elżbieta Skotnicka-Illasiewicz and Wlodzimierz Wesolowski 1995

All rights reserved. No part of this publication may be reproduced,
stored in a retrieval system or transmitted, in any form or by any
means, without the prior permission of the copyright holder. Please
direct all enquiries to the publishers.

British Library Cataloguing in Publication Data
A CIP catalogue record for this book is available from the British Library

ISBN 1-85866-021-1 Hardback
ISBN 1-85866-022-X Paperback

Library of Congress Cataloging in Publication Data
A CIP catalog record for this book is available from the Library of Congress

Typeset by Mayhew Typesetting, Rhayader, Powys
Printed and bound in Great Britain by Biddles of Guildford

Contents

List of Contributors		vii
Acknowledgments		ix
1.	Introduction *Ernest Gellner*	1
2.	Nationalisms, Classified and Explained *John A. Hall*	8
3.	Towards a Theory of Nationalism: Consensus and Dissensus *John Armstrong*	34
4.	A Political Theory of Nationalism and Its Excesses *Michael Mann*	44
5.	National Self-Determination from a Historical Perspective *Miroslav Hroch*	65
6.	Origins of the Constructivist Theory of the Nation *Nicholas Stargardt*	83
7.	Intellectuals, Ethnic Groups and Nations: Two Late-twentieth-century Cases *Chris Hann*	106
8.	Breaking the Mould? Quebec Independence and Secession in the Developed West *Hudson Meadwell*	129
9.	Institutional Plurality: Problem or Solution for the Multi-ethnic State? *Hans van Amersfoort*	162

10. Nations, Nationalism and European Citizens *John Keane*	182
11. The Significance of Preconceptions: Europe of Civil Societies and Europe of Nationalities *Elżbieta Skotnicka-Illasiewicz and Wlodzimierz Wesolowski*	208
12. Conclusion *Sukumar Periwal*	228
Index	241

Contributors

Hans van Amersfoort is Professor at the Institute for Social Geography, University of Amsterdam.

John Armstrong is Professor Emeritus of Political Science, University of Wisconsin-Madison.

Ernest Gellner is Professor Emeritus, University of Cambridge, and Director of the Centre for the Study of Nationalism at the Central European University.

John Hall is Professor of Sociology at McGill University, Canada.

Chris Hann is Professor of Social Anthropology at the University of Kent.

Miroslav Hroch is Professor of History at Charles University, Prague.

John Keane is Director of the Centre for the Study of Democracy, University of Westminster.

Michael Mann is Professor of Sociology at the University of California, Los Angeles.

Hudson Meadwell is Associate Professor of Political Science at McGill University, Canada.

Sukumar Periwal is Research Fellow at the Centre for the Study of Nationalism, Central European University.

Elżbieta Skotnicka-Illasiewicz cooperates with the Institute of Philosophy and Sociology, Polish Academy of Sciences, Warsaw.

Nicholas Stargardt is Lecturer in Twentieth-century European History at the University of London.

Wlodzimierz Wesolowski is Professor of the Polish Academy of Sciences, Warsaw.

Acknowledgments

A book of this sort is the work of many hands. As its editor, it is my pleasant duty to acknowledge those who have made our book possible.

I would first like to thank the contributors. Few books on nationalism can boast quite such a distinguished cast. The considerate promptness with which they provided their texts has made my editing job much easier.

I must also thank *Daedalus* for readily providing permission to reprint Professor John A. Hall's essay in this volume.

The impetus for the volume came from a conference on 'Theories of Nationalism' organized in Prague by the Centre for the Study of Nationalism of the Central European University. Many of the essays brought together here benefited from the comments and criticisms made by other conference participants; I would like to thank both them and the organizers of the conference, especially Guido Franzinetti, Leila McAlister and Kateřina Pekárková. The driving force behind the conference was also a constant source of encouragement for me as I edited this book, and it is with deep gratitude that I thank Professor Jiří Musil for his generous support.

It would be impossible to find a more supportive, encouraging and interested publisher than Pauline Wickham of the Central European University Press. I am very grateful for her help throughout the editorial process. My thanks also go to Liz Lowther and Sue Wilson of the CEU Press for their help, and to Stephen Ball for his superb copy-editing and valuable comments.

A fellowship from the Centre for the Study of Nationalism made it possible for me to prepare the text for publication with minimal distractions, and it is a great pleasure to me to thank the Centre's Director, Professor Ernest Gellner, for his support for the project and for his kindness in writing the introduction. I would also like to thank the

Centre's administrators, Robin Cassling and Gaye Woolven, for their ever-available and much-needed help.

This book is dedicated to George Soros for his unprecedented support for scholarship in Central and Eastern Europe. Mr Soros's philanthropy has made it possible for a whole generation of students from Central and Eastern Europe to gain greater access to the wider world of scholarship, and it is on their behalf that this book is dedicated to him, as a small sign of appreciation and gratitude.

Sukumar Periwal
Prague
December 1994

1

Introduction

Ernest Gellner

There are two great moral philosophies – the Platonic and the Kantian. They are radically opposed to each other. The Platonic one expresses what much later came to be called the morality of my station and its duties. It presupposes an organic society, within which morality consists of each part performing its appointed tasks. The organic structure is not arbitrary: it is inscribed into the very nature of things, so that the fulfilment of duty is at the same time obedience to the commands emanating from the very order of existence.

Kantian morality can hardly be more different. The commands of morality are not specific to each station, but universal, and generically directed at all men, indeed at all rational beings. They emanate from the nature of reason and are blind to, indeed utterly contemptuous of, the specific attributes of categories of men. They are equally blind to and contemptuous of the order of nature. Brute facts have no call to underwrite or impose commandments. Our obligations emanate from within us and are not sensitive to the biddings of contingent natural constellations.

For the comparative sociologist, these two moralities are the expressions of the most central polarity of sociology, the contrast between *Gemeinschaft* and *Gesellschaft*. Community imposes a morality of status; society imposes an ethic of equality and individualism. Sociologists fascinated by this polarity anticipated that, all in all, mankind would move from community to society. Liberals welcomed the transition, romantics deplored it.

For the purposes of this great debate, Marxists were but a species of liberal. In their formal vision, they were indeed more liberal than the liberals. The liberals-in-a-narrower-sense only anticipated and commended a minimal, night-watchman state, whereas Marxists looked forward to an erosion of the state altogether. The liberals-proper and the Marxists differed somewhat in the mechanism that they saw as the social agent of the emergence of universal individualist man, of the pure exemplar of *Gattungswesen*. The liberals-proper thought that the crucial agency would be the universal market and the services it performs for the attainment of human satisfaction; the Marxists, more sombre, thought universal and liberated man would emerge in the more tragic melting-pot of an impoverished proletariat, stripped by alienation of all specific attributes, and discovering, and implementing, true humanity through this historically imposed social nakedness.

It did not come to pass. The liberals and the Marxists shared the same error. The error was brought home to them by history, by facts, and not by logic. The logic of the liberals and of the Marxists was impeccable, but history did not conform to their logic. There was a third partner in the game, eventually more powerful than either of the other two – romantic nationalism.

Because the logic of the contrary expectation was so impeccable, nationalism has no right whatever, rationally speaking, to exist. The premises are correct, and the reasoning cogent. Nationalism feeds on cultural differences; it turns them into a principle of political loyalty and social identity (true). Cultural differences are systematically eroded by the processes which constitute the coming of modern society (true). So the more modern societies become, the less material there is for nationalism to work on. (The conclusion follows irresistibly from premises which are true.) Ergo, nationalism is on the way out. QED.

The facts are quite different. So where the devil did we go wrong? When we answer that question, we have a theory of nationalism.

The nationalist vision, and the social reality which engenders it, cut across the Platonic/Kantian dichotomy. Nationalism borrows its imagery and verbiage from the organic option, but is based largely on the social reality of anonymous, atomized society.

Societies did indeed move in the 'modern' direction, though (first important fact) not in a synchronized manner. Second important fact – the most important mechanism of atomization was neither proletarian impoverishment and alienation, nor a universal market prosperity. The real melting-pot arose from the new role of culture in industrial-technological society. A homogeneous humanity was engendered by the fact that work and indeed all social life in such a society is semantic: it consists of manipulating ideas and messages and people, not matter. Physical labour in the full sense, the application of human brawn to things, virtually disappears. Life and work consist of communication with countless anonymous strangers. Such communication must ignore context – previously by far the most important phoneme is speech – and must require the capacity to articulate and understand context-free signals. This is no mean skill and requires sustained formal education, as opposed to mere enculturation by the daily activities of a local group. In brief, everyone, or every effective participant, must have passed through school and be literate. This means that the idiom in which a man has been educated defines the limits of his social effectiveness, his employability, political participation, social acceptability. His education-transmitted, codified, standardized culture becomes by far the most important element in his 'identity', replacing any 'station'. An ethos of 'my station and its duties' becomes an absurdity.

But this shift from localized, life-transmitted folk cultures to a standardized, education-transmitted culture does not, as liberals and Marxists anticipated, produce one universal culture for all, practising some kind of Kantian morality. In historical fact, it engendered a series of internally homogeneous, externally bounded and hostile, cultural pools.

There are various obvious reasons, obvious at least with hindsight, why this should be so. The processes which led to modernization and its benefits did not take place at the same time or the same speed or in the same form everywhere. This led to an antagonism between the earlier and later arrivals. The earlier beneficiaries of the new order were not eager to share their perks with the late arrivals; and late arrivals soon discovered that it was advantageous to them, individually and collectively, to set up their own units, if they were to avoid a permanent or much prolonged status as despised second-class citizens of units dominated by earlier comers to modernity.

Kantian morality, the natural expression of the transition had it been free of these chasms between culturally differentiated groups – now soon to be called 'nations' – insists on the rational and the universal. The romantic reaction to this insisted that the essence of humanity was the specific and the emotional: specific feelings, not universal reason, is what makes us human. Romantic philosophy provided the conceptual tools for nationalism: man should not be a universal exemplar of Manchester commercialism or Versailles classicism, but rather, he should find himself in his *roots*, and roots communicated by sentiment not by reasoning. So nationalism took over the imagery of community.

But this is utterly spurious: the community it commended and advertised had nothing to do with the intimate, face-to-face community of the past. It was a large, anonymous, atomized 'imagined community', to use the title of Benedict Anderson's book on nationalism. But, although it was indeed a society and not a community, it had to stress the specificity which differentiated it, and not some universal humanity. This curious blend of the two original visions is at the heart of nationalism. Of course, the differences it picked on were sometimes borrowed from pre-existing cultural traits, and this is the grain of truth in the 'primordialist' position which attempts to defend the nationalist claim that the 'nations' had always been there (they had only been politically asleep, for some strange reasons, which may have included the malevolent machinations of their enemies).

So the moral vision of nationalism is a curious blend of the Kantian and the Platonic. For all its romantic organicist rhetoric, it cannot preach or require an ethic of my station and its duties: it cannot and does not require the fellow-nationals to be respectful of a rigid system of statuses. They are *brothers*, fraternity is obligatory and expected; the easy camaraderie of brethren rather than deference of rank is required. Nationalism arrived when, for instance, the Polish 'nation' ceased to be an association of gentry (happy to include Ruthenian-speaking landowners and to exclude Polish-speaking peasants), and became, instead, an association of members of Polish culture irrespective of landholding . . . But at the same time, this ethic is not *open*, and membership is indicated by powerful inner intimations indicating shared roots, or if you like, shared roots transmitted by authentic sentiments.

If roots are the tokens of authentic humanity, then rootlessness, cosmopolitanism, is the ultimate sin. And although of course nationalism is often bitterly hostile to neighbouring, rival root-communities, its strongest venom is reserved not for competing roots, but for those without roots altogether. Roots are indeed rural: the imaginary community invoked by the new ethos is territorial and has intimate links to the land. By contrast, there can be no roots in the city, least of all in mobile, specialized occupations. There are nations in Central and

Eastern Europe in which peasant ancestry, real or imputed, is a necessary condition of membership. The most influential novel in Czech nineteenth-century literature is *Babička*, i.e. 'Granny'. A Czech without a peasant granny is a contradiction in terms; no such thing has ever been heard of.

But of course the obverse of this populist nationalism is that the condition of being *déraciné* is the ultimate degradation, the exclusion not merely from nationality, but from humanity. This is the powerfully felt moral metaphysic of antisemitism: the Jew may be human for a Kantian, in so far as he shares rationality (in fact, the Talmudic tradition endowed him with special ability in exercising rationality, which seemed to be readily transformed into high performance in modern forms of it, whether in physics, philosophy, law or finance). But for the nationalist ethos, this no longer makes you human; on the contrary, it makes you suspect if it does not altogether exclude you from humanity. This vision was strongly internalized not only by those who used it to exclude and execrate others, but, just as strongly, by those who were its victims. Two thousand years of urban existence made peasant roots somewhat inaccessible, but Jewish nationalism nevertheless incorporated a powerful populist element: the kibbutznik is an artificial peasant. By inventing a perfectly real, not just imagined, community, with shared property, accentuated fraternity and closeness to the land, Zionism created not merely a fine military instrument which saved Israel in 1948 (as in tribal society, the social unit is at the same time a military one which is ready without additional training and *encadrement*), it also restored, with a vengeance, the imbalance in 'roots'. In fact, the synthetic *Gemeinschaft* of the kibbutz turned out to be more effective than the 'natural' *Gemeinschaft* of the blood clan: kibbutzniks do not fragment into sub-clans in defeat, nor disappear to take home the booty when victorious.

The impact of the nationalist ethos on Europe passed through a number of stages. The first, characteristic of the nineteenth century, was relatively humane, liberal, and one might even say timid. The nationalists were in alliance with the liberals against the non-ethnic hierarchical *ancien régime*, and the Herderian form of nationalism opposed an arrogant, confident universalism, and merely claimed a shared place in the sun for local, distinctive cultures. Czech Masarykian nationalism, for instance, linked the emergence or alleged re-emergence of the nation to a benign world-historical process in which authoritarian churches and states were replaced by liberal individualist ones, so that the nationalist vision (consistently or otherwise) was made into an ally or implementation of the universalist, individualist one. The fusion of the two visions was worked out in theory, in Masaryk's *Světová Revoluce* (1925), a book meant to legitimate the creation of the Czechoslovak state, but it was not resolved in actual political practice, with disastrous consequences.

The human, liberalism-prone nationalist was replaced by the virulent, aggressive form which reached its height during the interwar period. The pre-affluent economic crisis of capitalism accentuated inter-ethnic tensions. The gentle communalism of the Herderian type was transformed by the impact of Darwinism: the imagined community was not merely cultural, but also biological, genetic. It was all blended with the doctrines of biological competitiveness and the view of conflict and ruthlessness as a precondition of excellence and even mental health. Darwin mediated by Nietzsche is more dangerous than Herder. All of this was further exacerbated by the fact that during the first half of the century, perhaps in part because of the success of Marxism in inducing most men to think more in terms of industrialism, the old peasant/aristocratic tendency to link wealth and power with land was still dominant: *Lebensraum* was the slogan.

All this changed after 1945. The aggressive-romantic theory of how to run industrial society (return to hierarchy, authoritarian leadership) was not merely defeated in the *Weltgericht* of its own choosing – trial by combat – but far more conclusively refuted by the brilliant economic success of the defeated neo-militarists. Shorn of empire and territory, they did much better than the victors. History now inverted the medieval Spanish saying that war is both quicker and more honourable a way to wealth than commerce: successful industrial growth is a far more effective means to both power and wealth than warfare. It is easier and more effective, not to mention the fact that it is more comfortable and cheaper, to dominate Europe through the Bundesbank than through the Bundeswehr.

Nationalism gets its chance when the non-ethnic imperial structures collapse. The Habsburg Empire unfortunately collapsed at a time when the virulent, aggressive version of populist-romantic nationalism was at its height. The Masarykian vision of a nationalism aligned to liberalism failed dismally: it was only implemented in one country in Eastern and Central Europe anyway, and Masaryk's successor failed to defend it against the totalitarian enemy, not once, but twice over.

The collapse of a non-ethnic empire was however repeated, to everyone's surprise, at the end of the penultimate decade of the century. But the parallel is not complete. The interwar or Weimar period was one in which both the extreme Left and the extreme Right were confident and dogmatic. Happily, this is not the case now. Communism has left behind a strong desire for a pluralist civil society, in which truth, virtue and salvation are privatized: their privatization is even more important than that of the economy. The ideological danger is a vacuum, not the infallibilism which Masaryk and Russell discerned at once, and feared, in Leninism. But all this does not mean that nationalism may not once again re-emerge in its virulent form. In at least one country, it has done so with catastrophic results. But it has not yet happened generally. It may do so. The question is open, and must obviously be our main concern.

The essays assembled in this volume make a very significant contribution to our understanding of this problem. They do not all share the theoretical viewpoint I have sketched out in this introduction, and this is most desirable: the theoretical understanding of nationalism is an open and contentious field in which there is little that is firmly established. The current situation has stimulated the debate: we need both ideas and information.

2

Nationalisms, Classified and Explained

John A. Hall

Understanding nationalism is so obviously an urgent necessity that there is much to be said for the provision of a clearly delineated overview of the state of play among theorists of the subject.[1] What exactly do we know about a force whose impact on this century has been – against the expectations of mainstream social theory – greater than any other?

My overview will be active rather than passive. The use of the plural in the title gives away one central claim: no single, universal theory of nationalism is possible. As the historical record is diverse so too must be our concepts. This is not, it should be stressed, to suggest a move from universalism to complete particularism, from a general theory to national histories. On the contrary, middle ground can be cultivated by delineating various ideal types of nationalism, the characteristic logic and social underpinning of each of which are highlighted by a name, an exemplar and, somewhat loosely, a characteristic theorist.[2] But I move beyond classification to explanation: a second claim is that the patterning underlying different types is political rather than social.

The sort of analysis that is required is similar to that which now characterizes the study of economic development. Most obviously, it has come to be widely recognized that there are different routes by means of which economic development can be achieved. The initial path may not have been captured by Max Weber, but there is everything to be said for his insistence that it was original – in the sense that it was unconscious and unplanned. In contrast, all other forms of economic development have been imitative, seeking to copy something whose dimensions were broadly known. Such secondary imitation may, as in East Asia, benefit from entirely different qualities than those needed for invention: conformity may now matter more, for example, than rampant individualism.[3] Further, we now also appreciate that late development is far from a unitary affair. The heavy industrialization of late-nineteenth-century imitators – turned via Lenin's admiration for the German war economy into the general model of state socialism – seems to be markedly ineffective once the age of national mercantilism is replaced by an interdependent world economy, genuinely based on an international division of labour. We shall see that nationalism faces historical stages, albeit not to quite the same extent as does economic development. But it is important to stress a further analogy. The character of the stages of economic development is affected by history in an entirely different sense – that is, in terms of idiosyncrasy or accident. More particularly, the modern world political economy has been and continues to be deeply affected by the political style of the United States.[4] Similarly, some types of nationalism have been affected by particular historical combinations of analytic factors, whose conjunction may not recur.

NATIONALISM DEFINED, ITS MODERNITY EMPHASIZED

Just as differences in routes need not entail the absence of a singular sense of economic development, so too the variety of nationalisms does not rule out a unitary definition. Nationalism is considered here very conventionally.[5] It is the belief in the primacy of a particular nation, real or constructed; the logic of this position tends – beware this cautious note! – to move nationalism from cultural to political forms, and to entail popular mobilization. This is meant to be an omnibus definition, but it is as well to note two further presuppositions which distinctively prejudge key issues.

First, the definition is often linked to the view that there have been three great ages of nationalism: the foundation of new states in Latin America in the early nineteenth century, the enlargement engineered by Wilson at Versailles, and the much greater and more genuinely creative expansion of the international order as the result of decolonization.[6] There is indeed much to be said for the view that nationalism flourishes as the result of the collapse of empires, a view which makes us realize that the collapse of the Russian empire means that we are faced now with a fourth great moment in the history of nationalism. Nonetheless, the omnibus definition should not be linked to the idea that nationalism is in any absolute sense linked to separatism. Very much to the contrary, the spirit of nationalism can dominate established states. If the contemporary United States, as is possible, becomes mobilized, either as the result of incautious elite manipulation or of sentiment genuinely coming from below, around the conviction that Japan is an economic enemy, then this will deserve to be considered an example of nationalism.

Second, there seems to me to be everything to be said, despite the works of John Armstrong and Anthony D. Smith, for the view that nationalism is modern.[7] There have always, of course, been distinctive cultures, and particular upper classes have had some sense of shared ethnic solidarity. But the power of the nationalist idea – that people should share a culture and be ruled only by someone co-cultural with themselves – seems to me historically novel. The crude logistics of most societies in history – bereft of effective mass communication and cheap transport – meant that most human beings were stuck in highly particularized segments, quite unable to share a sense of destiny with people they had no chance of meeting.[8] In this connection, it is well worth noting that the actual sharing of destiny came much later than is often realized even to the core societies of northwest Europe. The much-cited findings of Eugen Weber's *Peasants into Frenchmen* have recently received stunning support from Susan Cotts Watkins's demonstration that fertility patterns in Western Europe become national only in the early twentieth century.[9]

The theorist who has realized the modernity of nationalism most fully is Ernest Gellner.[10] His contribution to the study of nationalism has been fundamental, and it is accordingly sensible – not least since my argument departs from his – to consider his basic interpretation of nationalism immediately, even though this goes against the chronology that otherwise characterizes the argument. Nationalism is seen by Gellner in terms of the logic of industry. At the basis of this theory is the insistence that an industrial society depends upon a common culture. This probably depends upon sharing a language, and certainly upon sharing an extended cultural code. The destruction of local cultures in Algeria meant an attack upon French and Berber and a favouring of mass education in Arabic; more serious problems, and far greater resistance, obtained in the Nigerian case. Two analytic points are being made here. On the one hand, industrial society is held to depend upon the ability to communicate in an abstract manner with people over space, strangers whom one has not and never will meet. On the other hand, massive social engineering is required because 'nationalism is not the awakening of nations to self-consciousness; it invents nations where they do not exist'.[11]

This ferocity of this phrase led to a magisterial rebuke from Benedict Anderson: 'Gellner is so anxious to show that nationalism masquerades under false pretences that he assimilates "invention" to "fabrication" and "falsity", rather than to "imagining" and "creation"'.[12] Whilst this is right, as is the related point that a history of imagining makes nation-building easier,[13] it should not be allowed to detract from the essential correctness of Gellner's point. There is no firm sociological mooring whatever to the nation,[14] not in language, not in religion, and not in ethnicity, and Gellner is quite right to insist in consequence that nation is far harder to define than is nationalism.[15] There is no reason to accept the sleeping beauty view propounded by nationalist ideology – that is, the view that nationalism is the awakening of something extant which had merely been dormant. Gellner needs to be defended quite as much on another point. A characteristic attack has come to be directed against his position, namely that it fails because it is functionalist. It is certainly true that functionalism cannot be intellectually correct; any theory of this type must be ruled out of court. Logically, functionalism takes a consequence as a cause, the expression of a societal need as a reason for the existence of institutions that seek to look after it. Life is not like that – I have plenty of needs, many of which go unmet – and neither is history. But proper specification of Gellner's theory can point to a mechanism explaining why attempts are made to meet these societal needs, and this ensures that the theory does not fail. The mechanism is simple. Many nationalist leaders in the twentieth century have been aware of the connection established by Gellner – that is, they are modernizers consciously aware of how to create industrial society. Such modernizers seek to break down the segments of the traditional order so as to create a common culture capable of integrating all citizens. Daniel Patrick Moynihan realized this in his famous complaint, when American ambassador to the United Nations, that many Third World nationalists had been trained at the London School of Economics. Certainly Jomo Kenyatta, who can serve as the exemplar of this type of nationalism, was trained there – and by no less a figure than Malinowski.[16] An interesting footnote in Jadwiga Staniszkis's *Dynamics of the Breakthrough in Eastern Europe* notes that A. Jakovlev changed his mind about the nationalities question in the erstwhile Soviet Union because reading Gellner made him convinced that nationalism had to be recognized in order to reach capitalist development.[17] This is perhaps less empirical support for Gellner's theory than direct creation of the evidence! But that is a distraction. The general claim that I am making is that Gellner's account of this type of nationalism is a great success; it goes a very long way to explaining the third wave of nationalism identified. It may well be that the theory derives from the periods that Gellner spent in North Africa in the 1950s and 1960s: it is that sort of experience which is being theorized.

CLASSICAL PATTERNS

One reason why Gellner's theory is not a truly universal one is that it fails to explain the very first emergence of nationalism in eighteenth-century Britain and France. The nature of the failure is obvious: nationalist sentiments are clearly in place before the emergence of industry. This type of nationalism can be explained in terms of the logic of the asocial society. This last expression is that of Immanuel Kant, referring to that multipolarity, unique in civilizational terms to northwest Europe, which led to endless competition between states.[18] The general character of this system has been theorized most powerfully by Otto Hintze and Charles Tilly.[19] Their finding is that wars make states quite as much as states make war. Continual competition between states leads to an arms race requiring ever greater funding. Kings are thereby forced not just to sit on top of the various cultural segments within their territories, but rather to interact with them ever more closely in order to extract ever greater funds. One way in which monies were extracted was through the provision of the services of justice. Another was through the increasing territorialization of social life: if one example of this was a burgeoning ability to provide order, that is, to successfully claim a monopoly of violence, another was that of an incipient economic nationalism which increased the customs and excise revenues on which monarchs relied. Over time, those states able to consolidate their territories into a single unit subject to bureaucratic rules fared best in warfare. Such national states often gained strength through cooperating with civil societies that they could not completely control: the absence of great despotic power did a great deal to increase their infrastructural reach.[20]

A characteristically brilliant essay by Michael Mann, the theorist of this type of nationalism, begins by noting that the eighteenth century bred marked increases in the communicative capacities of civil society.[21] These were pioneered from below in England by the creation of a unique pre-industrial commercial revolution and from above on the continent by both the military and economic demands of enlightened absolutism. The entry of the people onto the political stage accordingly became possible, rather against the expectations of such of its leading theorists as Adam Smith and David Hume. One such entry led to the creation of the United States, whose political culture remained overwhelmingly universalist despite the change from 'people' to 'nation' in the key founding documents of 1776 and 1789. The French Revolution was also universalist given that one could choose to become French, but the body to which people were to belong was on this occasion clearly that of a particular nation-state – with some Jacobins proving unwilling to trust those who had not learnt French.[22]

This concentration on the nation is best explained by the fact that civil society increased its capacities at the very time in which Europe was torn apart by the long War of the Atlantic – that is, the visceral struggle between Britain and France over the long eighteenth century. This meant that states were forced to extract historically unprecedented amounts from their societies.[23] One consequence of this was state reform, by the ending of 'old corruption' in Britain and by revolution in France. Another consequence was, however, the emergence of nationalism. It is of the crux of the matter that both processes were entwined, that the struggle for representation raised the question of identity.

A very full portrait of the processes, coming both from below and from above, involved for Britain has now been given to us by Linda Colley's *Britons*. This was a complex affair. A British nationalism certainly existed first, founded on the notion of a Protestant people under attack from Europe's Catholic monarchies.[24] But there was also an English nationalism, often directed against the Scots – not least as they did so well out of their connection with Britain.[25] In many ways, John Wilkes is the best exemplar of such nationalism, as he is the struggle for representation more generally.[26] He was an apologist for the blunt ways of John Bull, for roast beef and Yorkshire pudding, and for the liberties established in 1688. It was entirely characteristic that a typical procession of Wilkite supporters in 1768 assembled at a tavern named after William of Orange before setting out to vote for their hero under banners of Magna Carta and the Bill of Rights; equally many Wilkite songs were sung to the tunes of 'Rule, Britannia!' and 'God Save the King'.[27] All this was of course contrasted to the mannered artificialities of the French aristocracy and, somewhat later, to the geopolitical greed of Napoleon. It is scarcely surprising that the French replied in kind by inventing the image of Perfidious Albion.

Whilst there can be absolutely no doubt about the impact of the ideals of social mobility represented by Napoleon, we can best approach the next type of nationalism, dubbed here revolution from above, by noting recent scholarship on the logistics of the French armies.[28] It is not the case, as was once believed, that the French armies spread nationalism by design. Absolutely to the contrary, the fiscal crisis of the French state meant that its armies plundered huge amounts from territories it was forced to conquer – and continued to do so for years as such territories were made to pay for the occupying French troops. French rule was imperial, and it accordingly led to nationalist reactions.

The concept of a revolution from above is, of course, taken from Barrington Moore's great *Social Origins of Dictatorship and Democracy*.[29] It is of use here in highlighting a type of nationalism pioneered by states with previous histories, choosing to change their social structures in order to survive. If this is to say that the logic of state competition is at work here as it was with the previous type, the social base of this type of nationalism is distinctively different. This third type of nationalism has been recognized best by John Breuilly in his treatment of the Meiji reformers reacting to the incursion of Commander Perry and of their Prussian predecessors responding to the possibility that their state might actually disappear after its defeats at Jena and Auerstadt.[30]

I take as the exemplar of such nationalism Karl von Clausewitz, a member of the circle which included Scharnhorst and Gneisenau but better known to us than them because of his stature as the theorist of war.[31] That theory was necessitated by the appearance in 1793 of a force:

> that beggared all imagination. Suddenly war again became the business of the people – a people of thirty millions, all of whom considered themselves to be citizens . . . The people became a participant in war; instead of governments and armies as heretofore, the full weight of the nation was thrown into the balance. The resources and efforts now available for use surpassed all conventional limits: nothing now impeded the vigour with which war could be waged . . .[32]

The diagnosis that the reformers made after their own defeat stressed the need to completely change society if Prussia was to survive. The professional armies of Frederick the Great would never be able to compete against citizens in arms. It was accordingly necessary to abolish feudalism, and to contemplate arming the people so that something like the Spanish guerrilla resistance would become possible. Frederick William III disliked this latter proposal, but the possible curtailment placed on Clausewitz's career was occasioned by a different matter. In 1812 Prussia briefly made peace with Napoleon. Clausewitz was appalled that a peace had been made against the national enemy, resigned his commission and fought in the Russian army against the French. All of this perhaps reflects the fact that Clausewitz was something of an outsider. It may well be important that Clausewitz's family was not a member of the grand aristocracy: he himself depended upon state service quite as much as did the lesser Samurai of the Meiji Restoration.[33] But if on this occasion, the old regime – scared of the popular mobilization that the call to the nation entailed – won, in the long run Germany was created as the result of revolution from above.

The creation of completely new states in Latin America resulted from a very different type of nationalism, that curious compound of desire and fear blessed by opportunity that is exemplified in Simon Bolivar himself and particularly well understood by John Lynch.[34] The desire for independence had two sources. On the one hand, the ideas of the Enlightenment, gained more from the United States (whose importance as a model cannot be overly stressed) than from Spain, gave an impetus to ideas of freedom, reason and order. Much more important, on the other hand, was extreme disenchantment with a metropolis at once corrupt and underdeveloped. One element here was economic. Spain wished its colonies to produce bullion and to absorb its own manufacturing products, and to that end increasingly attacked local economic development, not least since Spain's involvement in European war increased its own fiscal needs. For a long period, trade was monopolized by a Spanish elite which consistently overcharged for imports whilst underpaying for exports. Another element was social. Attempts to increase control by sending out officials from Europe were particularly humiliating to local creoles whose standards of education and attainment were habitually far greater: 'the lowest, least educated and uncultivated European', Alexander von Humboldt observed, 'believes himself superior to the white born in the New World'.[35] Added to these sentiments was fear. The creole planters were a small minority sitting atop large Indian and slave populations upon whose continued quiescence their position depended. The revolt of Tupac Amuru showed them the dangers of an assault on their privileges in their own lands, but it was the use made by Toussaint l'Ouverture of the slogans of the French Revolution that really terrified them. Their adherence to Enlightenment ideals did not go so far as to countenance the loss of their land, let alone self-destruction. Hence, their own nationalist revolutions in the early years of the nineteenth century – suddenly made possible by Nelson's breaking of the link with the Peninsula and by Napoleon's invasion – were exceptionally socially conservative. Whilst sheer logistics entailed the creation of separate states, the mobilization of the people, generally characteristic of nationalist politics, was strenuously avoided.[36] This segmentation of social life has continued to characterize Latin America, not least since the relative absence of geopolitical conflict has not thereafter made it necessary for states to increase their infrastructural powers.[37]

In contrast, what is striking about risorgimento nationalism – at least, at first sight – is that it comes from below. This type of nationalism is extremely well known, not least because of Hroch's demonstration in his *Social Preconditions of National Revival in Europe* of the three-stage development from the collectors of folklore, to the ideologists of nationalism, to the final moment at which cultural revival becomes political demand.[38] Two particular forces fuelled movement from below. First, there was a notable increase in the educated in nineteenth-century Europe, an increase which often began before states sought to create normative integration within their territories.[39] Second, economic development moved many from the countryside to the city: the destruction of the traditional segmentary cultures of such people made them available for nationalist propaganda.[40] An important general point to be made about this type of nationalism is that it deserves to be considered liberal – that is, it stressed civic loyalty within a democratic regime rather than ethnicity. Both John Stuart Mill and Mazzini were famously among its numbers, and the conjunction of their names makes it clear that the hope of the age was that the setting free of oppressed peoples would usher in a reign of peace.[41] There is a blissful innocence about their particular dreams – which came to be exploded once non-historic nations, most notably the Irish, insisted on their right to a state.

Hroch's marvellous phenomenology of nationalism does not say very much as to why there was a transition from cultural to political nationalism. But it is not hard to see what is happening. Consider the career of Frantisek Palacky, the Czech historian who followed Herder in seeing the Czechs as a peaceful people oppressed by both Magyars and Germans.[42] Palacky had begun working for the Bohemian Museum in the 1830s, and his great history was begun in German. Increasing anti-German feeling, consequent on the state's attempt to make German the language of officialdom, led him in the 1840s to start writing in Czech. But it was the events of 1848 which pushed him into politics. The Czechs refused to join the National Assembly in Frankfurt, and felt deeply threatened by plans concocted there that might have led to their cultural demise. They participated instead in a counter-meeting in Prague, which firmly stressed that the best hopes for the Slavs, given their geopolitical position between Russia and Germany, remained with the Habsburgs.[43]

Reflection on this episode leads to two analytic points. First, the move from cultural to political nationalism was occasioned by blocked social mobility. This should not be seen, as wise words of Ernest Gellner emphasize, in purely economistic terms – as if people became nationalists in order to get better jobs, true though that sometimes has been.[44] What matters is the prospect of humiliation and the fear that one's children's lives will suffer. In the Habsburg lands the switch to political nationalism did not, in a sense, come from below: it was rather the desire of a modernizing state to conduct official business in a single language that suddenly placed some in the position of facing blocked or perhaps downward mobility. State intervention occasioned popular response.

The second analytic point is much more general, but it can be approached by asking bluntly whether the Habsburg enterprise was doomed by nationalism to collapse. General considerations suggest a negative answer, at least for a particular sort of Habsburg enterprise. By that I have in mind the Kremsier reform proposals of 1849, the key clause of which asserted that:

> All peoples of the Empire are equal in rights. Each people has an inviolable right to preserve and activate its nationality in general and its language in particular. The equality of rights in the school, administrative and public life of every language in local usage is guaranteed by the state.[45]

Had this been enacted, different nationalities may not have sought to escape the empire. The analytic point is best described with reference to Albert Hirschman's classic distinction between exit, voice and loyalty: when it is possible to have voice inside a system, exit loses its attraction.[46] Differently put, the nature of the political regime matters: nationalism has historically habitually involved separation from authoritarian polities. The general analytic point is then hopeful, given the problem of minorities: multinationalism may be possible, as Switzerland indicates, albeit limitations to the linguistic capacities of most human beings suggest that it is scarcely likely to become the norm.

The Habsburgs did not, of course, consistently take this liberal option.[47] The explanation of their failure has everything to do with geopolitics. First, defeat by Prussia allowed Hungary to gain its historic rights. The fact that Hungarians felt threatened by perhaps not forming a majority in their own lands led to that policy of forced magyarization which gave impetus to southern Slav nationalism.[48] Differently put, the creation of Austro-Hungary effectively ruled out federal reform. Such reform was probably unlikely anyway for a second reason. The Habsburgs were not prepared to retrench, to allow some territories to leave and to concentrate on economic development rather than geopolitical prestige. The *raison d'être* of the monarchy had been and remained that of being a great power. Still, it is noticeable that after 1867 the empire did not look set to fall apart. Its elements were clearly unable to agree, but geopolitical facts remained, and the Czechs did not yet look as if they were prepared to risk going it alone. What changed everything was defeat in war.

The last classic type of nationalism is integral nationalism. This has sometimes been seen as a reaction to Versailles, or more generally as a response that had logically to follow given that the drives for social integration of the new nations founded at that time were always likely to disadvantage minorities. Certainly there is a change in mood with integral nationalism: it is illiberal. There is no longer room for the belief that human beings, seen as possessing inalienable rights, need the carapace of a nation – but that all nations can develop together in a positive sum game. On the contrary, universalism is held to be a febrile myth: the fact that one should think with one's blood naturally turned nationalist quarrels into Darwinian zero-sum affairs. Ethnicity has now completely taken over from civic obligation.

The theorist of this type of nationalism is Ernst Nolte.[49] This form of nationalism was well in place before it received its ultimate form in German national socialism, and accordingly cannot be completely explained in terms of a reaction to Versailles. It may well be that integral nationalism is bred more generally by the trauma of defeat: it certainly seems to help explain the life and deeds of the *Action française* and its leader, Maurras – who invented the name of this type of nationalism and who stands as its best exemplar.[50] But this is too partial an explanation. We can see what has been missed from the explanation of its classical turn of the century form by considering carefully Max Weber's admonition in his 1895 inaugural address:

> We must grasp that the unification of Germany was a youthful spree, indulged in by the nation in its old age; it would have been better if it had never taken place, since it would have been a costly extravagance, if it was the conclusion rather than the starting-point for German power-politics on a global scale.[51]

In the context of his time, Weber's nationalism was of course liberal – although Poles familiar with Weber's wartime views as to how Germans should behave in the East are not likely to accord him that epithet.[52] Nonetheless, it is crucial to stress that the context of that time included the myth of imperialist mercantilism. A newly industrialized country like Germany had risen in part through trade, and its future could have been assured by continued adherence to that trading route; but some voices argued that secure sources of supply and of sale necessitated territorial possession. In a nutshell, Germans preferred to act as 'heroes' rather than as 'traders'.[53] The fact that Bethmann Hollweg listened to such voices was one element in the pattern that led to disaster in 1914.[54]

Something needs to be said about the social base of this integral nationalism. Studies of the popular leagues pressing for expansion to the East and for a *Weltpolitik* in late Wilhelmine Germany have shown us that these views were attractive to the educated, to those whose careers were associated with a German state of which they were proud – a fact which undermines Hobsbawm's influential view that nationalism turns nasty towards the end of the nineteenth century because it comes to be rooted in the lesser bourgeoisie.[55] This respectable but radical Right nationalism played some part in limiting the Wilhelmine state's room to manoeuvre in the years immediately prior to 1914, and this helped cause the outbreak of war.[56] The rules of diplomacy depend upon key state actors being part of international society: academic realism rests upon the presence of transnational identity. What radical nationalists at this time were demanding was an end to transnational identity so that national society could be favoured – in a world seen, and as much by Sidney Webb as by Maurras or Max Weber, largely in Darwinian terms.

This emphasis on the pre-1914 origins of integral nationalism is not meant to detract from its intensification after 1919. It is of course true that many of Wilson's borders are still intact, though this is in part because of the ethnic cleansings unleashed by the two great revolutions of the twentieth century. Nonetheless, one cannot help but note how disastrous was the Versailles settlement in East Central Europe. Regimes were created which were geopolitically unviable, lacking firm guarantees, prone to quarrel among themselves, and possessed of minorities whose suppression invited irredentist claims.[57] In a sense, this provided Hitler with a set of cards, the playing of which allowed for such viciousness that nationalism thereby gained a reputation from which it has not recovered.

REPRISE: FROM SOCIETY TO STATE AND REGIME

Any specification of different types of nationalism needs to be fairly close to historical reality if it is to fulfil its purpose, that of helping general thought and the understanding of particular cases. I believe that the typology offered to this point is close to reality, and I stand by it and by the claim that nationalism is not one but many. Nonetheless, I wish to look at the two obvious ways in which this typology might be criticized. A measure of disagreement with the second criticism will move my argument beyond phenomenology towards underscoring key theoretical points.

The first type of criticism is obvious: namely, that the typology should be expanded. John Breuilly's complete treatment of nationalism makes systematic use not just of 'revolution from above' but also of the distinction between separatist and unification nationalism, and it does so for social worlds with and without nation-states.[58] The most recent work of Ernest Gellner, keen to understand nationalism in post-communist societies, has made much of a brilliant essay by John Plamenatz to note differences within risorgimento nationalism between the German and Italian cases, definitively possessed of extant high cultures, and of the situation further to the East, where cultures were almost completely invented.[59] Finer analyses would also result from distinguishing more clearly between popular sentiment, the dreams of intellectuals, and the manipulative practices of politicians.[60] The validity and helpfulness of these distinctions do not, however, seem to me to be such that they could not be included within the typology presented, were greater space available to allow for its full elaboration.

The fact that there are so many types might well encourage exactly the opposite comment, somewhat in the spirit of Pirandello, to the effect that these types need an integrating general theory. This would, I suspect, be the response of Ernest Gellner, and this is accordingly a good moment to return to his theory. It is not, in fact, hard to see how one can diminish the number of cases. Some mileage can be had by extending the notion of industrialism in the logic of industry to include the capitalist development that provided the human *matériel* for risorgimento nationalism. Better still, I believe, would be to take the notion of blocked mobility, properly understood in the sense of humiliation, and say that it is an essential part of what is going on within the logic of industry.[61] This link is precisely at the heart of Gellner's real and best attempt to produce a general theory of nationalism – that is, a second and more general theory which does not fall foul of the functionalism of the industrial society school to which, as noted, he is recently somewhat prone.[62] More particularly, this connection is necessary for him, for otherwise the logic of industry could in principle take place within large empires; that is, it has no need to take on the national form. Differently put, the actors in this category seek to modernize apart from and even against metropolises that had discriminated against their talents. All this is to say that Gellner theorizes his own Czech background as much as he does North Africa, and that he has accordingly been unfairly treated to this point by being considered the theorist only of the logic of industry.

I can see the logic of this type of integrating argument, and can think of additional reasons to avoid dogmatism about my own concepts. For one thing, we can now see that the types represent in part stages, with the logic of asocial society, for example, being unique and thereby unavailable for later use. For another thing, it will soon be seen that integral nationalism in the contemporary world sometimes loses its bite because the drive for ethnic homogeneity is no longer so closely connected to economic mercantilism – nor is it now easy to so cage politicians that they are forced to ignore the realities of transnational society. Nonetheless, I still think that the logic of asocial society, revolution from above, desire and fear blessed by opportunity, and integral nationalism escape the integrating argument outlined.[63] In other words, I prefer my types of nationalism on phenomenological grounds: my exemplars are very different sorts of people, and they would have been uneasy in each other's company. But it is neither desirable nor necessary to leave matters at this point. For a certain amount of patterning is implicit within the types presented: explanation has rested less on social than on political factors, notably those concerned with state and regime.

We can begin by noting that Gellner's trinitarian view of human history is too simple: he is too much of an economic materialist, almost a Marxist in reverse, in imagining that history is structured simply by evolution from foraging-hunting to agrarian production and then to modern industry – powerful as these forces undoubtedly were.[64] More particularly, there are two notable ways in which modernity has been seen here to pre-date the coming of industry. First, civil society connections expanded in the eighteenth century, most spectacularly in Britain as the result of a commercial revolution which preceded the advent of the industrial era.[65] Secondly, multipolar state competition was born in the agrarian era and flowed into the industrial era: it was never a merely superstructural affair, being often powerful enough to disrupt the histories of economy and society.[66] States certainly mattered for nationalism. Most obviously, a long process of state building in northwest Europe created national states and territorialized social relations. Still more importantly, it was the fiscal needs of states, ever engaged in war, that led to those fights for representation that encouraged the emergence of national sentiment. Differently put, the forces of civil society, left to themselves, tend not to breed political action: what mattered was their interaction with the demands of states.

But the nature of regime has as important an impact as does the state *per se*. We know that working classes differed in their levels of militancy at the turn of the century according to the regimes with which they interacted: the presence of a liberal regime meant that class conflict took on an industrial rather than a political character, whereas the political exclusion characteristic of autocracy and authoritarianism concentrated attention on the state both because of its arbitrariness and its refusal to allow unions to organize.[67] Early realization of this point lay behind Max Weber's call for limits to Wilhelmine authoritarianism. Neither capitalists nor the state had anything to fear from liberal measures towards the working class: to the contrary, the more that class felt itself to be part of society, the less likely it was to embrace radicalism.[68] The same paradoxical principle – that openness increases cohesion – applies to nationalism.[69] The omnibus definition given at the start carefully noted that cultural nationalism tends to become political. In fact, we have seen that a liberal option was available within the Habsburg domains which, had it been adopted, would probably have satisfied the key nationalities by respecting their historic rights – which is to say that nationalism might not have become political. This option was ruled out by the Habsburgs, convinced that federalism would have undermined their geopolitical dreams. My guess is that this perception may have been inaccurate, as most certainly was the case with that of those Wilhelmine politicians who failed to sense that their working class could be coopted best by reform. Might not the empire actually have been strengthened, as Masaryk thought, if it had embraced this liberal option? Obviously, this question can never be decided. But there is much to be said for endorsing the ethic of eighteenth- rather than of nineteenth-century theorists: political arbitrariness creates much more anger than does social inequality. People prefer reform to revolution, the possibility of peaceful change to the dangers of the barricades. Liberalism thus diffuses conflict through society whereas authoritarianism concentrates it.

MODERN VARIATIONS

The first modern variation has already been encountered as the logic of industry, but analysis of the impact of the United States within its sphere of influence in the postwar era can enhance understanding of its character. Most obviously, decolonizing nationalism owed something to American dislike, for ideological and economic reasons, of European empires. This clearly hastened the end of the Dutch empire, and it was not without influence in the British case. Nonetheless, the logic of the situation in any case favoured decolonization. Empire became costly as soon as European troops had to be used, as was the case when faced even with relatively minor rebellions. The British, once deprived of the Indian army, understood this almost immediately, and quickly handed over territories to groups whose claims to represent 'nations' they often knew to be farcical. In contrast, the French fought longer and harder, and even dreamt of a greater France within which modernization could take place. One of Raymond Aron's most impressive, and influential, exercises in logic – demonstrating that this policy would significantly lower the standard of living within France itself – effectively destroyed that illusion.[70] All the same, the subsequent career of these new states was deeply influenced by the terms of the American system. Most importantly, the world polity for most of the postwar period has been extraordinarily conservative. A truly amazing obeisance was given to the norm of sovereignty, with the result being that very few boundaries have changed; if the United States supported this norm, it was, of course, as much in the interests of the post-colonial states themselves. This is not to deny that the American system sometimes coped poorly with the post-colonial world. The rules of the international market upon which it insisted helped advanced countries far more than those seeking to develop.[71] More importantly, it was prone to consider nationalism as if it were communism, thereby letting itself get trapped in Vietnam and landing itself with the Ayatollah Khomeini rather than settling for Mossadeq. Still, in historical terms the United States favours trade rather more than it does heroism, and its empire is now almost completely non-territorial. By and large, the Third World is less exploited than ignored.

The fact that the United States has been the sole genuine hegemon that capitalist society has ever possessed has had a fundamental impact on the states of the advanced world.[72] Trading has quite generally replaced heroism, economic ambition now mattering more than geopolitical dreams. Some mercantilist tricks are still practised by such states as Japan and France, and far more by the European Union in this present moment of uncertainty, but these are difficulties facing the world political economy rather than disasters likely to engulf it. The situation remains the exact opposite of that of the interwar years: the fundamental stability of the geopolitical settlement is likely to allow for compromise in the economic arena. If this decline of economic imperialism is likely to curtail any revival of integral nationalism, so too is the undoubted fact that the American system has encouraged the internationalization of key elites – who are most distinctively no longer so caged by nationalist pressure groups. But concentration on established states should not be so overdone as to detract attention from an essentially novel form of nationalism, that of nationalism by trade. The boldest theorist of this type is Tom Nairn, but Hudson Meadwell's recent arguments point in the same direction.[73]

Nationalism by trade is novel in seeking separation for regions of advanced societies. Nairn stresses that such nationalism is likely to do best when the region in question has good chances for economic prosperity: just as the six counties of Northern Ireland had no desire to be impoverished through connection with poor Catholic peasants, so too Catalans and Spanish Basques, perhaps even northern Italians, wish to protect their economic interests. A representative of this sort of nationalism is the leader of the Parti québécois, Jacques Parizeau, whose strategy is that of convincing the Québécois that they would be richer without the rest of Canada. The likely career of this sort of nationalism is hard to predict. There have been very few exits from liberal systems, and the diminished geopolitical need for centralized and unitary states makes it possible to allow for the introduction of federal and consociational deals capable of appeasing discontent.[74] If this has happened in Spain, it most certainly has not in Scotland – where the absence of a local assembly has meant that the majority has been governed for many years by leaders who are distinctively not co-cultural. But economic changes may increase the opportunities for this type of nationalism by diminishing the costs of transition that it would involve. If Adam Smith is right, the limitation of the size of the market decreases affluence: if one can separate and stay within a larger market, as in Europe but not yet for sure in North America, nationalism by trade starts to look a good bet. But if this happens, it is important to note that it does not matter much: political democracy and an open trading system are unlikely to be impaired by this sort of nationalism.

No survey of nationalism can omit mention of two unfolding situations – one obvious but the other potentially still more important, with both being as yet hard to conceptualize – which may give rise to novel types of nationalism. The first of these situations is that facing the post-communist world, and the second is that confronting many post-colonial states.

In retrospect, it is obvious that the Bolsheviks continued the work of the Tsars, thereby so delaying nation-building that its contemporary incidence is that much sharper and more determined. The peoples of the former Soviet Union itself were always likely to be attracted to nationalism for the imperial system which dominated them was led by Russians – whose depredations were not merely political and economic but quite as much ecological.[75] This suggests that there is something to Linz and Stepan's suggestion that the early calling of elections might have held together both the Soviet Union and Yugoslavia as it did

Spain.[76] It is certainly true that neither Gorbachov nor Milosevic accepted the need for immediate federal elections, whilst more generally it is important to recall that the intermarriage rate in much of Yugoslavia was beginning to undermine the clearness of ethnic divisions – thereby actually diminishing the historic backlog of hatred. Nonetheless, I doubt that this argument captures the specificity of the situation in Eastern Europe – and this despite an obvious sympathy for the general ethic lying at its core. It is vital to pay more attention to one key legacy of communism, namely that of its destruction of civil society. It is beginning to be accepted that this made liberalization of communist regimes virtually impossible. The slow decompression of authoritarian capitalist societies was made possible by pacts with organized forces within civil society; this strategy was simply not possible for those seeking to liberalize authoritarian socialism.[77] In other words, it is a mistake to mechanistically apply theories derived from the exit from authoritarian capitalism to the exit from socialism. Similarly, lessons about nationalism learned from Spain may well not fit post-communist reality. The destruction of civil society together with the vacuum created by the absolute collapse of the socialist project probably meant that the force of nationalism simply could not be contained. Consider in this context the social character of nationalist leaders in post-communism. It is very noticeable that former communists unable to make it in the market have been attracted to nationalism for the most self-interested reasons. One has the impression that Meciar at times scarcely believed in the manipulative tricks in which he was engaged.

A very great deal in this world remains open. What is noticeable at present is that nationalism in the territories of the former Soviet Union is, at least in comparison to those of former Yugoslavia, by no means utterly violent. The initial group of successor states are based on the union republics. Of course, it is extremely easy to point to the potentialities for matrioshka nationalism.[78] That this looks most likely in the North Caucasus may well have something to do with Georgia's decidedly integralist nationalism.[79] In contrast, matrioshka nationalism is somewhat curtailed in Russia by Yeltsin's adherence to democracy: the desire to exit is again held in abeyance by the possibility of voice. This factor too explains the remarkable success of the Ukraine in holding together different religions, languages and ethnicities within a single state.[80] This raises a final consideration. The softer, more federalist and more democratic route is made possible by the remarkable fact that geopolitical conflict has been controlled and limited in this part of the world since the end of the Cold War. Were Russia again to embrace heroism, the protection of powerful states would become vital. Such states would likely pay little heed to the demands of their own nationalities.

The considerations raised here bring us to the post-colonial situation. Anthony D. Smith is surely right to stress that nation-building and state-building in post-colonial societies have often been very difficult.[81] We need not accept his positive thesis – that European nations depended on a single ethnic core – to endorse the view that the absence of any shared political history and the presence of tribalism presents unique problems. The extraordinary stability that resulted from obeisance to the norm of non-intervention – endorsed by the Organization of African States even at the price of accepting Idi Amin – has a sting in its tail at this point. Acceptance of this norm has meant that there have been extraordinarily few inter-state wars within the Third World since 1945 – which should not for a moment detract from the vast numbers of deaths in civil wars.[82] A consequence of that state of affairs is that states have often been content to rest on top of differential segments rather than to rationalize their societies. In a horrible sense, Third World countries have not had enough war, or, perhaps enough war of the right type. They are quasi-societies, not nation-states.[83] Their states desperately need to be strengthened so that they can provide that basic order that we have come to take for granted.

This consideration suggests a worrying conclusion. It looks as though the ordering of world politics may be about to change. The norms of sovereignty and non-intervention are now at something of a discount, and it may well be that rules for intervention, made possible by a concert of the great powers, will now come to the fore. In one way, this is profoundly to be welcomed: it may make liberalism real. But perhaps in another way, this new development may not be such good news. There are many, many minorities whose cause could call for intervention: not just Bosnian Muslims, nor just Palestinians and Kurds, but, according to one recent survey, at least 250 other minorities currently at risk.[84] To give statehood to all such minorities would more than double the number of states in the world. Further, let it be remembered that there are perhaps 8,000 languages in the world, most of which could be used to put forward nationalist claims.[85] Given that not every language can have a state, one wonders as to the wisdom of interventionist policies which may weaken states that need to be strengthened. Thankfully we are not completely without intellectual resource at this point: if the break-up of Yugoslavia teaches us one thing for sure, it is that international recognition should be withheld from a state until it puts in place internationally acceptable protection for minority rights. Genscher failed to do this with Croatia. But this is a single point. The dilemma as a whole – between universal liberalism and the building of states, whose creation may still be humanity's best hope – is far too complex, at least for me, to solve.

NOTES

1. An earlier version of this chapter was given at a conference on 'Theories of Nationalism' organized by the Central European University in Prague. I am indebted to comments received and arguments made there, and in particular to N. Stargardt, S. Graubard, H. Meadwell, W. Wesolowski and, as always, to M. Mann.
2. The typology offered here incorporates and adds to that in P. Alter's fine but insufficiently known *Nationalism* (London: Edward Arnold, 1990). My argument as a whole resembles that of W. Mommsen, 'The varieties of the nation state in modern history: Liberal, imperialist, fascist and contemporary notions of nation and nationality', in M. Mann (ed.), *The Rise and Decline of the Nation State* (Oxford: Basil Blackwell, 1990). The looseness in question comes from citing some theorists in connection with a single type of nationalism when in fact their approach considers varied nationalisms. Injustices at this point are corrected in the course of this essay.
3. N. Abercrombie, S. Hill and B. Turner, *Sovereign Individuals of Capitalism* (London: Allen & Unwin, 1988).
4. A point made on many occasions, and with ever greater force, by S. Strange. See particularly 'The persistent myth of lost hegemony', *International Organisation*, 41, 1987.
5. Cf. E. Gellner, *Nations and Nationalism* (Oxford: Basil Blackwell, 1983), ch. 1; J. Breuilly, *Nationalism and the State* (Manchester: Manchester University Press, 1982), ch. 1; E. Hobsbawm, *Nations and Nationalism since 1780* (Cambridge: Cambridge University Press, 1990), pp. 9–13 and ch. 1.
6. J. Mayall, *Nationalism and International Society* (Cambridge: Cambridge University Press, 1990), p. 64. The excellence of this book is marred at this point by the declaration that 'there are no more empires to collapse and therefore very limited possibilities for further state creation by this route'.
7. J.A. Armstrong, *Nations before Nationalism* (Chapel Hill, NC: University of North Carolina Press, 1982); A.D. Smith, *The Ethnic Origins of Nations* (Oxford: Basil Blackwell, 1986).
8. P. Crone, *Pre-Industrial Societies* (Oxford: Basil Blackwell, 1990); M. Mann, *Sources of Social Power. Volume One: A History of Power from the Beginning to AD 1760* (Cambridge: Cambridge University Press, 1986); B. Anderson, *Imagined Communities: Reflections on the Origin and Spread of Nationalism* (London: Verso/NLB, 1983); Gellner, *Nations and Nationalism*, ch. 2.
9. E. Weber, *Peasants into Frenchmen* (London: Chatto & Windus, 1979); S.C. Watkins, *From Provinces into Nations* (Princeton, NJ: Princeton University Press, 1991).

10. E. Gellner's earliest statement is in his *Thought and Change* (London: Weidenfeld & Nicolson, 1964), ch. 7. A slightly revised version of his position appeared as 'Scale and nation', *Philosophy of Social Sciences*, 3, 1973. The most complete statement of his position is *Nations and Nationalism*. Important differences between these statements are noted by A.D. Smith, 'Ethnic persistence and national transformation', *British Journal of Sociology*, 35, 1984. Gellner's position continues to change, as can be seen from 'Nationalism and politics in Eastern Europe', *New Left Review*, 189, 1991; 'Nationalism reconsidered and E.H. Carr', *Review of International Studies*, 18, 1992; and 'L'avvento del nazionalismo, e la sua interpretazione. I miti della nazione e della classe', in P. Anderson (ed.), *Storia d'europa* (Turin: Einaudi, 1993).
11. Gellner, *Thought and Change*, p. 169.
12. B. Anderson, *Imagined Communities*, revised edn (London: Verso, 1991), p. 6.
13. Analyses of earlier imaginings are contained in Armstrong, *Nations before Nationalism*, and Smith, *The Ethnic Origins of Nations*. Cf. L. Greenfeld, *Nationalism* (Cambridge, MA: Harvard University Press, 1992). It seems to me that Gellner now accepts the spirit of this point: his most recent essays cited above make much of the difference between national awakening in Germany and Italy, already possessed of high cultures, and in the 'time zone' further to the East – where invention was, so to speak, complete.
14. I owe this point, that nationalism 'lacks sociological moorings and depends upon strong political projects', to N. Stargardt.
15. Gellner, *Nations and Nationalism*, *passim* but especially ch. 5.
16. Breuilly, *Nations and Nationalism*, offers several interesting comments on Kenyatta. A related article, at once powerful and disturbing, is that of S. Pederson, 'National bodies, unspeakable acts: The sexual politics of colonial policy making', *Journal of Modern History*, 63, 1991.
17. J. Staniszkis, *The Dynamics of the Breakthrough in Eastern Europe* (Berkeley, CA: University of California Press, 1991), p. 294.
18. J.A. Hall, *Powers and Liberties* (Oxford: Basil Blackwell, 1985).
19. O. Hintze, 'Military organization and the organization of the state', in F. Gilbert (ed.), *The Historical Essays of Otto Hintze* (Princeton, NJ: Princeton University Press, 1975); C. Tilly, *Coercion, Capital and European States, AD 990–1990*, (Oxford: Basil Blackwell, 1990). Cf. Mann, *Sources of Social Power. Volume One*.
20. These dimensions of state power were identified by M. Mann, 'The autonomous powers of the state: Origins, mechanisms and results', *European Journal of Sociology*, 25, 1984. For an attempt to remove confusions from these categories and to push them a little further, see J.A. Hall, 'Understanding states', in J.A. Hall (ed.), *The State* (London: Routledge, 1993).
21. M. Mann, 'The emergence of modern European nationalism', in J.A. Hall and I.C. Jarvie (eds), *Transition to Modernity* (Cambridge: Cambridge University Press, 1992). Cf. M. Mann, *Sources of Social Power. Volume Two: The Rise of Modern Nations and Classes, 1760–1914* (Cambridge: Cambridge University Press, 1993).
22. Hobsbawm, *Nations and Nationalism since 1780*, pp. 18–23.
23. Full details are available in the tables in Mann, *Sources of Social Power. Volume Two*, ch. 11.
24. L. Colley, *Britons* (New Haven, CT: Yale University Press, Haven, 1992), p. 18.
25. Colley, *Britons*, pp. 117–32.
26. J. Brewer, *Party Ideology and Popular Politics at the Accession of George III* (Cambridge: Cambridge University Press, 1972).

27. These details are taken from Colley, *Britons*, pp. 111–12.
28. T.C.W. Blanning, *The French Revolution in Germany: Occupation and Resistance in the Rhineland, 1792–1802* (Oxford: Oxford University Press, 1983); S. Schama, *Patriots and Liberators* (New York: Alfred A. Knopf, 1977). On this topic more generally, see D. Kaiser, *Politics and War* (Cambridge, MA: Harvard University Press, 1990), part three.
29. B. Moore, *The Social Origins of Dictatorship and Democracy* (Boston: Beacon Press, 1966).
30. Breuilly, *Nationalism and the State*, chs 9 and 13. Cf. Alter, *Nationalism*, pp. 34–7. Both these authors prefer the term 'reform nationalism'.
31. This paragraph draws heavily on P. Paret's superb *Clausewitz and the State* (Princeton, NJ: Princeton University Press, 1976).
32. C. von Clausewitz, *On War*, trans. M. Howard and P. Paret (Princeton, NJ: Princeton University Press, 1976), pp. 591–2.
33. Breuilly, *Nationalism and the State*, ch. 15.
34. I have relied most heavily here on G. Masur, Simon Bolivar (Albuquerque, NM: University of New Mexico Press, 1969); J. Lynch, *The Spanish-American Revolutions: 1808–1826* (New York: Norton, York, 1973); and L. Bethell (ed.), *The Independence of Latin America* (Cambridge: Cambridge University Press, 1987). J. Merquior's 'Politics of transition', *Government and Opposition*, 16, 1981, noted some time ago that Gellner's theory of nationalism failed to confront the first great wave of state creation; Gellner admits as much in *Nations and Nationalism*, p. 135. A first attempt to bring the Latin American experience into the centre of nationalist studies was made by B. Anderson: the revised edition of *Imagined Communities* changed the title of the fourth chapter to 'Creole Pioneers' in an attempt to underscore the importance of this historical experience.
35. J. Lynch, 'The origins of Spanish American independence', in Bethell, *The Independence of Latin America*, p. 25.
36. This point about logistics is strikingly made by Anderson, *Imagined Communities*, ch. 4.
37. K.J. Holsti, 'Armed conflicts in the Third World: Assessing analytical approaches and anomalies', Paper given at McGill University, 1993.
38. M. Hroch, *The Social Preconditions of National Revival in Europe* (Cambridge: Cambridge University Press, 1985). Gellner's 'L'avvento del nazionalismo, e la sua interpretazione' critically evaluates Hroch's argument, albeit so as to underscore nationalism's social roots. Later in this essay it will become clear that the weakness of both Gellner and Hroch resides in their downplaying of political determinants of nationalism.
39. L. O'Boyle, 'The problem of an excess of educated men in Western Europe, 1800–1850', *Journal of Modern History*, 42, 1970.
40. Hroch's work at this point is, of course, superb.
41. J.S. Mill, 'Of Nationality, as Connected with Representative Government', ch. 16 of his *Representative Government* [1861] in his *Three Essays* (Oxford: Oxford University Press, 1975). Mazzini's views are amusingly described in Hobsbawm, *Nations and Nationalism since 1780*, chs 1 and 4. Cf. Alter, *Nationalism*, ch. 3.
42. In so doing, I am following Breuilly, *Nationalism and the State*, p. 100.
43. A.J.P. Taylor's unsurpassed *The Habsburg Monarchy 1809-1918* (London: Hamish Hamilton, 1948), chs 5 to 7, gives details both of the particulars and the general context of this story.
44. Gellner, *Nations and Nationalism*, pp. 60–2.
45. This is cited in A. Sked, 'Historians, the nationality question and the downfall of the Habsburg Empire', *Transactions of the Royal Historical Society*, 31, 1981. I am much

indebted to this article, and to the same author's *The Decline and Fall of the Habsburg Empire 1815–1918* (London: Edward Arnold, 1989).
46. A. Hirschman, *Exit, Voice and Loyalty* (Cambridge, MA: Harvard University Press, 1970). Hirschman has recently claimed – 'Exit, voice and the fate of the German Democratic Republic: An essay in conceptual history', *World Politics*, 45, 1991, p. 194 – that exit is quintessentially a private matter. Nationalism shows that this need not necessarily be so.
47. O. Jaszi, *The Dissolution of the Habsburg Monarchy* (Chicago: University of Chicago Press, 1961); Michael Mann, *The Sources of Social Power. Volume 2*, ch. 10.
48. Taylor, *The Habsburg Monarchy*, p. 290.
49. E. Nolte, *Three Faces of Fascism* (New York: Holt, Rinehart and Winston, 1965). Cf. Alter, *Nationalism*, chs 2 and 4.
50. Alter stresses the importance of defeat in his *Nationalism*, pp. 46–6, in this following E. Lemberg, *Nationalismus* (Reinbek: Rowohlt, 1964). Sources used for Maurras include Nolte, *Three Faces of Fascism*; E. Weber, *Action Française* (Stanford, CA: Stanford University Press, 1962); and Michael Curtis, *Three Against the Third Republic*, (Princeton, NJ: Princeton University Press, 1959).
51. *Max Weber: Selections in Translation*, ed. W.G. Runciman (Cambridge: Cambridge University Press, 1978), p. 266. Cf. W. Mommsen, *Max Weber and German Politics, 1890–1920* (Chicago: Chicago University Press, 1984).
52. For details, see Mommsen, *Max Weber and German Politics, 1890–1920*, pp. 211–27.
53. W. Sombart, *Händler und Helden* (Leipzig: Duncker und Humblot, 1915). Cf. J.A. Hall, *International Orders* (Cambridge: Polity Press, 1994), ch. 4.
54. A particularly powerful appreciation of this point is given by Kaiser, *Politics and War*, part four.
55. The two most important studies of popular nationalism are G. Eley, *Reshaping the German Right* (New Haven, CT: Yale University Press, 1980); and R. Chickering, *We Who Feel Most German* (Boston: Allen & Unwin, 1984). The views of Hobsbawm are spelt out most fully in *Nations and Nationalism since 1780*, ch. 4, especially p. 118.
56. Mann, *Sources of Social Power. Volume 2*, ch. 21. I rely on Mann's argument for the rest of this paragraph. Cf. G. Eley, 'Some thoughts on the nationalist pressure groups in Imperial Germany', in P. Kennedy and A. Nicholls (eds), *Nationalist and Racialist Movements in Britain and Germany before 1914* (London: Macmillan, 1981).
57. K.J. Holsti, *Peace and War* (Cambridge: Cambridge University Press, 1991), chs 8 and 9; E.H. Carr, *The Twenty Years Crisis, 1919–1939* (London: Macmillan, 1939).
58. Breuilly, *Nationalism and the State*.
59. J. Plamenatz, 'Two types of nationalism', in E. Kamenka (ed.), *Nationalism. The Nature and Evolution of an Idea* (London: Edward Arnold, 1976). The essay is discussed in Ernest Gellner, 'L'avvento del nazionalismo, e la sua interpretazione'. Gellner's arguments echo those of Theodor Schieder, *Der Nationalstaat in Europa als historisches Phänomen* (Cologne: Westdeutscher Verlag, 1964).
60. I owe this point to W. Wesolowski.
61. Humiliation is also distinctively part of Latin American nationalism – which lacks, however, a modernizing impulse. Nationalism by trade, discussed below, is equally as prone to draw on such feelings, despite its overtly more instrumental approach.
62. This general theory is most clearly present in *Thought and Change* – which I find generally to be more convincing than *Nations and Nationalism*.
63. An extraordinary essay by P. Anderson, 'Science, politics, disenchantment', in Hall

and Jarvie (eds), *Transition to Modernity*, compares Gellner and Weber on nationalism so as to reach the conclusion that the former's theory is generically functionalist, failing to make the viciousness to which nationalism can be prone part of its conceptual apparatus.
64. E. Gellner, *Plough, Sword and Book* (London: Collins Harvill, 1988).
65. This is made particularly clear in E.A. Wrigley's *Continuity, Chance and Change* (Cambridge: Cambridge University Press, 1988). Benedict Anderson's sociology of nationalism differs from that of Gellner on this point: what matters to him is the advent of print culture rather than industry *per se*.
66. For a criticism of Gellner at this point, see J.A. Hall, 'Peace, peace at last?', in Hall and Jarvie (eds), *Transition to Modernity*.
67. There is considerable literature on this point. See, *inter alia*: D. Geary, *European Labour Protest 1848–1945* (London: Methuen, 1984); R. McKibbin, *The Ideologies of Class* (Oxford: Oxford University Press, 1990); Mann, *Sources of Social Power. Volume Two*; I. Katznelson and A. Zolberg (eds), *Working Class Formation* (Princeton, NJ: Princeton University Press, 1987); and T. McDaniel, *Capitalism, Autocracy and Revolution* (Berkeley, CA: University of California Press, 1988).
68. Weber made his views especially clear in his wartime reflections on the historical sociology of Wilhelmine Germany. These writings are available as 'Parliament and government in a reconstructed Germany', in his *Economy and Society*, trans G. Roth and C. Wittich (Berkeley, CA: University of California Press, 1978), especially p. 1391.
69. This point lies at the heart of Mann's brilliant *Sources of Social Power. Volume Two*.
70. R. Aron, *La tragédie algérienne* (Paris: Plon, 1957).
71. J.G. Ruggie, 'International regimes, transactions and change', *International Organisation*, 36, 1982.
72. Hall, *International Orders*, chs 3 and 4.
73. T. Nairn, *The Break-up of Britain* (London: New Left Books, 1977); H. Meadwell, 'The politics of nationalism in Quebec', *World Politics*, 45, 1993, and his essay in this volume.
74. I owe this point to M. Mann.
75. A. Khazanov, 'The collapse of the Soviet Union', *Nationalities Papers*, 1993.
76. J. Linz and A. Stepan, 'Political identities and electoral sequences: Spain, the Soviet Union, and Yugoslavia', *Daedalus*, 121, 1992.
77. R. Bova, 'Political dynamics of the post-communist transition: A comparative perspective', *World Politics*, 44, 1991, especially pp. 131–2.
78. I. Bremmer and R. Taras (eds), *Nations and Politics in the Soviet Successor States* (Cambridge: Cambridge University Press, 1993); R. Szporluk, 'The national question', in T.J. Colton and R. Legvold (eds), *After the Soviet Union* (New York: W.W. Norton, 1992); *National Processes in the USSR: Problems and Trends* (Moscow: USSR Academy of Sciences, Nauka, 1992); A. Khazanov, *Soviet Nationality Policy during Perestroika* (Virginia: Elek, 1991); and 'A country of countries', *The Economist*, 27 March 1993.
79. S. Jones, 'Georgia: A failed democratic transition', in Bremmer and Taras (eds), *Nations and Politics in the Soviet Successor States*.
80. B. Krawchenko, 'Ukraine: The politics of independence', in Bremmer and Taras (eds), *Nations and Politics in the Soviet Successor States*.
81. A.D. Smith, 'State-making and nation-building', in J.A. Hall (ed.), *States in History* (Oxford: Basil Blackwell, 1986).
82. Holsti, 'Armed conflicts in the Third World', provides figures on this point.

83. R.H. Jackson, *Quasi-states: Sovereignty, International Relations, and the Third World* (Cambridge: Cambridge University Press, 1990).
84. T.R. Gurr and J.R. Scarritt, 'Minority rights at risk: A global survey', *Human Rights Quarterly*, 11, 1989. This survey is cited by Holsti, 'Armed conflicts in the Third World'.
85. Gellner, *Nations and Nationalism*, pp. 43–50.

3

Towards a Theory of Nationalism: Consensus and Dissensus

John Armstrong

In Alexander Motyl's exploratory volume on the relation of nationalism concepts to Soviet developments, I suggested (pp. 32–8) that major obstacles prevent movement towards a general theory of nationalism. Since writing those lines (1988), two types of developments have led me to believe that my assessment of the rocky road to theory may have been somewhat too pessimistic. It may surprise some readers that I do *not* include the spectacular emergence of nationalism in the former Soviet Union among causes for measured optimism on theory. Overall, the dissolving Yugoslav polity has provided more evidence so far about the persistence and problematic nature of nationalism than have the ex-Soviet republics. Like many other specialists, I was not surprised by the demonstrated strength of national liberation movements in the Soviet republics and Moscow's East European satellites. It was, rather, the extreme weakness of the Soviet regime's response which was startling.

On the other hand, recent scholarly progress in recognizing the historic dimension of Anglo-American nationalism has exceeded my expectations. An outstanding event has been the publication (early in 1993) of Liah Greenfeld's *Nationalism* by Harvard University Press. Sociologist Greenfeld's inspiration evidently came in part from her experience in East Europe; but her innovation is making English and American brands of nationalism the cornerstone of an integrated historical process. As I discuss in detail elsewhere,[1] Greenfeld seems to me to exaggerate both the initial significance of the English experience and the benevolence of its United States offspring; but there is no gainsaying her accomplishment in moving the Anglo-American components of the historical process to centre stage. Secondly, the historical development of nationalism has been significantly clarified by the work of numerous scholarly conferences. In 1993 alone, I participated in three – a small sample of the universe of scholarly discussion on nationalism during the early 1990s. Two (the Fifth International Congress on Central Asia, Madison, Wisconsin, and the nationalism section of the Second Congress of Ukrainian Studies, L'viv) were more limited than another general examination of nationalism, in Prague. Yet all three conferences demonstrated awareness of the theoretical implications of their subjects and brought extraordinary expertise to bear on relating particular nationalist experiences to social theory. In the following notes I shall outline my observations concerning both the elements of consensus that appeared to be emerging and the recalcitrant disagreements.

It now appears that the notion of national identity as a *primordial* phenomenon has been generally discarded by scholars.[2] Few are prepared to reject the proposition that national identity (like other social constructs) originated at a specific point, however remote, in history. Nationalism – the conscious demand for political expression of the nation – originated, on the other hand, no earlier than the fifteenth century. As suggested previously, Greenfeld stipulates its emergence in sixteenth-century England, whereas impressive French works continue to assert a slightly prior emergence of French nationalism. Nonetheless, the notion that nations, or even 'ethnic groups', have existed forever is scarcely tenable among scholars. Some, indeed, consider that the notion of the primordial nation was always merely a popular delusion. But those who have had close contacts with learned but intensely nationalistic intellectuals know how difficult it was – even a decade ago – to overcome the misconception. Let me cite two examples of reactions to my book *Nations before Nationalism* (1982). On 22 May 1983, the popular Catalan-language periodical *Avui* published a review by Victor Alba entitled 'A transitory phenomenon'. Alba – a Catalan spokesman known in English speaking countries for his works on international communism – wrote:

> I happened to remark in passing – I retain no record of my motivation – that Catalonia had not always existed and would not eternally exist. My companions became indignant at this argument. It seemed to them as if, by affirming the transitory nature of the nation – that is, of whatever

nation, and in the final analysis the national form of organization of political society – one betrayed the foundation of nationalism in the here and now. . . . Now I have been confirmed in my viewpoint by a learned North American specialist on national questions. . . . [who shows how] some nations persist, and grow stronger, others vegetate, still others are absorbed, destroyed, or vanish.

A second, less specific illustration struck me in the oral response of several German colleagues (including historians) to my extended treatment of *Stamme* ('tribes') as creatures of medieval ecclesiastical and political divisions rather than as direct descendants of pre-historic Teutonic groupings. Yet a monumental work of anthropological historiography, Reinhard Wenskus's *Stammesbildung und Verfassung: Das Werden der Frühmittelalterlichen Gentes* (1961) had conclusively demonstrated (as numerous subsequent works by the Freiburg historical school testify) that the latter-day *Stamme* are medieval inventions. To a considerable extent, therefore, one may agree with British scholars Eric Hobsbawm and Benedict Anderson that, like other human identities, national identity has been an invention.[3] The principal remaining disagreement is over the antiquity of some inventions and the repertory of pre-existing group characteristics that inventors were able to draw upon.

Before briefly considering such disagreements, I must point to what appears, at least superficially, to be another area of dissensus, the significance of *ethno-religious identity*. My position has been, for at least twenty years, that there is a fundamental continuity between identities of diaspora groups (as religions of the *millet* type) and their modern expression as political nationalisms. Every historian recognizes that such expression (for example, in Theodore Herzl's Zionism and the Armenian Hunchak party) emerged only during the late nineteenth century. As the late Hugh Seton-Watson (with whom I repeatedly discussed the issue during 1975–6) wrote, after tracing the influence of proto-Zionists during several centuries, 'the influence of Judaism on the life of Israelis, and on the formation of Israeli national consciousness, can certainly not be explained in terms of party maneuvers, or limited to professed believers. . . . the religious heritage thus directly reinforces national consciousness.'[4]

In the light of very recent events it would be hard to argue that such continuity of religion and national identity, even in its political expression as nationalism, is limited to diasporas. Liah Greenfeld directly links the origins of English nationalism to the Tudor reformation. Others, notably J.G.A. Pocock,[5] have seen the persistence and expansive tendency of English nationalism as arising from contact with Roman Catholic resisters and Protestant dissidents in the Celtic fringe. The intractable conflict in Northern Ireland daily substantiates this analysis. In the former Soviet Transcaucasus, some strife – between Georgians and Ossetians, and among Georgian clans – is intra-Orthodox; but the Abkhazian–Georgian conflict and Armenian–Azeri warfare occur along fault lines historically separating Muslims and Christians.[6] The effects of such fault lines in producing (directly or indirectly) conflicts across the Black Sea in former Yugoslavia are even more obvious. Not only do Croats, Serbs and Bosniaks speak the same language – even its dialect boundaries cut across the intermingled settlement of the three groups, which are distinguished almost entirely by diverse religious heritages (notably, written expression of identical locutions in the Latin, Arabic and Cyrillic alphabets). Of course, there are contrasting examples: tranquil relations between Protestants and Catholics in Hungary and the Czech Republic, Catholics and Orthodox in Ukraine. But the contention here is not that ethno-religious nations are the *norm*, but that religious divisions remain *one* significant basis for identity. *If* this non-restrictive position comes to be accepted generally, one major source of recent disagreement concerning the direction nationalism theory should take will be eliminated.

Whatever disagreement persists on ethno-religious divisions as part of a continuum with national identity, before and during the dominance of nationalism, there is general agreement that the latter, as an ideology, diffused first to Central Europe, and then to other regions. In its diffusion, nationalism resembles other modern political movements – political parties, mass elections, parliaments, constitutionalism, Marxism, and bureaucracy in the Weberian sense. Like other institutional and ideological innovations, nationalism is heavily influenced by the culture of receiving societies, yet retains, especially in its formal and superficial aspects, the marks of its Western European origins. Given this general scholarly agreement, it is apparent that the appropriate theoretical approach is *developmental* – that is, examination of national identity and nationalism as historical processes. Such an approach differs sharply from comparisons in the simpler sense of derivation of nomothetic theses via 'concatenated theory', which has been defined as 'a set of logical empirical generalizations that possess a common focus; however, the logical relationships between such generalizations are not specified'.[7] By pursuing the developmental approach (which does involve intersocietal comparisons of a more complex nature), students of nationalism *can* endeavour to specify logical relationships, in the mode of the great nineteenth-century sociological schemas of theorists like Marx and Weber.

One reason some have rejected the concept of a persistent ethno-religious syndrome has been insistence on *language* as the prime indicator of nationalist cleavage. Such insistence implies the corollary that (since a single standardized linguistic code is a recent development even in 'old' nations like France) nationalism cannot pre-date the late eighteenth century. If, on the other hand, we accept arguments (outlined previously) that nationalism originated either in France or England by the sixteenth century, language as an indicator cannot have been decisive.[8]

Certainly, elite nationalist spokesmen have endeavoured to demonstrate the importance of language differences, regardless of the real influence of linguistic differences at the mass level. Intensive efforts by politicians, journalists, literary figures, philologists, folklorists and historians led (during the nineteenth and early twentieth centuries) to the emergence of a group of East Slav dialects as 'Ukrainian', of certain South Slav dialects as 'Macedonian', and of 'Slovak' as a major West Slav language. In these Slavic examples, also possibly among emerging Turkic national languages, and potentially in the re-emergence of Occitan, what makes the artificiality of language invention most evident is the lack of objective criteria for distinguishing marginal dialect elements on the ground. A large Pripet territory cannot be assigned by any unambiguous linguistic criteria either to the present Ukrainian dialect group or to Belarus.[9] In Macedonia, as Horace Lunt has expertly explained, there are no completely objective boundaries between 'Bulgarian' and 'Serb' dialects, but only a series of indeterminate transitions – that, at least for the time being, open the way for a third, 'Macedonian', national option.[10] Ultimately, official usage, notably in the common school, creates a consciousness of belonging to one national group or the other; but it is politics that, even earlier, determined official usage. However, as Reinhard Weinskus shows, during more remote periods spontaneous popular perceptions distinguished between sharply differentiated language groups, notably in boundary situations – for example, 'Tiutsch' (German) contrasting to 'Wends' on the east and 'Welsch' to the west and south. Such early perceptions rarely led to political consciousness, which ordinarily accorded with divisions cutting across language boundaries. During the last two centuries, however, lingering awareness of such sharp linguistic divisions has often constituted a convenient, though far from indispensable, starting point for elites manipulating national identity symbols.

Emphasis on language derives in part from two aspects of nationalism that, I think, nearly all scholars find significant. One is the Romantic movement that endowed most nationalist ideologies with an aversion to rationalized programmes and imbued adherents with contempt for rational planning as contrasted with self-sacrifice, 'heroism' and emphasis on will-power. The Romantic movement led nationalists to glorify the archaic, the traditional (or pseudo-traditional), and (in Europe) the peasant.[11] It is scarcely an accident that the Grimm brothers, noted for their revival (and invention) of romantic fairy tales, also played a major role in developing the isogloss technique for delineating linguistic patterns. Since isoglosses are appropriate only as lines between dialects spoken by territorially stable peasant populations, the 'scientific' aura of the technique provided a potent reinforcement for Romantic exaltation of the peasantry. Hence it is not surprising that this combination became a dominant component of most Central European nationalisms during the nineteenth century. Recent events in Yugoslavia have demonstrated the lingering potency of the claim that territorial divisions should accord with the folkways of peasant settlement (even though, as noted earlier, in Yugoslavia the distinguishing folkways have not been linguistic in the usual sense of the term). Although Bosniaks (Muslims) demonstrated their majority status in an election and a referendum during 1991–2,[12] Serbs spread throughout the poor hilly areas have been able to enforce their claim by ruthless irregular warfare that Serb peasants excel in. Thus a combination of historical circumstances produced an outcome in nationalist competition incompatible with the norms of democratic procedure.

From the perspective of Western Europe and North America, Romantic emphasis on the peasantry (as late as the 1930s significant in the USA through literary currents like the Southern 'agrarian school') has rapidly become quaint. Even in much of Eastern Europe peasants are ceasing to be a dominant force. One might infer that nationalism, as we have known it, will therefore soon become more prominent in the agrarian Third World than in more developed regions. The continued strength of nationalism in a highly urbanized country like Weimar

Germany suggests, however, how adaptable the ideology of nationalism can be.

Consideration of the role of peasants in nationalist constructs implies a significant role for economic factors and class divisions in explanations of modern nationalism. Somewhat similarly, I was led to begin my discussion of nations *before* nationalism with the treatment of factors derived from material production during earlier centuries, namely sedentary versus nomadic lifestyles. Consequently, it never occurred to me that ideas divorced from material circumstances could constitute the sole explanation for national identity or nationalism. Nevertheless, the *principal* source of disagreement among scholars searching for a general theory is the *way* in which material and ideal factors interact. My strongest objection (spelled out in the Motyl article, and also cogently expressed by Shmuel Eisenstadt) has been to the treatment of national identity and nationalism as epiphenomena. Like many other social constructs, these serve human needs far beyond the material realm. However, it would be just as objectionable to assert that such constructs can be understood apart from changing material circumstances.

Much depends, of course, on how one defines material and nonmaterial circumstances. Liah Greenfeld rejects nationalism as an expression of purely material interests, defining it instead as an expression of status concerns, equivalent to pride or vanity. Other interpretations, however, consider status concerns to be indicators of material interests. For example, examinations of intellectuals' attraction to nationalism have focused on competition between persons of differing backgrounds for scarce positions in communications media, education and bureaucracies. From the material standpoint, such competition centres on officials' pay and perquisites, and use of public office to attain less formally authorized rewards. In an interpretation emphasizing ideas, status satisfaction becomes, on the other hand, psychological: personal attainment of prestigious roles, public recognition of one's background as equally or more suitable for authoritative posts. Moreover, apart from actual status attainment, the nationalists' ideology assures them that their identity reference group, although for the time being suffering discrimination, is equal or superior to others. To such psychological satisfactions is joined the less tangible assurances derived from the *Weltanschauung* aspects of nationalism. As Peter Berger suggests, identity creeds, whether ethno-religion or modern nationalism, reassure their adherents in the face of the inescapable human condition of mortality.[13]

At this point it should be obvious that the most intractable disagreements among students of nationalism derive from fundamental philosophical differences. One can plausibly attribute extreme materialist interpretations to deeply ingrained beliefs that human personality is extremely malleable and that, consequently, human society is perfectible. Such positions, although explicitly advanced by Marxist materialists, are by no means confined to that ideological persuasion. Early in modern history, Anglo-American societies became imbued with millennial concepts of recreating the Biblical 'city on a hill' on this earth, in our own time.[14] As the fervour of evangelical religion weakened, millennial convictions of the feasibility of transforming human personality by using the impressive material advances of the last two centuries replaced Biblical religion. Most such interpretations identify industrialization as the critical step towards such perfectibility. Liberal states based on industry and commerce are contrasted with pre-industrial polities whose principal activity was preparation for war. Thus contemporary interpretations can readily perceive recent nationalist moves for independence when they are directed against authoritarian regimes, but recoil at the notion of separation from liberal regimes. From such a standpoint, current tendencies for separatism, as in Quebec, can be overcome if nationalist supporters come to perceive the commercial advantages of remaining in a larger polity.[15] When one contemplates the relative feebleness of Scottish separatism, compared with the extreme pressure of Slovenes for independence because authoritarian Belgrade hindered their economic development, the interpretation appears plausible. Yet the most conspicuous recent case, Catalonia, is ambiguous because resistance of that industrial and commercial nation to separation from the broader Spanish market, overt only after Franco's demise, restrained moves for independence before authoritarianism had passed away. Moreover, equally industrialized Basques have remained sharply divided on independence even under a democratic regime.

Clearly, one will not decide between the materialist interpretation and the view that contemporary history has demonstrated the bankruptcy of attempts to attain societal perfectibility via economic progress by citing aggregated examples like those mentioned. Ultimately, social scientists and historians will draw on the resources of philosophy (of various schools) and the sociology of knowledge (in its Kuhnian and Foucaultian versions as well as Frankfurt 'critical theory') to try to comprehend the human predicament at the start of the twenty-first century. While nationality specialists await guidance from such an overarching inquiry, it seems to me that our areas of agreement and disagreement suggest one useful line of practical investigation: scrutiny of biographies of individuals involved in their search for national identity. In contrast to most sociological and political science studies of nationalism, which reanalyse aggregate data or rely on survey samples, close biographical examinations are (for a limited number of cases) available to historiography and in current situations when political circumstances preclude adequate survey research. Of course, such biographical study cannot, even if aggregated, provide valid samples. But the investigations can scrutinize psychological aspects of national identity that, in my opinion, have been most neglected. As exploratory investigations, biographical research would be conducive to more systematic, comprehensive hypotheses, essential steps in our understanding. Hypothesis-testing would, of course, take much longer. I conclude, therefore, that the range of emerging scholarly consensus is encouraging, but that decisive theoretical advances depend on further research, requiring many years if not decades.

NOTES

1. Forthcoming in *History and Science*.
2. Among political scientists, Arend Lijphart, *Democracy in Plural Societies* (New Haven, 1977), pp. 17ff, has been influential in emphasizing 'primordial' loyalties of ideological, religious and regional nature as contrasted to material-interest pressures. Very recently (*Foreign Affairs*, November-December 1993) he has termed nationalism not only as 'primordial', but as 'deeply rooted in human nature'. Conversely, Miroslav Hroch (and the Czech historian Frantisek Graus) appear to share my position that nations *did* exist before nationalism; but I infer that both would accept the concept that nations were invented (or at least that *nationalism* was) at some point in the past. On the origins of the French nation, and subsequent nationalism, see especially Colette Beaune, *The Birth of an Ideology: Myths and Symbols of Nation in Late-Medieval France* (Berkeley, 1991), which places the origin of the nation in the late fifteenth century, but of French nationalism (more conventionally) in the late eighteenth century or even 1812; and Miriam Yardeni, *La conscience nationale en France pendant les guerres de religion* (Louvain, 1971), which identifies a 'consciousness' apparently equivalent to nationalism by at least the sixteenth century.
3. Eric Hobsbawm and Terence Ranger (eds), *The Invention of Tradition* (Cambridge, 1983); Benedict Anderson, *Imagined Communities: Reflections on the Origin and Spread of Nationalism* (London, 1983).
4. *Nations and States* (Boulder, 1977), p. 403.
5. 'The limits and divisions of British history', *American Historical Review*, LXXXVII, 1982, especially pp. 325–34.

6. For elaboration of the 'fault-line' thesis, see my 'Toward a framework for considering nationalism in East Europe', *Eastern European Politics and Society*, II, 1988, pp. 280–305.
7. Lawrence C. Mayer, *Comparative Political Inquiry: A Methodological Survey* (Homewood, IL, 1972), p. 61. After quoting Mayer in *The European Administrative Elite* (Princeton, 1973), p. 312, I employ concatenated theory to hypothesize certain elements fostering administrative intervention attitudes throughout modern political systems. I do this, though, *after* tracing the origins and elaboration of such administrative interventionism in the histories of the four major European systems. I do not contend that such a genetic approach is always preferable or feasible in comparisons of national identity (notably during the pre-nationalism era). I do, however, insist that students of nationalism should bear in mind the approximate chronological origins of the phenomenon, which probably requires one to accept either Greenfeld's developmental interpretation, or some other interpretation on origins advanced by her competitors.
8. I think that both Greenfeld and I perceive *early* nationalism as a predominantly elite construct; hence the issue of its development into a mass phenomenon is not crucial for us, as it may be for other interpreters. I do, however, regard it, as discussed below, crucial to determine how elites at all stages of the emergence of nationalism have manipulated pre-existing language patterns.
9. F.T. Zhylko, *Narysy z dialektolohii ukrainsk'koi movy* (Kiev, 1955), especially end map.
10. 'Some sociological aspects of Macedonian and Bulgarian', *Papers in Slavic Philology*, 1984; and review in *Slavic Review*, XLI, 1986, pp. 1–13.
11. Historically, peasants have occupied a quite different position in Islamic societies, particularly in relation to the nostalgia that is often the starting point for elite symbol manipulation. See my *Nations before Nationalism* (Chapel Hill, NC, 1982), pp. 16–27.
12. See the analysis in United States, Commission on Security and Cooperation in Europe, *The Referendum on Independence in Bosnia-Herzegovina* (Washington, 1992), pp. 6, 8, 23.
13. Peter L. Berger and Thomas Luckmann, *The Social Construction of Reality* (Garden City, 1966), pp. 46, 96.
14. See especially Catherine L. Albanese, *Sons of the Fathers: The Civil Religion of the American Revolution* (Philadelphia, 1976), pp. 8–9, 80. It should be noted that the old Puritan (Calvinist) concept relied for perfectibility on the minority pre-elected by God, hence it did not posit a malleable human nature.
15. I have no intention of proposing a propositional inventory such as Robert A. Levine and Donald T. Campbell present in *Ethnocentrism* (New York, 1972), an impressive effort to cover societies at all levels of development. My propositions (which, I hope, will lead to a more complete and refined list) are designed to be applicable only to nationalist movements in relatively 'advanced' societies.

4

A Political Theory of Nationalism and Its Excesses

Michael Mann

I here present a politically driven history of nationalism and of its excesses, concentrating on its emergence and development in Europe. I argue that nations and nationalism have primarily developed in response to the development of the modern state. Though I will sometimes concede that this or that aspect of the nation had either economic or ideological causes, on the whole I shall reject the materialist and culturalist theories of nations and nationalism which tend to be dominant today, and revert to a more old-fashioned theory based primarily on political institutions. It is sometimes said such a theory cannot account for the passions that nations have aroused (Calhoun, 1993: 219). This is probably because most earlier political accounts tended to focus on the gradual 'top-down' extension of state sovereignty among the people. I will, on the contrary, stress the role of turbulent, passionate, popular political movements – which later forced some 'top-down' regimes themselves to become far more passionate and aggressive nationalists. We will see that moderate nationalism is a product of the drive towards democracy. Aggressive nationalism is a perverted form of that drive.

A nation is a community affirming a distinct ethnic identity, history and destiny, and claiming its own state. Nationalism is an ideology whereby a nation believes it possesses distinct claims to virtue – claims which may be used to legitimate aggressive action against other nations. Like most writers, I adhere more to a 'modernist' than to a 'perennialist' or 'primordialist' view of nations. They are not old. They arose only from the eighteenth century (one or two writers prefer the seventeenth century), first in Europe and America, then elsewhere (Kohn, 1967; Anderson, 1983; Gellner, 1983; Hroch, 1985; Chatterjee, 1986; Hobsbawm, 1990; Calhoun, 1993; the main 'perennialist' dissidents are Armstrong, 1982; and Smith, 1986). Since in pre-modern times the culture and organization of dominant classes were largely insulated from the life of the masses, political units could rarely be defined by a common culture, as occurs in a nation (Mann, 1986: 527–30; Gellner, 1983: ch. 1; Hall, 1985; Crone, 1989: ch. 5). And everyone concurs that the ideology of nationalism is distinctively modern. So I concentrate on modern Europe, where nations first surfaced and dominated.

However, we must start a little earlier in time, with two 'proto-national' phases before the full emergence of nations and nationalism: the *religious* and the *commercial/statist* phases. The expansion of literacy was key to both, since this provided the necessary infrastructure through which culture might be more broadly shared. In the religious phase, beginning in the sixteenth century, Protestantism and the Counter-Reformation expanded literacy across the spread of each vernacular language and downward across middling classes. A single written vernacular spread out from the 'home counties' at the expense of other dialects and languages, increasing a sense of shared cultural community. The Protestant Reformation involved a degree of popular religious mobilization against ruling classes and church hierarchies. The Counter-Reformation and the Protestant princes then sought to control this mobilization from above. Where different Churches organized different states or regions, their conflicts might then generate 'proto-national' sentiments reaching the lower classes, as in the Wars of Religion. Yet these tendencies were limited since the Catholic and some Protestant Churches were transnational, and since state, linguistic and Church boundaries only sometimes coincided. The state was not yet relevant enough to social life to stably form the focus of many persons' identities or ideologies.

In the second 'commercial/statist' phase, begun in the late seventeenth century, commercial capitalism and military state modernization took over much of the expansion of literacy. In Britain and Holland commercial capitalism predominated, in Austria and Prussia the military state – while France mixed both fairly equally. Business contracts, government records, army drill manuals, coffee house discussions and academies of notables and officials secularized and spread slightly downward literacy and culture. Social identities could be standardized across larger social spaces and to a limited extent across the classes. Since all states were now ruled by law, rudimentary notions of 'civil citizenship' diffused across state territories. Yet since capitalism, upper-class literacy and Churches all remained somewhat transnational, national identity remained limited. Anderson's (1983) much-touted 'print capitalism' could as easily generate a transnational or a federal West as a community of nations. The nation still did not mobilize society though it was now technically possible for it to do so.

This centuries-long process could also slowly and steadily solidify local and regional communities. Interaction networks expanded as agriculture commercialized; local religious practices became more shared across the classes; customs, marriage patterns and cultural practices stabilized. Local-regional mobilization across the classes became more technically possible. By the late seventeenth century the local-regional community often seemed to mobilize entire 'ways of life'. Thus it might seem strong, deeply rooted, honoured by time, a seemingly 'ethnic' identity. Yet the other limits of such communities remained imprecise, since the scope of the interaction networks generated by emerging standardization of languages, economic markets, marriage markets, churches and cultural practices might all differ. Pre-modern ethnicity was also inherently local and concrete, rarely capable of uniting complete strangers – the hallmark of the 'imagined community' that is the modern nation (Anderson, 1983).

The merging of these two 'proto-national' elements – the bounded but weakly rooted state, and the vibrant but poorly demarcated local-regional ethnic community – into fully fledged and sometimes aggressive nations took place in the three phases I label *militarist, industrial* and *modernist*, lasting from the late eighteenth into the late twentieth century. But different types of nation emerged. Firstly, nations differed in their sizes vis-à-vis existing states. British and French nations were coterminous with existing states – and so the nation proved *state-reinforcing*. Yet in the Austrian, Ottoman and Russian Empires nations proved smaller than state boundaries and they became *state-subverting*. There was also a temporary third size since across Germany and Italy the nation was at first bigger than any existing state. It developed a *state-creating* (or 'pan-state') role – though as one state (Prussia, Piedmont) succeeded in swallowing up the others, the nation then became state-reinforcing. Secondly, nations differed in their forms of popular mobilization, being mobilized 'bottom-up', popularly and democratically, or 'top-down', controlled from above by authoritarian or semi-authoritarian regimes. Why did nations develop, but in these varied forms?

Only a small part of the answer can be found in capitalism. True, the emergence of industrial capitalism expanded the interaction networks and the literacy of civil society, enabling identities to stabilize over larger social spaces. But there was little in the capitalism of this period to encourage a distinctively *national* civil society. Capitalist markets remained fairly transnational across the eighteenth and nineteenth centuries: smuggling exceeded the trade regulated by eighteenth-century mercantilism; capital and labour moved increasingly freely across frontiers up to the 1870s; and industrialization spread faster across peripheral and frontier regions (the Low Countries, Bohemia, Catalonia, etc.) than in state cores. Early industrialization reduced state regulation of labour relations: increasingly, labourers, artisans and merchant capitalists settled their relations with little recourse to national politics. It is true that from the 1870s state protectionism, subsidization and regulation began to grow, but industrial capitalism remained largely transnational in its organization and effects. We shall see that in the second, 'industrial' phase economic development did impact on the nation, but largely indirectly, by bolstering up the state. The nation is not so intimately related to capitalism or industrialism as is often argued.

The key lies rather in the state. Pre-eighteenth-century states had done little beside fighting and preparing for wars. Only where entwined with Churches did they penetrate much of social life. Yet under the pressure of the Military Revolution (from the sixteenth century), reinforced by persistent eighteenth-century wars, their military activities began to significantly affect social life. Around 1700, European states still absorbed only around 5% of GNP in peacetime, 10% in wartime.[1] By 1760, this had risen to 15–25%; by 1810, 25–35%. Virtually all the increases went on financing wars. By 1810, the armies were calling up about 5% of the total population. These extraction rates are identical to those of the First and Second World Wars and to the highest rates in the world today – those of Israel and Iraq. No modern state (outside the Soviet and fascist blocs) has loomed larger than the states of the Napoleonic War period.

Such figures enable us to appreciate the scale of the eighteenth-century transformation. From being fairly insignificant, states now loomed over the lives of their subjects, taxing and conscripting them, attempting to mobilize their enthusiasm for its goals. As state extraction increased, it became more regressive – since the dominant classes were the moneylenders and could better resist increased taxes. This was class exploitation, made transparent at the level of the state. Thus subjects became aroused out of their historic political indifference into anger and violence against naked exploitation. They petitioned, demonstrated, rioted and sometimes rebelled – showing as much emotion as any critic of political explanations could ask for – in their demand for political citizenship for 'the people' and 'the nation'.[2] After prolonged social struggles, such labels were usually restricted for much of the nineteenth century to bourgeois and petty bourgeois males drawn from dominant religious and ethnic groups, but later the peasantry, the working class, minorities – and eventually women – joined people and nation.

However, let me draw back from a single-factor explanation of the entire process. Local-regional ethnic communities also played their role in generating capacities for political mobilization: family and neighbourhood organization was prominent in many popular movements of the time; while in countries like Britain and France a more-or-less shared language and religion helped protest to focus on the broader nation. But the clarity of focus on the nation as coterminous with the state cries out for a predominantly political explanation. Self-conscious nations emerged from the struggle for representative government, initially born of the pressures of state militarism. Whatever atrocities were later committed in the name of the nation, its emergence lay with those democratic ideals of this period that we most value today.

The militarist phase also produced our two main nation sizes – state-reinforcing and state-subverting – as well as the third, temporary, state-creating nation. Britain (apart from Ireland) and France were examples of state-reinforcement, since the linguistic community was securely located in the state's territorial and class core, and since the emerging political nation was virtually coterminous with state boundaries. Reformers and revolutionaries alike focused on transforming the central state, to make it more representative. Their activities only served to strengthen the salience and centralization of that state. When they succeeded in making it more representative, it became a more unitary nation-state, its activities (principal among which remained warmaking) increasingly mobilizing national sentiments.

But Empires like the Austrian, the Ottoman and the Russian were essentially confederal, blending many languages, religions and provinces, most with autonomous political histories and organization. Fiscal and conscription pressures here produced very different outcomes. When Austrian taxes and borrowing arrangements proved insufficient for modern warfare (and the Habsburgs declared bankruptcy in 1811), higher exactions had to be negotiated with regional notables represented in provincial Diets and staffing provincial administrations. Thus reformers within the Habsburg domains sought less to transform the central state than to strengthen regional political autonomies against the central state. The drive here was towards what we would call federalism. 'Patriotism' became associated more with the single province than with the whole empire. Indeed, in the 1780s Joseph II's administrative and fiscal rationalization had provoked the first self-styled 'patriot' movements in Europe – one in the most advanced province, the Austrian Netherlands, the other in a backward one, Hungary. Thus these 'national' revolts cannot be traced to a certain level of industry or capitalism. Instead what the two shared was powerful provincial political organization, in the Netherlands among all propertied classes, in Hungary confined to the nobility. The Habsburgs – or the Romanovs or the Ottomans – *could* have dealt with dissent by establishing a federal form of representation – the United States and Switzerland had pioneered such constitutions. But these dynasties were absolutist, opposed to representation. Thus, right up to the twentieth century, only mixtures of two political alternatives were available to most ethnic minorities: centralized authoritarianism, and limited, centrally controlled regional autonomy – a kind of pseudo-federalism.[3] Since regionalists deeply opposed the former, they increasingly sought to expand the latter, first into genuine federalism involving regional autonomies, then (when the empires would not concede this) into state-subverting nationalism.

Again, this is not intended as a single-factor explanation. The core of these 'province-nations' was usually reinforced by more than one among a distinctive language, a religion and a distinct economic market, all tending to cement and expand ethnic solidarities. Yet virtually everywhere, nationalist movements focused on existing political units, provinces with distinct assemblies or administrations centred on old political units. Gellner (1983: 45) has observed that there were vastly more languages and ethnic or cultural groups than there were nationalist movements. We cannot predict which few nations successfully emerged on the basis merely of 'ethnicity'. The presence or absence of regional administration offers a much better predictor. This suggests a predominantly political explanation.

In Germany and Italy states were much smaller than proto-national identities. 'Germany' existed as the mutually intelligible dialects of educated people, as a paper-thin political federation (in which Austria was actually the leading player) and as a vague sense of the past. But it had over 300 states plus 1,500 minor principalities in 1789; 39 still survived in 1815. By a historical quirk, most (including Prussia) had a quite secure fiscal basis: their dynasties owned larger private estates and/ or had institutionalized stabler tax-collecting systems than had most other European states. Thus Germans were not goaded on as much by the military-fiscal-representation cycle to transform and so increase the salience of their states. The expansion of German literacy was thus more 'apolitical', producing a Romantic movement exploring language, emotions and the soul more than reason and politics. Schiller defined German 'greatness' as 'delving into the spiritual world'. Schiller and Goethe wrote: 'Forget, O Germans, your hopes of becoming a *nation*. Educate yourselves instead . . . to be human beings' (Segeberg, 1988: 152).

German attempts to grammaticize and codify their own language were also imitated across central Europe by Poles, Magyars, Czechs and other Slavs. But this had more political consequences, encouraging state-subversion. For example, most Czechs spoke dialects of a mutually intelligible language, giving them some sense of shared community. But few yet thought of this as a singular 'national' identity: Czech was the language of the private household and local community, German of Habsburg capitalism and state. Those involved in the latter often classified themselves as 'Germans', despite having Czech surnames (Cohen, 1981). But to standardize Czech was to make it potentially available for the public realm as well, increasing its significance as a source of social identity. Philologists did not attack states, yet they encouraged community identities, subtly subverting state boundaries.

The French Revolution and the ensuing wars escalated some of these tendencies. Fiscal and manpower needs forced limited reforms, inching states towards more universal 'national' principles of administration, military service and representation. The scale of war mobilization – 5% of total populations conscripted, perhaps half agriculture and manufacturing surpluses fed into the war machines – meant whole 'peoples' were organized to fight each other. Negative national stereotypes of the enemy became more widely shared in Britain and France (Colley, 1986; Newman, 1987). And as initial French 'liberation' turned into French imperialism, widespread revolts became legitimated by national stereotypes: Germans characterized themselves as open, upright and God-fearing, Spaniards described themselves as dignified, honourable and devout, and both styled the French as sly, frivolous and unreliable.

But who could the new patriots turn to? Local notables – nobles and clerics mobilizing peasants – could lead guerrilla warfare in backward Spain and mountainous Switzerland and the Tyrol. Elsewhere, big armies mobilized by large states were required to kick out the French. That meant submission to the Prussian or Austrian monarchies. The Prussian regime had been shocked by defeat at the hands of Bonaparte towards stuttering reforms, harnessing proto-national sentiments to absolutism. There developed the first significant 'top-down' national identity, that of Prussia–Germany, harnessing national (and also Evangelical religious) sentiments to loyalty to a strong semi-authoritarian state. Between 1815 and the 1870s, as Prussia absorbed Germany, this top-down nationalism became more unitary (despite an ostensibly federal *Reich* constitution) and state-reinforcing.

The Habsburgs could not choose such a national solution, however top-down: they were dynasts ruling a confederal empire. When somebody was recommended to the Emperor Francis as a patriot for Austria, Francis replied 'He may be a patriot for Austria, but the question is whether he is a patriot for me' (Kohn, 1967: 162). Russian and Ottoman rulers confronted the same problem. Habsburg dynastic power was fully restored in 1815. But war-induced fiscal pressure continued to evoke regional-national autonomy movements. Through the next (and last) century of their rule the Habsburgs were assailed by nationalists asserting that a people, defined by ethnic-linguistic culture, but ruled by foreigners, should have its own state. These state-subverting nations triumphed – the Magyars in 1867, the rest in 1918. The triumphs of Ottoman provinces in Europe occurred through the same period; those of most Russian provinces had to occur twice, in 1918 and 1991.

The emergence and triumph of the state-subverting nations were not directly caused by the development of capitalism or industrialism (as Marxists and Gellner, 1983 argue). Hroch (1985) gives the most careful account of nationalism in terms of economies and classes. He studied nationalist societies in eight state-subverting small nations across Europe. He found commercial and manufacturing groups under-represented in nationalist societies, urban professionals over-represented – especially where markets were most developed. Yet if we look right across Europe we find greater variability. The Austrian Netherlands and northern Italy (not studied by him) were commercialized and urbanized at the time of their first patriotic ferment (as were the Czechs by the time ferment reached them). But Poland, Hungary, Slovakia and the Balkans hosted nationalist movements while they were still far more agrarian and backward. There was probably a threshold level of market-aided literacy and communication below which patriots could not credibly organize – as Hroch concludes. But above that threshold there was diversity. Indeed, Hroch's 'bourgeois' nationalist societies were not always the most significant actors. In the 1848 revolution, most leaders of provincial 'national' movements were nobles seeking representation only for themselves (Sked, 1989: 41–88). State-subverting nationalism later also acquired a peasant base. What common class motivation could lead such disparate movements to proclaim themselves nationalists (asks Sugar, 1969)? Nationalists said little about classes or capitalism or industrialism. Why, then, should we believe them reducible to these forces?

My explanation centres rather on the political economy of the state: its growing fiscal and manpower costs, and its office-holding benefits. As elsewhere, discontent concerned taxation, conscription and rights to hold public office. But here it was expressed territorially, by region. British discontent might produce class riots which local gentry and yeomanry could handle. But territorially based discontent (which the British experienced only in Ireland) led to revolts by provincial notables, wielding militias and sometimes regular troops, with initial sympathy from lower-level clerics, mobilizing intense local-regional ethnic sentiments. Linguistic issues increasingly arose: what should be the language of the public sphere, especially of government, and what languages should be taught in schools? As Gellner (1983) argues, literacy was cultural capital, bringing rewards through employment in army, civil administration, law courts and capitalist economy. In the Austrian lands, as capitalism and states expanded, non-German speakers were blocked from administration and law courts – or so the revolutionaries of 1848 claimed (Sked, 1989: 41–88). Yet linguistic nationalism was not just an instrumental demand. As clerics and philologists standardized local vernaculars, these became the cement of public as well as private interaction networks, reproduced in elementary schools, churches and market exchanges. Language gradually became coterminous with the sense of a regional cross-class ethnicity. Politics concerned identities as well as interests, deepening the emotions they could mobilize.

I have argued so far that nations essentially originated as movements for democracy. Reformers were confronted by a choice: to democratize a central state, or to reduce the powers of a central state and seek federal government based on more democratic regional governments. Since none of the three major empires would accept genuine federalism, Europe saw the development only of state-reinforcing and state-subverting nationalism. Across the whole of Europe federal representative government, democratically regulating the relations between regions, could not be established. We still live with the consequences of that non-event.

As is often observed (for example by Mommsen, 1990), nationalism was not yet very aggressive. Nonetheless, harbingers had already appeared. It was those most concerned to establish 'rule by the people' who most severely repressed their domestic foes once in power. They legitimated this in a particular way. French revolutionaries had legitimated the Terror by denying the royal family, aristocrats and (non-juring) clerics membership in the nation, which they said was 'one and indivisible'. Thus there was no place in the nation for particularism or conflict: political disputes were to be resolved not by compromise, but by exclusion and force. Terror was purity, compromise was corruption, proclaimed Saint Just. His American counterparts killed 'Loyalists' (to the British) precisely because they were not 'Patriots'. Excluding certain groups from the nation later proved to be one of nationalism's two killing-fields. Yet the numbers killed here were small, and the goals were ostensibly liberal. The French revolutionaries also invaded the rest of Europe in the name of *la grande nation.* Inter*national* wars later proved nationalism's second killing-field. Yet the French believed they were liberating not subordinating nations. When Bonaparte turned this into imperialism, he played down nationalism. Moreover, during this period few reformers were democrats. By the 'people' or 'nation' they usually meant only male property-owners. Though citizenship was extended, most reformers could rely broadly on traditional methods of controlling the masses, without resorting to terror or to chiliastic ideologies. Most nations comprised respectable men, using fairly moderate methods.

From the mid-nineteenth century to the First World War, in the *industrial* phase, states shifted gear in two ways, largely under the pressures of industrial capitalism. First, the notion of popular sovereignty took fire among subordinate classes mobilized by the spread of industry, commerce and commercialized agriculture. By 1914 west of Russia, suffrage was widely diffused among middle-class males and it was widely accepted that full male (and probably female) suffrage would eventually come. The more reactionary ruling classes had adapted democratic arguments: the energies of the masses could be mobilized by themselves in a 'top-down', semi-authoritarian national state, of which the German *Kaiserreich* was the prototype. This also increased their attachment to centralization, denying genuinely federal forms of representation. Nationalism – having arisen 'on the Left' – moved rightward.

Second, state functions rapidly expanded. Though military functions remained important, there were few wars before 1914 and states were for the first time performing major civilian functions. These centred on communications systems needed by an industrial society – canals, roads, post offices, railways, telegraph and, most significantly, schools. By the 1880s, expenditures on these were rivalling military expenses, by the 1900s they exceeded them. These infrastructures enhanced the density of social interaction – but being largely confined within the state's territories they subtly 'naturalized' social life. During the twentieth century, welfare and fiscal policies redistributed resources between regions, age-groups and classes, reducing inequalities and further solidifying the nation. Perhaps the most impressive evidence comes from Watkins's (1991) analysis of fertility, illegitimacy and marriage age rates. She shows that from the 1870s right through to the 1960s regional variations in these rates declined, as each nation-state acquired a distinctive, homogeneous, national demographic profile. Without anyone intending it, and even in the intimate sexual sphere, social behaviour had been 'naturalized'. Both popular sovereignty and state activities had furthered the nation as an experienced community, linking the intensive and emotional organizations of family, neighbourhood and ethnicity with more extensive and instrumental power organizations.

Yet the expanding scope of state activities still left around 40% of budgets going on war and preparation for war. Military virtues were still a valued part of masculine culture; women were valued as the bearers and nurturers of future warriors. Now that these states were becoming more representative and more national, it is often asserted that in the industrial phase the whole population began to identify their interests and their sense of honour with those of their state against other nation-states, endorsing aggressive nationalism. A rival class theory looks to see exactly who was represented in these states. It concludes that full political citizens – primarily the middle class – were the bearers of aggressive nationalism in alliance with old regimes.

Yet to conceive of oneself as a member of a national community does not necessarily mean supporting aggression against other nations. Even though nation began to be associated in this period with 'race', racism was predominantly used to justify *European*, not national, imperialism (against 'non-whites' elsewhere on the globe). Only some versions of nationalism showed aggression towards other Europeans. In Britain the old radical 'Protestant' conception of the popular nation, now more secular and still quite pacific, contested against conservative imperialist conceptions, while some Liberals advocated a softer imperialism. French Republicans, Monarchists and Bonapartists offered rival conceptions of the meaning of 'France', some aggressive, others quite pacific. Classes and minorities who experienced the sharp end of domestic militarism tended to oppose aggressive nationalism. But then so did much of the enfranchised middle class – and the much-maligned petty bourgeoisie – since few wanted war or higher taxes or had reason to hate foreigners. True, aggressive nationalism had broadened its appeal, but this was predominantly in a rather specific and 'statist' way. Hundreds of thousands of administrators, teachers and public sector workers now depended for their livelihood on the state; hundreds of thousands of young middle-class men passed through its institutions of higher education; while millions of young men of all classes were disciplined by a military cadre into the peculiar morale, coercive yet emotionally attached, that is the hallmark of the modern mass army. These three bodies of men, and their families – not broader classes or communities – provided most of the fervent nationalists – as studies of prewar pressure groups reveal (summarized in Mann, 1993: ch. 16). They were 'super-loyalists' or 'nation-statists', with an exaggerated loyalty to what they conceived to be the ideals of their nation-state. These state ideals varied. British officials might be attached to liberal ideals, French to Republican ideals, Spanish and Italian officials to rather varied ideals (since their regimes were rather mixed ones). German pressure groups, centred on state officials, proclaimed an authoritarian and increasingly racist nationalism whose violent rhetoric and agitational style was moving beyond control by the old regime (Eley, 1980). But since all states were militarist, their servants were generally mobilizable at least to an ostensibly 'defensive' militarism. This fervent 'statist' form of nationalism was to become highly significant in the twentieth century.

Nationalism came to possess a further feature in the more reactionary states west of Russia, especially in the German Empire, in Spain and in the Germanic and Magyar cores of the Habsburg domains. As confrontation between their ruling classes and the Marxian (or anarchist) proletariat grew, it took on 'national' hues. Since the proletariat organized by socialists and anarchists came to see itself as transnational, the ruling class associated itself more with the nation – as mobilized in 'top-down' fashion by an authoritarian or semi-authoritarian state. Thus the dominant classes began to define the proletariat as disloyal to the nation. The German term, *Reichsfeinde*, 'enemies of the Reich', serves to convey the rather statist flavour of this condemnation. The *Reichsfeinde* were not just the socialists, but also Poles, Danes and other nationalities inside the Reich, and more occasionally Catholics and Jews. In contrast, the nationalists began to think of themselves – as in the title of Chickering's excellent (1984) book – as 'We Men Who Feel Most German'. 'Integral' nationalists in Spain, Portugal and France also began to claim that leftists and regional-nationalists (like Catalan or Basque autonomists) were traitors to the nation-state. Only they themselves represented the true, integral nation. It was a disturbing revival of the earlier revolutionary tendency to exclude whole categories of people from full membership in the nation. After the First World War it began to legitimate terror.

Though the rise in nationalism was a cause of the First World War, it was not one of the most important ones. Elsewhere I have argued that more decisive were traditional geopolitics, the almost casual militarism of some old regimes and the chaotic decision-making structures of the states – to which nationalist agitation, however, did make a contribution (Mann, 1993: ch. 21). The war produced an immediate explosion in voiced nationalist sentiments. But it is easy to exaggerate this. A shallow 'spectator sport militarism' was here baptized as many millions of men and women cheered on 'their boys', sang patriotic songs and handed out white feathers – at no real cost to themselves. A few million young men were sufficiently caught up by an early patriotic frenzy to sign on in moods varying from enthusiasm through resigned duty to fear of social ostracism. But this produced insufficient recruits. Conscription became necessary.

Frontline moods also differed considerably. By 1917 there remained a small core of enthusiastic 'nation-statist' soldiers for whom the later myth of *Fronterlebnis* may have been reality, a smaller core of dissidents-becoming-revolutionaries (their proportions were reversed in the Russian armies) and a vast majority desperately tired of war, fearful of death but obeying orders as the safest way of keeping their heads down. The First World War also saw relatively few excesses in the name of the nation. Its horror derived more from weaponry and tactics than from atrocities, while the atrocities committed were mostly the traditional ones of rape, pillage and murder of civilians. Enemy combatants were treated quite well. Up to 1918, nationalism remained surprisingly mild.

My third, *modernist* phase begins with the peace settlements of 1917–19. They redrew the map fairly authoritatively. Though there were discontented 'revisionist states' – the Soviet Union (at first), Germany and Hungary, and to a lesser extent Italy and Bulgaria – boundaries were clear and internationally guaranteed. There were border clashes between government forces and/or fervent minority nationalist paramilitaries around German frontiers, between Poland and the Soviet Union and around Trieste, but these died away (though they left important influences on domestic politics). German and Italian nationalist aggression was to revive in the 1930s, but the 1920s saw war-weariness and low-profile diplomacy.

Yet domestically it was a different story. The war and the peace settlements destroyed most of the authoritarian and semi-authoritarian old regimes of Europe, and with them went the centrepiece of institutionalized control over the masses. Churches, armies, lesser monarchies and notable conservative parties remained, but all were under pressure to compromise with the lower classes through parliamentarianism, institutionalized labour relations and land reform. The dislocations even to nominally victorious regimes like those of Italy or Romania were also severe, since lower-class expectations had been aroused by wartime promises of a better society. Neutral Iberian regimes were weakened by other forces (though Spanish military disasters also played a role).

Across the whole of central, eastern and southern Europe, not a single parliamentary regime was already stably institutionalized – unlike almost the whole of northwest Europe. Either parliamentary regimes had not previously existed, or they had relied upon state executive interventions at the top and patron–client party corruption at the bottom. This political system was now in crisis since postwar constitutions reduced state executive powers, and as socialist and populist Christian parties threatened patron–client parties from below. Under the strain conservatism split, into parliamentarianism and an authoritarian radical Right. In their different ways each represented a coming to terms with popular sovereignty. Conservative parliamentarians accepted party democracy; the radical Right far surpassed the old regimes in 'top-down' political mobilization, building up mass street-fighting parties, often founded upon the immediate postwar paramilitaries. The radical Right stood for a kind of perverted democracy, its legitimacy and mobilization based essentially on 'the nation', yet advocating anti-democratic constitutions. Throughout the entire centre, south and east (except for Czechoslovakia), the competition between the two rightisms had a single result: authoritarianism triumphed, either as parliamentary conservatives themselves launched coups, or as they were swept aside by quasi-fascist radical rightists. By 1938 modern authoritarianism was entrenched across two-thirds of the continent.

The victorious authoritarian rightists had two main bases of support. One was class. Since they promised to suppress working-class movements, in most countries the higher the social class, the more support they got. Yet the relationship was not strong and contemporary research stresses the extent to which fascists in particular managed to recruit among *all* social classes, if with two exceptions: though they recruited many workers, they could rarely penetrate the organized working-class core (though they did in Hungary and Romania), and certain religions or minorities were highly resistant (there were not many Catholics who were Nazis, nor Basques or Catalans who were Nationalists or Francoites). Authoritarian Rights claimed indeed to be *national* movements, and this was substantially true.

But, second, this nation had a more limited core: extreme 'nation-statists' with a close relationship with the state. Over-represented were adherents (and sometimes priests) of state religions,[4] soldiers or veterans, state civilian employees (including public sector manual workers), and students, professors and graduates of state higher educational establishments.[5] Adding these together normally gives us a majority of leaders and militants and a sizeable minority of all members. There were also complex regional patterns of support often revolving around a 'national' axis: if a region might claim to embody the 'core' of the nation-state, or if it felt the need for strong defence by the state, then it provided more support for authoritarian rightism – like Old Castile, certain rural regions of Romania or German border regions.

Thus authoritarian rightism, including fascism, was essentially an aggressive, statist and class-biased form of nationalism. Authoritarian rightist movements in *every* country now argued that socialists and anarchists were traitors to the nation since they favoured internationalism and fomented class conflict, thus weakening the nation. They generally charged liberals, and ethnic and regional minorities less strongly with the same treason. Such traitors made democracy unworkable, they claimed. The people must rule, but as a 'purer nation', and by more 'organic', 'integral' means than a corrupt, chaotic democracy of competing parties. Only the Nazis went as far as mass slaughter of those they claimed could not be assimilated to the nation – Jews, Slavs, gypsies and the mentally defective (though their wartime collaborators in several countries became equal partners in the slaughter).[6] But apart from its racism Germany was not unusual. With a few exceptions (Pilsudski in Poland, Primo de Riveria in Spain, Pats in Estonia, Metaxas in Greece) authoritarian rightist regimes legitimized the suppression and selective killing of their domestic opponents by denying them membership in the nation. The Left had their own popular exclusionary slogans. These were more varied, since leftists also mobilized class exclusions – Stalin, for example, proclaimed his enemies to be class traitors. Yet several leftist movements, especially in southern Europe, claimed to mobilize 'the people' against the rightist 'nationalists'. In the Spanish Civil War the Republicans deployed three main discourses – Republican constitutionality, the transnational proletariat and revolution, and 'the people' or 'the popular forces'. Their enemies, especially landowners and priests, might be shot because they were rebels, or not in the working class, or not of the people. But the other side not only claimed to mobilize 'the nation' – they actually defined themselves, and were usually described by others, as 'the Nationalists'; and their various factions were labelled as 'National-Catholic', 'National-syndicalist' etc. They killed large numbers of Republicans, both during and after the war, in the name of 'Spain' against 'anti-Spain' (Juliá, 1990; Aguilar, 1993). In this period nationalism found its main domestic killers – mostly authoritarian rightists. Apart from Nazi racists, they rarely argued that 'ethnicity' defined the nation. Opposed class and political movements, religious deviants and troublesome regionalists were 'foreign', outside the nation. But anyone could repent and join the nation – even the Nazis believed socialists and liberals could repent. Voluntary actions, not birth, defined membership for these highly aggressive nationalists. Politics, not ethnicity, generated most of the extraordinary emotional intensity, the barbarity conducted in the name of morality, of the modernist period – while the great exception, the Holocaust, embodied more racial than national ethnicity.

In foreign fields rightist regimes behaved more variably. Almost all developed ideologies of national superiority over foreigners – from Aryan supremacy to 'Hungarism' to *Hispanidad*. But most showed geopolitical caution. Not Germany or Italy, of course. But most Eastern European regimes went into the Second World War for what they believed was pragmatism (Hitler and Mussolini would win, so join the winning side). Franco and Salazar stayed out altogether, though Franco almost went in. And when they went in, most nations' soldiers did not commit all that many atrocities.

There were two main types of exception. First, Germans and Japanese, both with a highly racial notion of the nation, committed massive atrocities. The Germans did not only perpetrate the Holocaust against Jews. The German army on the Eastern Front let die 47% of its Russian POWs, whom it considered *Untermenschen*. But only 3% of its Anglo-American prisoners perished, since its racism accorded them membership in the Aryan race, if not in its national core (Bartov, 1985). Again, the worst slaughter must be explained more in terms of racism than nationalism. But the second exception returns us to politically driven nationalism. Across Eastern Europe there were atrocities between the remaining imperial states and their minorities denied political representation – Russians versus Poles and Ukrainians, Serbs versus Croats, some Baltic peoples versus Jews (as supposed agents of Russian Bolshevism). In contrast, nationalist sentiments were far milder further west. In the democracies, neither state-reinforcing nor state-subverting nationalism committed more than a handful of atrocities across the period of the Second World War. Popular sovereignty was here achieved. Thus nationalism and ethnicity (outside of racism used against persons of non-European origin) were fairly harmless.

The victors took more care over the peace settlement than their predecessors had in 1918 (Maier, 1981). The Soviet Union and the Western allies not only settled borders and ringed them with armies, they also institutionalized state socialist and democratic regimes. Democracy returned later to Greece, Portugal and Spain. All the new democracies worked well enough to defuse aggressive nationalism, whether state-reinforcing or state-subverting. In Spain especial care was taken over the regional question. Only those treated the worst under the Franco regime, the Basques, have retained much terrorism, and even that has steadily diminished as democratic federalism has advanced.

The Soviet bloc was not democratic. Its regional nations, dispossessed by a mixture of authoritarianism and pseudo-federalism, had little immediate hope of rising up again. For forty years they merely kept their heads down. This also happened under the somewhat more liberal Tito regime in Yugoslavia. But, as before, state-subverting nationalisms became violent where imperial regimes began to grow vulnerable yet still would not grant representation. When those regimes collapsed (from within in the Soviet case – not from the efforts of regional nationalists), a region clearly belonging with another established nation-state – like East Germany – could simply join it. Similarly, an oppressed historical nation-state – like Poland – could simply declare independence. Greater problems arose where an ethnic group, usually with past regional administrative institutions but without clear ethnic boundaries or actual historic state, had been inserted amid others, perhaps similarly placed.

A genuinely 'federal' association of ethnicities was clearly the best solution. Yet this was largely discredited by virtue of the pseudo-federalism of the exploiting imperial predecessor. Federalism had not been considered a feasible solution in 1918 for this reason (except, highly imperfectly, in Yugoslavia), and it has also collapsed at the beginning of the 1990s. On both occasions groups retreated down to the ethnic level where they believed the normative solidarities of ethnicity – language, religion and customs – might generate the political trust necessary for democracy. Each locally dominant 'people' thus sought to found its own representative state. Yet it was also expected to respect minorities, who might be the 'people' of the neighbouring state. Emergent peoples have had no prior democratic institutions, centralized or inter-regional, available for either task. They are proving brittle, tempted into grounding their representative institutions 'organically' (and so often non-democratically) on the core ethnic people, excluding minorities from full membership. Territorial incursions, mass migrations and 'ethnic cleansing' may result. The downward spiral may only be halted not by contractual federalism among the peoples but by inter-governmental agreements. These will probably produce mutual guarantees of minority rights – less ideal than genuine inter-regional federal democracy. But this may stem the slaughter.

In contrast, Western states that successfully institutionalized democracy – especially inter-regional, federal democracy – have experienced little nationalist violence even when beset by deeply rooted inter-ethnic disputes. Switzerland is quite stable. Belgium, Canada and even Spain may indeed break up – but if so, with very few fatalities. Northern Ireland may represent the worst scenario in the democratic world: a struggle between rival ethnic communities in a democracy which is yet highly centralized, with no effective federal institutions. The unitary Westminster and local government system has not been able to adequately represent the minority Catholic community, in an environment where the intimate lives of both communities remained highly segregated. Thus, in the worst years, just after the British resolve to hold onto the province clearly wavered, hundreds have died. But this is far fewer than where centralization has been buttressed by authoritarianism. Neither Yugoslavia nor the Soviet Union institutionalized either democracy or genuine federalism, yet they contained rival ethnic communities, many with their own historical political institutions. Massive state-subverting ethnic violence is thus resulting: a product of centralized authoritarian regimes in decline. This was so in the nineteenth century. It remains true today.

My politically driven account of nations and nationalism has argued that both their milder and their aggressive aspects originated and developed in response to the drive for democracy. An ability to gradually institutionalize representative institutions over a period of time developed rather mild nationalism, able to rally citizens behind their regimes at times of war, but rarely to commit nationalist atrocities. Failure to institutionalize democracy generated exclusionist nationalism, able to commit atrocities against persons defined as being outside the nation who might live inside or outside the national boundaries. These definitions of the nation were fundamentally political rather than ethnic, except where racism (with rather different and more particular sources) was invoked. State-subverting nationalism seems to have had a more ethnic base, yet it developed in drives for regional representation and was defused towards mildness by inter-regional, federal democracy. Yet complete repression of such drives by an authoritarian regime which then fails may lead to a downward spiral of nationalist aggression, involving territorial displacement and ethnic cleansing. Mild nationalism – whether state-reinforcing or state-subverting – is democracy achieved, aggressive nationalism is democracy perverted. The solution is, therefore, to achieve democracy – especially federal, inter-regional democracy. Unfortunately, this is easier said than done.

NOTES

A previous version of this essay was published as Working Paper No. 57, Instituto Juan March de Estudios e Investigaciones, Madrid, 1994.

1. All figures on state finances and manpower, and all generalizations about state activities prior to 1914, are drawn from the research I have conducted on the history of five states – Austria-Hungary, France, Great Britain, Prussia/Germany and the United States – reported in Mann, 1993: chs 11–14.
2. Some would argue that this process occurred rather earlier in England. Kohn (1967) and Greenfeld (1992) believe English conceptions of nation and nationalism arose in the seventeenth-century struggle against monarchical taxation (reinforced by a religious populism).
3. Only the Magyars forcibly, and the Finns peacefully, obtained more from the dynasties.
4. Though Catholic Churches usually resisted fascism, they were usually supportive of other forms of authoritarian rightism.
5. I am at present assembling all the available data on who supported authoritarian rightism in the countries of interwar Europe. There is no up-to-date published survey of all the evidence, though Linz (Linz J.J., 1976) commented very shrewdly on data then available to him, and various articles in Mühlberger, 1987, and Larsen et al., 1980, are good on individual countries.
6. I here include only the relatively few collaborators and allies who were also fervent racists – a very large number of Austrians, minority factions among Hungarians, Romanians, Slovaks, Croatians, Ukrainians and in the Baltic states, and very small numbers elsewhere. The peculiarity of Nazi racism was that it killed Europeans. The reasons for this lie outside my scope here (in any case it is not easy to explain).

REFERENCES

Aguilar, P. 1993 'Guerra civil y nacionalismo', unpublished paper (Madrid: Instituto Juan March).
Anderson, B. 1983 *Imagined Communities: Reflections on the Origin and Spread of Nationalism* (London: Verso).
Armstrong, J. 1982 *Nations before Nationalism* (Chapel Hill: University of North Carolina Press).
Bartov, O. 1985 *The Eastern Front, 1941–45. German Troops and the Barbarization of Warfare* (London: Macmillan).
Calhoun, C. 1993 'Nationalism and ethnicity', *Annual Review of Sociology*, 19.
Chatterjee, P. 1986 *Nationalist Thought and the Colonial World: A Derivative Discourse?* (London: Zed Books).
Chickering, R. 1984 *We Men Who Feel Most German: A Cultural Study of the Pan-German League, 1886–1914* (Boston: Allen & Unwin).
Cohen, G. 1981 *The Politics of Ethnic Survival: Germans in Prague, 1861–1914* (Princeton, NJ: Princeton University Press).

Colley, L. 1986 'Whose nation? Class and national consciousness in Britain, 1750–85', *Past and Present*, 113.
Crone, P. 1989 *Pre-Industrial Societies* (Oxford: Basil Blackwell).
Eley, G. 1980 *Reshaping the German Right* (New Haven, CT: Yale University Press).
Gellner, E. 1983 *Nations and Nationalism* (Oxford: Basil Blackwell).
Greenfeld, L. 1992 *Nationalism: Five Roads to Modernity* (Cambridge, MA: Harvard University Press).
Hall, J.A. 1985 *Powers and Liberties* (Oxford: Basil Blackwell).
Hobsbawm, E. 1990 *Nations and Nationalism since 1780* (Cambridge: Cambridge University Press).
Hroch, M. 1985 *Social Preconditions of National Revival in Europe* (Cambridge: Cambridge University Press).
Juliá, S. 1990 'Guerra civil como guerra social', in *La Iglesia Católica y la Guerra Civil Española* (Madrid: Fundación Friedrich Ebert).
Kohn, H. 1967 *Prelude to Nation-States: The French and German Experience, 1789–1815*, 2nd edn (Princeton: Van Nostrand).
Larsen, S.U. et al. 1980 *Who Were the Fascists?* (Bergen: Universitets Forlaget).
Linz, J.J. 1976 'Some notes toward a comparative study of Fascism in sociological historical perspective', in W. Laqueur (ed.), *Fascism: A Reader's Guide* (Berkeley: University of California Press).
Maier, C. 1981 'The two postwar eras and the conditions for stability in 20th century Western Europe', *American Historical Review*, 86.
Mann, M. 1986 *The Sources of Social Power. Vol. I: A History of Power from the Beginning to 1760 A.D.* (Cambridge: Cambridge University Press).
Mann, M. 1993 *The Sources of Social Power. Vol. II: The Rise of Classes and Nation-States, 1760–1914* (Cambridge: Cambridge University Press).
Mommsen, W.J. 1990 'The varieties of the nation state in modern history: Liberal, Imperialist, Fascist and Contemporary notions of nation and nationality', in M. Mann (ed.), *The Rise and Decline of the Nation State* (Oxford: Blackwell).
Mühlberger, D. 1987 *The Social Basis of European Fascist Movements* (London: Croom Helm).
Newman, G. 1987 *The Rise of English Nationalism* (New York: St Martins Press).
Segeburg, H. 1988 'Germany', in O. Dann and J. Dinwiddy (eds), *Nationalism in the Age of the French Revolution* (London: The Hambledon Press).
Sked, A. 1989 *The Decline and Fall of the Habsburg Empire 1815–1918* (London: Edward Arnold).
Smith, A.D. 1986 *The Ethnic Origins of Nations* (Oxford: Blackwell).
Sugar, P.F. 1969 'External and domestic roots of Eastern European Nationalism', in P.F. Sugar and I.J. Lederer (eds), *Nationalism in Eastern Europe* (Seattle: University of Washington Press).
Watkins, S.C. 1991 *From Provinces into Nations: Demographic Integration in Western Europe, 1870–1960* (Princeton, NJ: Princeton University Press).

5

National Self-Determination from a Historical Perspective

Miroslav Hroch

Since the 'ghost of communism' disappeared, the West seems to have been facing a new one: the ghost of nationalism and self-determination. Is it only a ghost or does it represent a real danger? This contribution does not pretend to answer this particular question. Historians have to explain, not to denounce or to pass judgments. As an object of scholarly analysis, self-determination is neither 'good' nor 'bad': it has to be understood as a specific type of social and political claim. This claim results from the following model: subject A feels in a subordinate position regarding subject B and tries to abolish this subordination. This call for self-determination is, in fact, a call 'from below', and, as usual, it is uncomfortable for those 'above' – that is, for those in power. By rejecting claims from below as 'nationalist', a priori, we would be taking up a position from above.

Self-determination was not 'invented' by Lenin or Wilson, as some trivializing journalists say, even if the term itself became customary after the October revolution. Self-determination (and the claims for it), as a political activity and, ultimately, as a historical change, is the final stage of a historical process and of a specific kind of political or social movement which has its roots in the nineteenth century.

To call these movements 'nationalist' is to simplify a complex problem, as well as to create misunderstandings. By nationalism *strictu senso*, I understand something else: that state of mind which gives an absolute priority to the values of one's own nation over and above all other values and group interests. For this reason, I find it preferable to call such activities national movements and to define them as organized efforts to achieve all the attributes of a fully fledged nation. National movements, as a concrete activity performed by concrete individuals, constitute a more appropriate object of research than the vague locution 'nationalism'. Nationalism, defined as a state of mind, was naturally present in national movements, but only as one of the many forms of national and regional identities to emerge in the course of these movements. What about the place taken by national movements in space and time?

My point of departure is a very empirical observation: from the Middle Ages, as a result of a long development, there existed at the threshold of emerging modern society seven established nation-states in Europe – England, France, Spain, Sweden, Denmark, Portugal and the Netherlands – all of them having their 'own' state, ruled by ethnically homogeneous elites (including the aristocracy and the emerging industrial and commercial bourgeoisie) and having a highly developed national culture and literary language. We can also observe two emerging nations having a developed culture and an ethnically homogeneous elite but without having formed a nation-state: the Germans and the Italians.

At the same time (that is, around the year 1800), we find more than twenty 'non-dominant ethnic groups', spread across all the territory of the European continent including the territory of some of the nation-states mentioned above. In other words, 'exogenous' ruling classes dominated ethnic groups which usually occupied a compact territory but lacked their 'own' (that is, belonging to their own ethnic group) ruling class and continuous cultural tradition in their own literary language. (Indeed, sometimes such a literary language did not even exist.)

Sooner or later, some members of the non-dominant ethnic group started to focus on their own ethnicity and to conceive of their group as a potential nation. They compared their situation with that of fully established nations, and formulated their goals. These goals were rather different in a variety of cases and they gradually changed: nevertheless, we can distinguish three groups of demands, corresponding to the three main aspects of national existence:

1. The development or improvement of national culture based on a local language which had to be used in education, administration and economic life.
2. The creation of a complete social structure, including their 'own' educated elites and entrepreneurial classes.

3. The achievement of equal civil rights and of some degree of political self-administration.

The relative priority and timing of each of these sets of demands varied and we can use them as suitable criteria for a typological differentiation of national movements.

This contribution is, however, focused upon only one group of national demands: the political ones. It was at this level that the demand for self-determination emerged. It must be stressed at the outset of this discussion that the demand for self-determination, for full independence, emerged at a very late stage in most European national movements.

For greater clarity, I would add two further introductory remarks. First, between the starting point of any given national movement and its successful conclusion (the achievement of all attributes of a fully formed nation), three structural phases have to be distinguished. During the initial period, Phase A, activists devoted themselves to scholarly inquiry into the linguistic, historical and cultural attributes of their ethnic group. But in all cases they were far from having any political goals. In Phase B, a new range of patriots emerged who sought to win over as many of their ethnic group as possible to the project of creating a future nation. Once the decisive part of all strata of the population shared their national identity as a specific value, a mass movement was formed, a stage which I have termed Phase C.

Secondly, although this chapter is specifically concerned with the development of the nation-subject in the central and eastern part of Europe, we must not forget that national movements also emerged in Western Europe. Yet I must stress one crucial typological difference: 'Western' national movements were characterized by having started Phase B under the conditions of a constitutional regime as well as under the conditions of a civil society, while the comparable Phase B of 'Eastern' national movements proceeded within the context of late-absolutist feudal regimes in the Habsburg empire, the Ottoman empire, Tsarist Russia, Prussia and Denmark. In the following analysis, the term 'Eastern' implies, not only geographical, but above all typological characteristics.

How strong were the political demands represented in different national programmes? Observing their participation in Phase B, we can distinguish two categories of national movements:

1. National movements where the political demands dominated their Phase B, accompanied by sometimes weaker, or later formulated,

linguistic and social demands. This was the case for the Polish, Norwegian, Serbian and Greek national movements in the 'East', and for the Irish and Scottish national movements in the 'West'.
2. Not only in the East, but also in the West European national movements, linguistic and cultural demands dominated during Phase B, usually followed by political demands but not before the transition to the mass movement in Phase C was achieved. This was the case for the majority of national movements. Nevertheless, the timing of the emergence of the political programmes was very different.

The structure of national programmes and their results were not exclusively decided by the individual wishes and demands of the leading patriots: some objective and specific circumstances have to be taken into account, which can be categorized in three groups:

- the political system under which the national movement proceeded during Phase B and Phase C;
- the social structure of the non-dominant ethnic group;
- previous developments: the history of this specific group.

How important was the political regime in the given state? Concerning Phase B, it is not enough to say that it was a late-absolutist regime. We have to distinguish between, on the one hand, the 'legalist' system of the Habsburg empire, where the ruling elites camouflaged their dominance by historical claims and contracts concluded between Habsburgs and the representatives of non-dominant ethnic groups, and, on the other hand, the Ottoman rule based on unconcealed and repeatedly demonstrated conquest and force. Although not as brutal, the practice of Russian rule was similar. While the political opposition in Phase C could find and use 'lawful' arguments against the Austrian ruling elite, in the Ottoman and Russian empires, any political opposition was a priori illegal. In entering the field of politics, national movements had to take into account that they would be confronted with persecution.

The social structure of the non-dominant ethnic groups at the eve of the modern age was very different. Some of them – Magyars, Poles, Norwegians and Greeks – were societies with an almost complete social structure corresponding to the stage of economic development of their given territory. The remaining majority lacked some important classes and groups, above all the higher ones. In some extreme cases, the non-dominant ethnic group consisted only of a rural peasant population (Lithuanians, Estonians, Slovenes and Belorussians).

Even though political demands emerged during the decisive modern stage of the nation-forming process, we also have to take into account previous developments. From this point of view, the consequences of these developments were rather different, in both their juridical and political aspects. Three main situations can be distinguished.

Firstly, where the non-dominant ethnic group lived under the conditions of its former independent medieval state, it could look to a past when it had its 'own' ruling class and its own national culture. This statehood was nevertheless weakened and suppressed during the early modern period through conquest or forced contracts. Certain institutions remained and a certain memory survived: strong ones in the case of Poles and Magyars, weaker in the case of Norwegians, Czechs and Croatians. A special case is that of Finland, which was given an autonomous status as a land after the Russian conquest of 1809.

Secondly, where the non-dominant ethnic group had once possessed a medieval state but this state had been destroyed and survived not in institutions or 'rights' but only in memory, this memory could be resuscitated as a political argument. This situation was the case for Greeks, Serbs, Bulgarians, Lithuanians and Ukrainians, and has its parallels in Western Europe (Catalans, Basques, the Flemish and the Welsh).

Thirdly, there were instances where the non-dominant ethnic group had never achieved the level of statehood and the tradition of a written language was also very weak. This was the case for Estonians, Latvians, Slovenes, Slovaks, Belorussians and, with the abovementioned reservation, also the Finns.

Naturally, we must first ask how relevant these differences were to the nation-formation process and whether we can combine all three objective conditions (political system, social structure, and history) to explain the difference in the strength of the political programme.

What we usually call the political programme of national movements was by no means a stable or homogeneous set of demands. As such, these variable demands cannot be reduced merely to the plea for self-determination. The demands differed in their relevance, intensity and structure. Without pretending to put forward a general political theory, I distinguish on the basis of empirical observation three levels or stages of national political programmes, which could be simply described by the following terms: substitution, participation and secession. Even though these levels or stages were not isolated in the everyday reality of national movements, it is convenient to analyse them separately.

Substitution. The elementary level of political programmes could be observed where only partial elements of politics entered into the national programme, thus forming the basic precondition for the two higher levels of demands. Among such elements, the most important ones were: the attempt to keep the unity or cohesion of the ethnic territory, and to step over political borders where members of non-dominant ethnic groups lived in the territory of two or even more political and administrative units. The formation of the image of the 'fatherland' as a psycho-geographical fact was part of the first steps of national agitation.

Linguistic and cultural demands temporarily substituted some functions of political aims, especially where an oppressive regime did not allow political activities: until the 1850s in Austria, until 1905 in Russia. A further form of substitution was included in the emerging historical consciousness rediscovering and remembering the glorious past. Patriotic agitators stimulated yearnings, sometimes nostalgic, sometimes militant, for some kind of restoration of old political institutions.

Participation. National participation was often discussed as far back as under the conditions of the old regime, and its first claim was almost everywhere directed towards participation in local (municipal) administration. These demands corresponded not only to political possibilities and opportunities but also to given social structures. Where members of non-dominant ethnic groups also lived in towns, as in Bohemia or in Hungary, for example, or had the opportunity to immigrate to the towns, as in the Baltics, Finland and in the western part of Ukraine, the idea of participation in municipal self-government grew stronger. The struggle for positions in the town hall was usually the first political experience of national movements. Connected to this was the struggle for positions in the municipal or local administration. The demand for participation in the territorial assemblies of representatives was naturally conditioned by the existence, or non-existence, of such assemblies within the given territory, and by the degree of civil rights given to the population by the ruling nation. Only in Hungary could the demand for political participation be used under the old regime in some continuity with the political demands of the old estates. Everywhere else, the struggle for participation emerged with the introduction of a constitutional regime: in Austria after 1860, in Russia in 1905. In the

Austrian case, the struggle was directed to two levels of representation – Reichsrat and Landtag. In Russia, only the central assembly was offered.

Where the national movement could count on the majority of the population in a given territorial (administrative) unit, the first goal of the struggle was to achieve a majority of national representatives in the Diet. This was, nevertheless, complicated by the fact that the elites of the ruling nation were over-represented there. The national movements, concerned with inequality (Czechs, Slovenes and Ukrainians) responded to their under-representation by demanding a reform of electoral laws: democracy entered into their political programmes.

The probability of getting some influence through participation in the central parliament (Reichstag, duma, Reichsrat, etc.) was near zero. In Russia the influence of small nations was made minimal in advance by their inferiority in numbers. In Hungary, the participation of non-Magyars was limited by the unproportional allocations of seats to them. Only in Cisleithania-Austria were some chances for participation offered to Poles and Czechs because of their numbers.

National leaders also tried other ways to advance the interests of their nation. The demand for representation in central offices, ministries and the like was part of the national programme, even if sometimes these demands were not publicly articulated. Successful advancement into the ranks of state elites offered not only more prestige for national movements but also an opportunity to present their demands more effectively.

Similarly, the struggle for participation was not an end in itself. Participation enabled activists to push forward national demands concerning language, culture and social goals. Linguistic demands became a part of the political struggle: high schools with the local language of instruction, full linguistic equality in administration, in courts of justice and in economic life – all this now depended on the ability of national representatives to persuade the competent institution in which they participated. The same went for social demands, such as improving the social status of the new middle classes, developing the just distribution of taxation, participating in decisions on public expenses, subventions, technical innovations etc. Naturally, even the central focus of some national movements – how to achieve the full social structure – became a matter of politics.

To summarize in general terms, the struggle for political participation included four groups of demands: municipal self-government, entry into all levels of state and regional administration, participation in legislative power including courts of justice, and participation in executive power.

Secession. Participation, even if successfully gained, represented, however, only one part of the political programme. Having no possibility to influence the central decisions through participation, national leaders tried to minimize the power of the centre and to get more space for independent decisions. The only possible way seemed to be to enhance the shared national identity through greater autonomy within 'their' territory.

On the level of theoretical consideration, the demand for autonomy appeared in parallel with the struggle for participation in legislative and executive power, or even before it. As a reality, autonomy was usually achieved later, after participation had been established. The idea of autonomy was accepted as the basis for the programme of 'Austro-Slavism' in 1848: according to it, the whole monarchy had to be reconstructed and divided into autonomous territories delimited by their ethnicity. This programme failed, as well as all later demands that were based on traditional historical territories.

The strongest tradition of territorial autonomy was kept in Hungary and related to the former medieval state. It is no wonder that the Magyar national movement, after having been temporarily defeated in the revolution of 1848–9, achieved full political autonomy through the installation of Austro-Hungarian dualism in 1867. The Polish calls for autonomy in Austrian Galicia were also partially successful. On the other hand, Czech and Croatian demands for more political autonomy, which also were based upon the memory of a medieval state, remained limited to the traditional institution of the Landtag, which was only provided with rather small competencies. This example illustrates the existence of a remarkable coincidence between the programme of political autonomy and the results of the first stage of the nation-forming process during the Middle Ages. All 'autonomist' national movements in the Habsburg empire occurred upon the territory of 'their' medieval state, and the territory that was claimed was defined by its historical border. The Habsburg monarchy was not an exception. The Serbian struggle for autonomy and consequently for independence, similar to the Lithuanian programme of autonomy from 1905 (and to the Finnish and Ukrainian ones, etc.) was also based upon the image of a historical national territory. However, in this case the border was not at all exact, in contrast to the case of the Habsburg empire.

Until the Second World War, both in Austro-Hungary and in Russia, the demand for autonomy remained the central point of the secessionist component in the programme of national movements. With the exception of the Magyars, whose national movement successfully ended by achieving a semi-state status, no relevant political group demanded full independence, and even in the Polish camp, autonomy seems to have been – after the defeat of the revolutions of 1848 and 1863–4 – the main goal. In Russia, only the Finnish national movement achieved some kind of autonomy, substituting an originally regional autonomy with a national one. Among other national movements, only in the Lithuanian case do we find a rather isolated voice demanding independence during the revolutionary year of 1905.

These dates demonstrate that all theories of 'nationalism' which define national goals as the struggle for independence, do not correspond to empirical facts. As products of ignorance and unacceptable simplification, they cannot be treated seriously.

Nevertheless, there have been some cases where the course of national movements seems to have corresponded to the concept of state-related nationalism. It is that minority of national movements in which the political programme became a central goal of the movement only during Phase B. This group includes national movements in the Balkans and Norway. The results were different: only the Greeks achieved full independence immediately, while the other movements – the Norwegian, Bulgarian, Serbian and Romanian ones – had to accept autonomy for some decades. These five cases do not offer a sufficient basis for generalization, only a partial one concerning the specificity of the nation-forming process in the Balkans. This specificity will be interpreted in the concluding part of this discussion.

National movements are sometimes reproached for having given higher priority to national goals than to civil rights. It is difficult to accept such a reproach, based as it is more upon moralistic prejudices than upon facts. All 'Eastern' national movements are, as explained above, typologically defined by the fact that their Phase B proceeded under the conditions of the old regime – that is, they were in progress synchronically with the emerging civic opposition against the regime. Naturally, under such conditions, both the linguistic and social programmes of national movements also included demands for the equality of all inhabitants, but they usually did not explicitly include civil rights. Opposing old state-elites, the leaders of national movements also opposed the old absolutist system, even if they did not – sometimes for opportunist reasons – verbalize this opposition. Also, in this respect, the linguistic and social programmes temporarily played a substitutional role for the political programme: as an opposition against the old regime.

This relation changed as a result of the emerging political programme during the bourgeois revolutions – 1848 in Central Europe, 1905 in Russia. The national leaders, formulating political demands for participation, or even autonomy, asked at the same time for constitutional and civil rights. However, their position became complicated by the fact that the liberal party of the ruling nation-state in Austria, and the democrats and socialists in Russia also fought for the same goal. Insofar as their constitutional concept did not include equality for non-dominant ethnic groups, the liberal/democratic struggle partially clashed with that of national movements. These conflicts proceeded as a clash between two options, two competing ways towards modernization: as such, it is not fair to accuse all participants in national movements of being 'counter-revolutionaries'. The conservative faction was, in fact, strong only in the Slovenian and Croatian national movements, but there were also specific liberal factions within these movements.

The Balkans also present some specificity in this respect. The demands for autonomy and for independence were usually so strong that they overshadowed any strategies concerning the political system that might be gained. The Greeks very soon considered the constitution as an important task, while in the Serbian, Romanian, and later also Macedonian and Albanian movements, this problem was not discussed before political success was achieved. There might be some parallel in the fact that the ruling elites in the Ottoman empire did not develop any relevant liberal programme during the nineteenth century.

The differentiation of political programmes which occurred everywhere where the transition to Phase C succeeded – in Russia naturally with limited publicity – started usually as a differentiation between national radicals, who inclined more to democratism, and national conservatives, who remained in a conservative-liberal position. Even if the dynamics of power between these two camps were, at the beginning (especially if it occurred during Phase B), usually in favour of conservatives, the power relation changed almost everywhere in favour of democracy. This trend was especially strong in those national movements where the only way towards participation for the non-dominant ethnic group was to give political rights to lower social classes – that is, to support the concept of democracy. It can generally be said that the way towards the democratic programme was easier in the case of non-dominant groups with an uncompleted social structure; while those national movements under the control of quickly emerging national ruling classes (Magyars, Poles and Greeks) inclined towards a marginalization of democracy.

Finally, it is necessary to stress the fact that the majority of national movements in Central and Eastern Europe achieved at least an independent status, even though this goal was not included in their national programme, which preferred less ambitious goals. The key turning point came from external factors: as the results of the First World War and the October revolution. Even at the beginning of the war, only a few politicians aimed towards the independence of their nation. The breakdown of the Tsarist system in Russia, and later the break-up of Germany and Austria-Hungary, opened the door to statehood even in such areas as the Baltic, where independence became by a coincidence of events the only alternative to communism.

Nevertheless, once achieved, independence was generally accepted and celebrated as a positive turn and as a positive milestone in national history. It is surprising – and requires explanation – how quickly the idea of national independence was accepted by the masses as self-evident. Since this time, the idea of the right to self-determination also became self-evident to a substantial segment of the population in those national movements that still had not achieved full independence, such as the Slovak, Croatian and Ukrainian movements.

From this point of view, we have to observe the fact that the population of all newly independent states accepted the loss of their independence during the period of 1939–48 as a collective humiliation and tragedy, without regard to the character of political oppression. By the time of the next suitable occasion, when new national movements emerged in the time of 'perestroika' (and even earlier), the notion of an independent state was included in national demands everywhere: this consensus across all borders is, perhaps, the main difference between the new and 'classical' national movements.

Even though the pre-history and the course of national movements differed distinctively, their outcome was in almost all cases surprisingly identical: sooner or later, they achieved political independence (as full statehood or as part of a federation) based on the call for self-determination. Trying to explain these transformations from the initial status of a non-dominant ethnic group, through national movements, up to the nation-state, we might quote classics like Hans Kohn: 'Every people awakened to nationalism sees political self-determination as its goal', presupposing that this 'awakening to nationalism' corresponds to the later part of Phase C. This would, however, be a vague observation, as he is at this point unable to explain: (a) why people successfully 'awaken' to nationalism; (b) where and why there existed a coincidence between Phase C and the call for self-determination; and (c) why national movements differed so very much in their timing and in the structure of their programmes.

My concluding remarks will take into account three groups of objective circumstances which were described in the introductory part: (1) the political, economic and social situation in multinational empires and the changes therein; (2) the social settings of national movements; and (3) historical developments previous to the national movement, including 'memory', traditions, institutions.

Political, economic and social conditions in the empires. To what degree did the emergence of political demands in national movements depend on the general political and social conditions in the given empire? Naturally, it was easier to formulate political demands under a constitutional regime, such as that of the Habsburg monarchy after 1860, than under an oppressive regime such as those of the Russian or Ottoman empires, but there existed no complete correspondence. Even under oppressive conditions in Russia and pre-constitutional Prussia, the Polish national movement declared its political goals including independence, as did the Magyar national movement before 1860. On the other hand, the Slovenes and Ukrainians in Galicia needed a long time to formulate a political programme, even under a constitutional Austrian regime. The extremely oppressive Ottoman empire could not keep Serbs, Greeks and later also Bulgarians away from political activities.

We could ask to what extent political oppression provoked political activities on the side of national movements. The political oppression of non-dominant ethnic groups also existed, however, in earlier times and it became nationally relevant whenever the oppressed population (or its educated part) was able to 'translate' this oppression into national terms and formulate answers in political terms. This 'ability' did not depend upon the political regime, but has to be explained by other factors.

Before we characterize these factors, we have to consider the role of unequal economic development inside the multi-ethnic empires. The difference between an internal core and a periphery, which could be found in each empire, significantly influenced the structure of social demands and could probably be taken into account as a factor of political mobilization. Unfortunately, up-to-date comparative research does not offer a satisfying amount of empirical data to answer, for example, the question of how far the political programmes of national movements at the internal core of the territory of an empire differed from those on its periphery.

The social settings of national movements. Observing the social structure of non-dominant ethnic groups during Phase A and Phase B of national movements, we can distinguish two different types:

1. National movements based upon an almost complete social structure. Thus we find among their participants members of the ruling classes as well: landlords and nobility in the Polish or Magyar national movements, entrepreneurs and members of the high bureaucracy in the Greek and Norwegian national movements, leaders of local administration and merchants in the Serbian national movement.
2. National movements without such a complete social structure, representing non-dominant ethnic groups limited sometimes to the rural population (Estonians, Lithuanians, Ukrainians and Slovenes), or also with the urban lower-middle classes (Czechs, Slovaks, Latvians and Finns).

If we compare the social composition of these two groups with the two types of national movements that we distinguished in our introduction, depending on their participation in political programmes, we observe a convincing coincidence. National movements with a full social structure (that is, with their 'own' national ruling classes), prioritized political demands only in Phase B, while national movements without a complete social structure preferred linguistic, cultural and social demands during Phase B and elaborated their political programme later, during Phase C. This comparison allows us to conclude that the social structure of non-dominant ethnic groups was a factor which decisively influenced the structure of national programmes.

This generalization seems to be confirmed by another set of empirical data concerning the development of Phase C. National movements belonging to the second group did not develop the secessionist level of political programme until the social structure of their nation was completed by an emerging bourgeoisie and a high bureaucracy.

Naturally, at this point one should ask why national movements with uncompleted social structures (which was the distinctively more frequent case) preferred the linguistic programme, but the limited length of this chapter does not allow us to answer this question.

Prior historical developments. What about the role of traditions? Nation-formation was a historical process and national identity was always accompanied by some elements of historical 'memory'. The development of political demands, their timing, and internal structure partially depended upon the previous development of the non-dominant ethnic group since the Middle Ages. It was an advantage if the national movement could present its demands for participation or for autonomy as a continuation or reconstruction of an old but partially oppressed statehood, as was the case for the Poles, Magyars, Czechs, Norwegians and Croatians. Sooner or later, these movements argued for their 'historical right' which had been violated by the ruling nation-state.

Even in those cases where the medieval state had been totally destroyed and the reality or function of statehood interrupted for some centuries, national movements were able to regenerate their historical consciousness and to formulate their political goals with references to their original statehood – naturally with strong mythological elements. We find such attitudes both in the case of national movements with completed social structure (Greeks and Serbs), and in the case of those with uncompleted ones (Ukrainians, Lithuanians and Bulgarians).

During Phase C, the programme of historical rights aimed towards the autonomous status of a national territory limited by historical borders. These historical borders were, however, never fully identical with ethnic ones: the territory claimed by historical right always included more or less numerous minorities. This was the main reason for some kind of continuity of national and nationalist conflicts, even though the secessionist demands of national movements were fulfilled.

The situation of 'nations without history' was in this respect different. Their national movements could not use arguments based upon their own political tradition and this probably contributed to the belated formulation of political programmes, especially at the secessionist level. Until the First World War, the call for self-determination was, in Slovene, Slovak, Estonian, Latvian and Belorussian eyes, irrelevant.

CONCLUDING REMARKS

Concluding these observations, we can put forward two general theses:

1. The strength and timing of the call for self-determination did not depend upon the intensity of political oppression and had no correlation with the level of linguistic and cultural demands.
2. Self-determination became stronger and more successful in national movements which were based on a complete social structure of their non-dominant ethnic group and which could use some institutions or traditions of their statehood from the past. If these two conditions coincided, the call for self-determination and statehood was developed and accepted even during Phase B, as it was for Poles, Magyars and Norwegians.

Up to now, one important factor of national integration has remained unnoticed: the nationally relevant conflict of interests. Even if this factor predominantly belongs to the social sphere, it has also to be taken into account in connection with political programmes, at least in one specific respect: as a conflict resulting from claims for political power.

National movements sooner or later included two anthropological constants: the need to identify with a group and the need for power. This conjunction was not limited to national movements: it can also be observed in the formation-process of nation-states. In the case of national movements, it had some specific features.

Insofar as a national movement focused its programme upon linguistic, cultural and social demands, the power aspirations of its leaders were limited to influence and authority: that is, they expected more prestige than power. Another specific feature has to do with the fact that national movements occurred under conditions of some kind of 'cultural autocephalism': deciding the norms of literary language and the ways of its intellectualization, the national leaders enjoyed an unlimited authority without having to submit to the authorities of a nation-state. For similar reasons, when identifying with the ethnically defined nation-to-be, national leaders resigned themselves to a struggle for political power at the state level, where it was monopolized by the members of the ruling nation. Their demands for the introduction of their language into schools and administration remained up to a certain point without political relevance, because the relation between the state elites and the leaders of the national movement was not a competitive but a hierarchical one.

However, this hierarchical relationship changed at a certain point: this occurred when the national leaders formulated their programme of political participation, which, as we know, also adopted and integrated linguistic, cultural and social demands. Let us stress again that the timing of this turn was conditioned by the introduction of constitutional regimes and by the completion of the social structure of the non-dominant ethnic group on its way to becoming a fully formed nation.

The relation between the completed social structure and the political programme of a national movement was not accidental and can be explained when we put it into the coordinates of power-competition. The members of the ruling classes – landlords, high civil servants and rich entrepreneurs – acquired, even under the old regime, some experience in the struggle for power. They were then able to 'translate' their group interests into the language of political power, and some of them – in Poland and in Hungary – still kept up the old tradition of the estates as political 'nations'. As long as they participated in Phase B, they brought these experiences with them and formulated their interests in political terms as in national ones.

In both types of development, the struggle for participation integrated national leaders into the sphere of power competition. In so doing, national leaders came to identify their interests with those of the national group: this 'service conception' of power acquired a national colour. The competition for political power was motivated by the intention to ameliorate and to improve the position of their nation, to decide their national fate. In the case of earlier completed social structure, this understanding of power (viewed as a duty or service) accentuated above all the group interests of the ruling elites. The leaders related the service conception of power primarily to their own class and verbalized its interests as national ones. This attitude strengthened the radicalism of their political demands, as can be observed in the Magyar, Polish and Greek cases.

Both forms of the struggle for political participation – the earlier (Phase B) and the belated (Phase C) – nevertheless had one thing in common: national leaders were not allowed to compete under equal conditions, because they were in the position of a non-dominant ethnic group. Being a minority, they could never achieve decisive power positions through participation even if they mobilized the majority of their own national group. Under the political conditions of a constitutional regime, they were allowed to publish their demands and to discuss their claims, but the realization of these claims did not depend upon participation. Their position always remained subservient to the numerically stronger representation of the ruling nation.

Autonomy seemed the only way out from this frustrating situation: in a territory, defined as 'national', leaders would be protected, to some degree, against state power. In those cases where the national movements achieved an autonomous status, a new power-mechanism started to work. The 'service definition' of power weakened, while the concept of political power was related to parties and individuals. Political differentiation occurred sooner or later in every national movement during Phase C and was accompanied by internal struggles for political power. However, all participants in this internal political dispute accepted one specific rule of the game, as a relict of the service concept of power: they stressed the priority of national demands over all other group interests (though their interpretation of national interests could differ), because they observed their nation as still being threatened by a common enemy – the ruling nation.

This argument became one of the stereotypes of national movements and also entered into the emerging phraseology of nationalism, but it was not unfounded. Some degree of inequality remained even under conditions of autonomy: the power of national leaders was limited to decisions taken at the national territory level, while more important decisions were made at the level of state institutions where the ruling nation kept its dominance. This phenomenon of domination could not be eliminated by autonomy.

Things having developed in this direction, a new attitude towards the ruling nation emerged: the search to legitimize the right for self-determination. The dominating institutionalized power of state elites was respected more as a power based upon force, rather than as a legitimate power based upon authority. Up to the time when the multi-ethnic empire seemed strong enough to suppress all secessionist movements by force, relations towards this empire remained apparently loyal. Almost all leaders of national movements, even though they did not give up their struggle for political power, were so accustomed to this stabilized relation of inequality that the idea of independence was probably beyond their imagination. As we know, only in relation to the Ottoman empire was the attitude of leaders different: here they tried immediately to achieve full independence.

The sudden collapse of the remaining three empires called the latent idea of self-determination into being. Loyalists could, under these changed conditions, become radical secessionists overnight, because the eventuality of secession (even if not necessarily in the form of an independent state) was kept in their political expectations, since the social structure of the nation was completed and since the autonomist demands had become a part of their political programme. Nevertheless, the role of individual decisions, based upon the protection of individual and group interests, could influence and differentiate the final outcome of this struggle.

To complete our picture, it is necessary to add that some national movements did not achieve full independence and in some case they did not demand it: Slovenes, Slovaks, Croatians, Ukrainians, Macedonians and Belorussians. However, their national movements continued – though with different intensity – and followed analogous patterns with the final effect of achieving full independence seven decades later.

Standing face to face with the fact that all 'Eastern' national movements at least achieved their statehood, it would be a wrong perspective to condemn them and the contemporary development towards self-determination as 'anachronistic' or anti-democratic. We ought indeed to criticize and to refuse nationalism as a way of thinking, and force as a method of struggle for power and for 'national interests', but we have to accept the fact that current national movements, based upon conflicts and tensions similar to the 'classical' ones, regard the right for self-determination as the only just solution to their problems, even if it were to produce new tensions and injustice.

6

Origins of the Constructivist Theory of the Nation

Nicholas Stargardt

Many people expected the fall of the Romanovs to herald the break-up of the Russian empire, just as the fall of the Habsburgs in November 1918 did in fact mark the collapse of Austria-Hungary.[1] But the successors to the Romanovs reconstituted their far-flung territories under the ideological fiction of founding a multinational federal state. The Bolsheviks were neither the progenitors of this constitutional concept, nor in the pre-revolutionary period had they been at all well disposed towards it. The multinational state and such associated principles as cultural autonomy and federalism were ideas particularly strongly if also unsuccessfully championed by Austrian Social Democrats. To be sure, they too had no monopoly over them. In the mid-1880s, the Ukrainian federalist M.P. Dragomanov started to draw up blueprints for reforming the tsarist empire, which he hoped would contain irredentist nationalism. Max Weber enthusiastically discovered his writings in 1906.[2] But the Austrian Social Democrats stood out in Central Europe at the turn of the century for the tenacity and rigorous consistency with which they advanced the federalist cause. It is their programme and theoretical ideas that this chapter seeks to excavate.

The Austrian Social Democrats started from the assumption that the population of Central and Eastern Europe was – to borrow from the vocabulary of ethnic nationalism – too 'mixed' to allow for the formation of independent nation-states without great violence and injustice. As one of the most outstanding writers on the subject put it in 1908:

> Those can only practise self-determination who form a 'self', a homogeneous entity. Otherwise, self-determination turns into its opposite, into the domination of the one over the other, autonomy turns into heteronomy, self-rule into rule over foreigners, social welfare into political war.[3]

The polarization and violence that marked out the travails of the 'successor states' established at Brest-Litovsk, St Germain and Versailles amply and tragically bore out this clinical diagnosis. Even in the doldrums of the early 1980s, the Czech Socialist Republic was still officially sterilizing gypsies, and this in a country which had gone through the Nazi extermination of European Jews and gypsies and the postwar expulsion of the German population.[4] And these questions are with us again. There are still large Magyar minorities in Romania and Slovakia. If Hungarian politicians have so far eschewed this potential source of populist legitimacy, that may be because they do not have to look far down the Danube to see the terrible costs incurred by nationalist conflicts which spiral out of control.

When the Soviet Union broke up, the fifteen constituent republics into which it split coincided only very loosely with prevailing 'ethnic' notions of fifteen nations. More than 30% of the populations of Estonia, Latvia, Moldavia, Georgia, Uzbekistan, Turkmenistan and Kirgizia were non-nationals according to the 1979 census. Kazakhs represented a mere 36% of the inhabitants of their own republic.[5] At his most extreme, Stalin had ordered the mass deportation of Chechens, Balkars, Tatars, Ingush people, Kalmyks, Karachais and Volga Germans. But well before the Second World War the borders of the Soviet Republics had often been gerrymandered in order to prevent ethnic homogeneity; some of the most notorious examples were in the Caucasus. Postwar trends of regional migration exacerbated this dispersal of populations and cultures.

Non-Russian Soviet citizens, however, only enjoyed the right to education and services in their national language within their designated republics or autonomous cultural regions, leading scholars to talk of the 'Russification' of non-Russians residing outside their 'home' republics.[6] Whatever the 'assimilationist' and 'centralizing' intent of Soviet administrators, it is also true that they did not invent all the nationalist conflicts which have erupted subsequently, let alone those which still might. However deficient its Soviet implementation, the principle of cultural autonomy is separable from those other hallmarks of Stalinist political practice: the mass deportation of populations, forced labour and mass murder.

In the pre-1917 period the very idea of cultural autonomy and a multinational federation was anathematized by both Lenin and Stalin. A careful reading of Lenin's pronouncements on the national question reveals not only an absence of any specific theory about the nation but, until 1919, the optimistic calculation that promising the right of nations to secede in principle might prevent them from taking it up in practice.[7] It was possibly in the same spirit that Stalin, persuaded by Lenin to go to Vienna in 1912 in order to study and criticize the Austro-Marxists' federalist schemes, compared them scathingly with full-blooded nationalism:

> National autonomy presupposes the integrity of the multinational state, whereas self-determination transcends this integrity. . . . Self-determination endows a nation with sovereign rights, whereas national autonomy endows it only with 'cultural rights'.[8]

In any event what remains of interest in this polemic is not so much Stalin's own theory of the nation – if one can dignify his tract with such a status – as the fact that he later put into practice some of the central principles he rejected here, federalism and national cultural autonomy, typically without ceasing to boast the superiority of Soviet practice in holding together a multinational state over the failure of Austro-Marxism and the dismemberment of the Austro-Hungarian empire.[9]

From 1897 onwards, the 'nationalities question', as it was called, dominated Austrian politics. In the summer and autumn of 1897 a major crisis erupted. In late November, crowds blocked the Ringstrasse in Vienna for several days while inside parliament German, Czech and Polish members came to blows and had to be dragged out of the house by police. This tumult was triggered by the question of the *Amtssprache*, the official language for internal bureaucratic communication. With a centralized and quasi-absolutist form of government, appointments to the civil service and hence the language in which the civil service conducted its own internal affairs became the focus of university students' ambitions and so aroused passions among educated Czechs, which otherwise might be difficult to understand. In particular they objected to having German as the official medium for internal government decisions in Bohemia. Count Badeni, a Polish aristocrat who exhibited a devastating penchant for combining authoritarian decrees with reforming tendencies on his appointment as prime minister in 1895, had tried to meet long-standing Czech calls for equality. The previous administration had already accepted that the government should communicate to the public in both Czech and German in 1880. But Badeni's decision to recognize Czech and German as languages of equal status in the crown lands of Bohemia and Moravia stipulated further that all officials would have had to learn both languages by 1901. He immediately raised the prospect that the German stranglehold on official appointments would be broken.

The pan-Germans of the *Deutschnationaler Verein* and German Liberals were incensed at such tangible concessions to Czech nationalism and embarked on a six-month-long mass campaign in the German parts of Bohemia, promptly sparking off a counter-campaign by the Young Czech movement. Demonstrations and counter-demonstrations were held in Prague. Meanwhile, Badeni's reliance on the political support of large Conservative agrarian interests and his blatant disregard for parliamentary procedure finally alienated the other major German Austrian parties, the Christian Socials (a Catholic pro-peasant and small business party similar to but considerably more conservative than the German Centre Party) and the Social Democrats (also modelled on its German namesake). In the face of such an array of popular forces, the Emperor dismissed Badeni. He was succeeded by a series of weak ministries who also tried — especially in 1900 and 1903 under Körber and in 1909 under Bienerth — to carry through some sort of language reform. Like Badeni their proposals were blocked in parliament and the reforms failed. Like Badeni also they resorted to administrative *fiat* to continue the daily running of government.[10]

It was in this unpromising situation that popular participation and, within highly unequal forms, representation in political life began. Rapid increase in urban populations, mass circulation newsprint, the sprawling railway network and industrial development all played their part in this change, though exactly what that part was is a question I shall leave to the social historians. But it can scarcely have been accidental that nationalist politicians were most vocal in Bohemia, the industrial heartland of the empire which had been left out of the 1867 compromise between German and Magyar elites. As in Germany, so in German Austria the 1890s saw the eclipse of older patrician parties such as the Liberals by new populist ones, the pan-Germans, Christian Socials and

Social Democrats. In the Czech areas the Young Czechs replaced the 'Old' who had happily worked with Conservative regimes. After the *débâcle* of 1897, the separatist Young Czechs found a range of rival groupings flanking them on both sides, including Thomas Masaryk's Realists who stood somewhere between them and Social Democracy. Following the introduction of universal male suffrage for the Reichsrat in 1907, the Christian Socials and Social Democrats became the largest parties. But as various observers and participants noted, mass politics was nationalist politics, to the virtual exclusion of social and economic issues by any other name. Where liberal nationalists in Italy and Germany had set out to overcome particularism in order to construct a central state, in Austria integral nationalists would increasingly erode the central state in order to consummate their particularisms.

Within this constellation the Social Democratic Party enjoyed the unenvied distinction of being the only seriously supranational party. The party had been founded in the winter of 1888–9 at Hainfeld through the union of the Czech and German labour associations. Until the Badeni crisis this supranational identity had not been challenged. It is true that some of its German Austrian leaders had been strongly influenced by German nationalist ideas. Victor Adler and Engelbert Pernerstorfer had helped to draft the Linz Liberal programme of 1882, a programme which one of its other authors, Georg von Schönerer – a leader who would in his turn be feted by Hitler as the mentor of National Socialism – swiftly purloined for the pan-Germans. But those like Adler who turned towards Social Democracy were scrupulously careful to align their estimation of German *Kultur* with liberal and democratic humanist values. And it was in this spirit of liberal universalism that German Social Democratic and Marxist texts were translated into Czech in the 1890s. The vocabulary of class might yet, it was hoped, provide a supranational identity.[11]

But it was not only Social Democrats who were inventing a new rhetorical repertoire. From 1897 onwards the word 'betrayal' was also given a new political meaning: no longer the betrayal of the ruling royal house or the Austrian state, but 'betrayal of the nation'. Czech and German Social Democrats might respond to finding themselves the butt of the same barb in different tongues by coining such phrases as the 'International of the nationalists'. But the epigram did not catch on, perhaps because, like the 'International of the arms industry' and the 'International of the warmongers', the idea lacked any common core apart from mutual hostility. By the turn of the century, nationalist conflict was passing beyond high politics and the issues of the *Amtssprache* or official appointments. Indeed an ironic reversal of positions occurred here. German nationalists, who had been the most vociferous opponents of learning Czech, now began to advocate it as a means of increasing German influence in Bohemia and Moravia; in their turn some Czech groups began to think it better to deal with a unilingual administration rather than with German officials who spoke Czech as well.[12] However reluctantly, Social Democracy had to engage more positively with the 'nationalities question' itself if the basis for class politics was to be restored.[13]

One of the first victims of this increased nationalism was 'Austrian patriotism'. From at least the alliance with Germany of 1879 on, any politics which preached the virtues of centralism was listened to by Slav nationalists as a sermon in favour of German domination; to pan-Germans, on the other hand, Austria's future lay within the German Reich.[14] With only slight irony, Victor Adler could remark in 1899, 'Today we have reached the point in Austria that to say someone is a good patriot is the greatest insult.'[15] The vagaries of what he described as despotism mixed with slovenliness, equally incapable by turns of just rule and unjust repression, had left the central state suspended in a social vacuum.[16] After the division of the Empire into the Dual Monarchy in 1867, the only coherent official identity marking the Austrian lands – Cisleithania[17] – derived from the river which separated them from Hungarian territory.

Into this apparent void of state patriotism Austrian Social Democrats now found themselves being prodded. The first proposal that the party should show the splinters of German Austrian Liberalism and the regime how they could realistically and rationally reform the empire was made under the immediate impact of the Badeni crisis. Its proponent was one Ludo Moritz Hartmann, a prominent historian of medieval Italy who only joined the Social Democrats in 1901. Hartmann began to correspond with Max Weber at this time, providing an invaluable intellectual and political link which flourished during the First World War and continued through to Hartmann's appointment as the first ambassador of German Austria to Berlin in 1919. The connection with Weber is a theme to which we shall return.[18] Hartmann's Fabian predisposition towards constitutional reform was enthusiastically endorsed by the *doyen* of orthodox Marxism, Karl Kautsky, himself born into a Czech–German family in Prague and educated in Vienna during the 1870s. Writing from his vantage point in Berlin, Kautsky drew an unfortunate parallel, comparing the Austrian state's current dire need for the support of Social Democracy in order to overcome the centrifugal forces of nationalism and the services rendered to it by Radetzky in crushing the revolutions of 1848.[19] From London, Eduard Bernstein swiftly pointed out to his old friend that the Austrian nationalities issue actually had nothing to do with the final crisis of world capitalism.[20]

Within Austria, even the generally cautious Victor Adler was far more circumspect about embracing the old regime without first extracting full-scale democratic reform. The Austrian party's first and probably most logical response in 1897 was to reorganize itself on a federal basis, devolving most practical organizational questions to its national sections. At the top of the agenda of the first united Cisleithanian congress held two years later at Brno was the nationalities question.

The policy adopted at Brno in 1899 was a programme for the transformation of Austria into a 'democratic federation of nationalities'. Social Democracy demanded that 'all the autonomous territories of one nationality should combine to form a nationally homogeneous association, which should have complete self-administration in national affairs.'[21] This programme, as a number of historians have justly noted, stood in a direct line of descent from the formulations of the Kremsier Reichstag of 1848–9, as well as from the ideas of two of the main thinkers of the second half of the nineteenth century, Jan Palacky and Albert Fischof.[22] As even one of the programme's sharpest Social Democratic critics, the historian and economist Otto Bauer, conceded, the programme 'opposed the centralism of the German bourgeoisie as well as the Crown land federalism of the feudal nobility'.[23] Just what this meant we shall see in a moment.

The final statement at Brno remained intentionally vague on two topics. One was what the programme coyly called the question of a 'language of mediation' – in other words, the *Amtssprache* which had undone Badeni. Indeed some of the less sensitive German Austrian delegates could not resist pointing out to their Czech comrades that the international language of the labour movement, the class struggle and the congress itself was German.[24] The other area of vagueness concerned the spheres of competence allocated to national and federal governments. The original draft had defined national affairs as 'linguistic and cultural', a view dismissed by the Czech socialist leader Nemec as too narrow. He demanded that economic questions should also be settled on a national basis.[25] But, as we shall see, subsequent thinking on the subject by the German leaders of the party continued to concentrate on separating social and economic questions from national ones.

At Brno, only one voice was raised in favour of what would in fact become the dominant Social Democratic position over the next decade.[26] This alternative view propounded the idea that national autonomy should be organized not on the basis of 'the population living in one territory but as the sum total of individuals claiming a particular nationality'.[27] This 'personality principle', as it came to be known, was a completely novel constitutional idea and became a hallmark of Austrian Social Democracy in the 1900s; there was also nothing intrinsically socialist about it.

In fact the inventor of the 'personality principle' was a civil servant who worked in the parliamentary library and was attempting to reconcile Marxist sociology with a neo-Kantian interest in the law, and who had published several tracts on the national question under a couple of pseudonyms.[28] Through his interest in transforming and conserving the Habsburg empire in accord with his notions of universal law and democratic representation, Karl Renner quickly became one of the leading figures in Austrian Social Democracy.[29]

Renner's guiding principle was the need to separate the nation and the state. In his administrative blueprint national functions would be restricted to education and culture, while the state would deal with social and economic issues as well as joint finances, justice, defence and foreign policy. Both state and national administrations would be organized along federal lines. The state was to be decentralized into eight 'culturally mixed' but geographically and economically integral regions or *Gubernia*. National associations would be recognized as legal entities and would mirror the state administration at every level. But enrolment in their registers would be a personal choice. These separate national and state institutions would meet at the local and the federal levels. By making the local administrative unit (the *Kreis*) the most important point for the delivery of services, Renner pointed to a mechanism that would unite a 'good nine-tenths of Austria in single language' areas. In the heterogeneous remainder, a double or triple system of cultural administration would have to apply within the same *Kreis* – in Renner's example, German and Czech Budweis (now České Budějovice). In such cases state and national activities were supposed to be kept strictly apart, with the national associations restricted to cultural matters.[30] 'We must,' Renner wrote in a later work,

> draw a double network on the map. . . . We must cut across the functions of the state. We must separate national and political affairs. . . . We must organise the population twice; once along the lines of nationality, the second time in relation to the state.[31]

In some respects, Renner's proposals were not new at all, and nor were the objections to them. Recognizing that any allocation of national rights had to follow linguistic and cultural boundaries rather than the historical and dynastic lines of the old crown lands went back to the proposals Jan Palacky had put to the ill-fated Kremsier Reichstag in 1848 and 1849.[32] By contrast, other Czech and Polish nationalists had persisted in defending the integrity of the seventeen crown lands as a territorial basis from which to agitate for full national independence, a position to which Palacky himself would return in old age. Even at Kremsier it had been evident that German proposals to strengthen the *Kreise* and make them the primary unit of 'national autonomy' contained a covert centralizing intent. Much as contemporary European federalists might wish to devolve authority to the regions as a means of weakening the powers of the nation-states, so in Austria-Hungary building up the *Kreise* was seen as inherently undermining the autonomy of the crown lands.[33]

Thomas G. Masaryk, who was to found and preside over the Czech republic, shared many of the federalist ideas espoused by the Social Democrats in the period before the First World War.[34] He agreed with them in rejecting the concept of historic privileges contained in the idea of Bohemian *Staatsrecht*. Like the Social Democrats, Masaryk and his young follower, the future Czech foreign minister and president Edvard Beneš, wanted to transform Cisleithanian Austria into a multinational federation. Beneš at least also endorsed the concept of the *Kreis* as the locus to separate mixed population areas and to minimize conflict. Finally, Masaryk's Realist Party and the Social Democrats agreed on the central part to be played by democratic and social reform in revamping the central state. Where the Czech Realists disagreed fundamentally with the Social Democrats was over the replacement of territorial division on the basis of the old crown lands with Renner's 'personality principle'.[35] But even here a degree of movement is discernible. At their 1912 Congress the Realists amended their programme and adopted the 'personality principle' as a way of protecting the minority rights of Czechs living outside Bohemia, in particular the large communities in Lower Austria and Vienna.[36] But in their scheme of things this could only serve as an extra-territorial adjunct to the Bohemian crown lands, never replace them. The dividing line between the territoriality of the crown lands and the local cultural autonomy of the *Kreise* became the touchstone of the difference between what we might call federal nationalists and federal centralizers.

Neither group wanted to do away with the structure of the Austro-Hungarian empire. Indeed, Beneš explicitly rejected the old Czech separatist programme on the grounds that 'one cannot seriously think about establishing a Czech state if one third of the population of the country [that is, the Germans in Bohemia] is ready to fight against it with all means'.[37] Both groups would find themselves at the end of the First World War at the head of states whose foundation they had opposed in the prewar period. In 1918 Renner published the definitive version of his federal solution, and on 18 November 1918 by an accident of history he became the first Chancellor of German Austria, a state whose creation he had resisted up to the end.[38] In a further irony and in a still more fraught situation, he would be returned to power as the head of state of the Second Republic by the Soviet forces in 1945, presumably at the behest of his old critic on the national question, Joseph Stalin.[39] The two foreign ministers who would lobby the *entente* powers at St Germain over the fate of the Sudeten Germans during the summer of 1919 were Edvard Beneš and Otto Bauer.[40]

In rejecting Renner's 'personality principle', Masaryk and Beneš were also rejecting the narrow definition of national interests which Renner and Otto Bauer were trying to develop, in particular the separation of social and economic interests from national ones.[41] Renner and even more Bauer were perfectly aware of the role that economic interest and class formation could play in the development of nations, and equally conscious that national subjugation could prevent economic development. But they hoped that it might be possible to delimit nationalism by allocating different sorts of interests to different spheres. The metaphor which Renner used was the place of religious affiliation in a secular state, respected, tolerated and tolerant in turn because it was also stripped of non-religious authority. All of the central elements of state power, except education and cultural affairs, would remain in the hands of a democratically elected federal government.[42] If religious tolerance had only become possible in Europe once the precept of *cuius regio eius religio* had been overcome, Renner was fond of saying, then national tolerance was only to be had by separating the nation from the state.[43]

In practice, this Renner–Bauer programme received some interested attention from reform-minded civil servants in the 1900s, but it was far too democratic and socialist for the 'Greater Austrian' reformers associated with Popovici. As we have seen, it was still too centralist for even moderate nationalists; in the summer of the Badeni crisis, Karl Lueger, the leader of the Christian Socials, coined the epithet '*Die k.-k.* [imperial-royal] *Sozialdemokratie*'.[44] The Emperor finally accepted federal and democratic reform on 16 October 1918, precipitating a series of revolutionary events which led to his abdication four weeks later.[45]

The need to attenuate nationalism into cultural spheres was deeply embedded in any distinctively Social Democratic vision of Austrian politics. The party had been forced to take account of nationalism only because it had brought supranational class politics to a standstill. After Badeni, parliamentary politics had become overshadowed increasingly by what Victor Adler characterized as negative and irresponsible demagoguery. He hoped that democratic reform would reopen the possibility of responsible politics and in particular the opportunity to tackle social and economic problems without their being swamped by nationalist conflicts. As Adler wryly explained,

> We cannot fight against a class state which does not show any signs of life. ... A strange situation arises in which we are calling for a state, a living modern state, while at the same time we are perfectly aware that this will not be our state. We differ from all other countries of Europe by fighting merely for a basis on which to carry on our struggle.[46]

In this respect Adler's diagnosis of the ills of late Habsburg Austria was strikingly similar to, though also more pessimistic than, Max Weber's analysis of the shortcomings of Wilhelmine Germany. Their proffered remedies also had points of similarity: democratization and social reform.[47] Both men saw such institutional engineering as a mechanism to strengthen the loyalty of the population to the central state. Neither achieved his objectives. As Otto Bauer concluded a trifle dogmatically in the wake of the transformative experience of the First World War and the nationalist revolutions of 1918, 'Adler led the struggle for democracy in the belief that democracy could remodel the old Austria whereas in reality it had to blow it apart.'[48]

Three factors seem to have informed Social Democratic choices in favour of their particular version of federalism. These factors were class politics, the economic size of the country, and great power nationalism.

Renner recognized that economic conflicts could be 'dressed up' as national conflicts; because Germans dominated industry and Slavs agriculture, the clash of interest between them could be depicted as a national rather than an economic one. But the whole thrust of Renner's work was directed at separating them.[49] 'The content and strength of national interest', he explained in 1902,

> is not the same for all members of a nation. The national interest of the worker is entirely different from that of the small businessman, the peasant, the official and the manufacturer. What is at stake is to depict the intersection of a plurality of national and economic interests. . . . *All* co-nationals do share *specific* common interests, although this does not in the least imply that they are more important than all [their] other interests, including economic ones.[50]

As a neo-Kantian, Renner was convinced that only interests which were universally and equally shared by a community merited the coercive legal authority of the state. As a Marxist he uncritically accepted the notion that a class model of society explained the pattern of economic interests. From these two assumptions it followed that *only* common cultural matters, such as education, merited recognition as national rights.[51] Reading these texts now inevitably raises the question as to how much of Renner's thought is separable from turn of the century Marxism. I think we can distinguish between his programme and his rather positivistic class analysis. As a number of writers have argued over the last decade, class politics did not necessarily have to depend on Marxist arguments about the fundamental reality of class structures. In the rise of class-based politics the character of different states and political languages may have played greater and more direct causal roles than economic or sociological factors.[52] From this perspective, it is at least possible that had Renner's programme been carried through then it might have created the political and institutional conditions for its own social success.

Renner extended his argument about the intersection of class and national interests to justify the appropriateness of his 'personality principle' to an age of industrial capitalism. Whereas the old feudal nobility had championed the historic crown lands, and the bourgeoisie the idea of the nation-state, the working class had been forced to migrate from the land, continually disrupting pre-existing patterns of settlement in the search for work. From its point of view, territorial divisions would only break up the economic unity of regions and in any case would quickly become out of date through labour migration.[53] Beneš might retort that the national group which was most scattered through Cisleithanian Austria and which would therefore benefit most from a non-territorial federation was the Germans.[54] But as the Realists' own 1912 programme recognized, this was not the case; there were large Czech communities in Vienna and Lower Austria. As we saw, this problem was one which recurred in the Soviet Union, though without the Austro-Marxist safeguard of personal cultural rights.

Linked to this image of class interest was the question of the territorial size of a viable economy. That the Habsburg empire was functionally necessary from an economic point of view was something which Renner took for granted, rather than sought to justify at length. In his *magnum opus* of 1907, *The Nationalities Question and Social Democracy*, Otto Bauer argued the case in terms similar to those in which Rosa Luxemburg had rejected Polish independence from Russia; in a capitalist world in which free trade was giving way to protection, small states and nations would be too economically vulnerable to survive without coming under the imperialist sphere of influence of one of their large neighbours.[55] By the time Rudolf Hilferding wrote *Finance Capital* three years later, the link between the size of a state's economic territory, capitalist development and great power conflict had been firmly established in many Marxist and some liberal minds.[56] In the much altered circumstances of 1918 and 1919 Otto Bauer wielded these arguments to very different effect. Bauer was the first Social Democratic leader to recognize that the non-German parts of the Habsburg empire would settle for nothing short of full independence, and to draw the conclusion that if Austrian Germans wanted to go on being members of a large industrial state then they had to join the German Republic. But for allied objections at the St Germain Peace Conference, the *Anschluss* might have been brought about in 1919 under two Social Democratic administrations.[57]

Mild and technical discussions of economic scale all too easily shaded into highly emotional appeals to great power politics, especially in turn of the century Vienna. Here Renner's and Bauer's views diverged quite sharply. Renner was primarily committed to reforming the Habsburg empire, Bauer to creating room occupied by nationalist agitation for socialist politics. Renner attacked the *Anschluss* programme of the pan-Germans for '*deserting the position*, a national and cultural desertion of the colours'; '*whatever the cost*' German Austria had a historic mission to keep the South and East Slavs with the West 'and not to drive these peoples into the arms of all-devouring Russia'.[58] Although in other respects Bauer supported Renner's programme until 1914, he was convinced that the 1905 revolution had removed any such tsarist threat and like other left-wing Social Democrats was shocked by the outbreak of the war.[59]

Renner was not alone in sounding the clarion of Russophobia. Such a blending of anti-absolutist rhetoric with belief in the cultural superiority of Western and Central over Eastern Europe had been widespread in Liberal and Social Democratic circles in Germany for decades.[60] In particular, Renner's position here is difficult to distinguish from that of the German nationalist and left liberal Max Weber. Even after the collapse of the Habsburg empire in December 1918, Weber still thought Bismarck had been right to leave the Habsburg empire intact, thereby preserving 'an institution which sacrificed the participation of ten million Germans in the Reich in order to neutralise thirty million non-Germans politically'.[61] Two years earlier Weber had run together Renner's own central arguments when he wrote that:

> A pure separation of the nationalities of Austria-Hungary into independent nation-states is in part already impossible for geographic reasons; in part it would make economic or political nonsense of the state boundaries. Here only a federation of nationalities under a supranational state is ever possible.[62]

But what Weber did not go into at all was how such 'a federation of nationalities under a supranational state' was to be constructed. Here we may take his silence as further dependence on the ideas of the Austrian Social Democrats – with whom through Hartmann he had maintained a regular contact during the war. Both Renner and Weber had frequent recourse to the argument that only a large state could protect the rights of small nations, whilst both – inevitably – preferred to belong to a large and powerful German one.

Renner, who was after all far more concerned that small nations should actually enjoy full legal equality than Weber, also hoped that his blueprint of the multinational state might provide the principles not just for an equitable settlement in Austria but for a just and stable international order:

Nature recognizes neither the equality of individuals nor the equality of nations. Equality is a creation of law. . . . Thus, the smaller nations have every reason to abolish the inequality of their natural existence, their defencelessness and helplessness beside larger nations by joining a supranational association based on law. Such an association cannot eliminate their natural inequality, but it can guarantee their continued existence and ability to act in the world.[63]

But what did Renner think a nation was? Were nations formed through some sort of process or were they ever-present if only intermittently active? He might assert acerbically that 'ethnology and ethnography are indispensable scientific props for the nationalist politician', but he did not himself set out a different theoretical answer to these questions.[64] Like Karl Kautsky earlier and Lenin later he seems to have been content to rely on Herder's definition of the nation as a 'linguistic community' without further elaboration. It is here that Renner's younger colleague Otto Bauer went way beyond the existing range of writings on the national question. Bauer's position was much more circumspect and it coalesces with his far more ambivalent attitude towards nationalism and the future of Austria.

Where Kautsky and Lenin, rather like Marx, fairly unselfconsciously elided capitalist development and the rise of nation-states,[65] Bauer repeated the famous question of the French philosopher and historian Ernest Renan: what exactly is a nation? In 1882 Renan had cast a highly sceptical eye over the view, popular then as it is now, that nations stemmed from race, religion or language. 'How is it', he asked,

> that Switzerland which has three languages, two religions, three or four races is a nation when Tuscany, for example, which is so homogeneous is not? Why is Austria a state but not a nation?[66]

Merely by repeating Renan's question, Bauer committed himself to a similar historical answer.[67] He would argue that nations were far more contingent entities than the communities of shared culture and language to which most nationalists at the turn of the century pointed; or rather – as Bauer set out to establish at considerable length – that those very shared cultures were themselves highly contingent historically. The mere creation of the Herderian 'community of language' (*Sprachgemeinschaft* in Bauer's notation) itself depended on various 'modernizing' influences, including the breakdown of peasant subsistence farming and the drawing of isolated rural areas into regional economic relationships so that dialects became more homogeneous. Bauer posited a second stage, the creation of a 'cultural community' (*Kulturgemeinschaft*) as mediating between the advent of a linguistic community and the attainment of national identity. In this second stage, the focus was directed to the development and dispersal of 'high cultures' and with them a 'correct' or 'high' language. In a passage, which has regained a certain topicality, Bauer explained that:

> No one can doubt whether an educated person is German or Dutch, Slovene or Croatian; national education, the national language, mark off from each other even the most closely related persons. By contrast, the question as to whether the peasants of some village or other should count as low Germans or Dutch, as Slovenes or Croats, can only be decided in a somewhat arbitrary fashion.[68]

In Bauer's account these high cultures first appeared in Europe as aristocratic products. With capitalist development they were acquired, as the contemporary German expression ran, by the 'educated and propertied bourgeoisie'. Finally, following industrialization and urbanization, the struggles of the labour movement represented a bid for full entry into cultural life:

> The ruling and possessing classes alone appropriate national cultural goods. The Social Democratic Workers' Party wants to make national culture the product of the work of the whole people, the property of the whole people.[69]

Flying in the face of much contemporary Marxist talk about proletarian internationalism, Bauer insisted that socialism could only increase national differentiation because 'it will distinguish whole peoples from each other by the diversity of national education and civilisation'.[70] Behind these prophesies lurked another Kantian idea, namely that the interaction of individuals creates bonds despite their asymmetries of power and differences of interest. From Bauer's point of view, cultural communities were united by the reciprocal interaction of their heterogeneous elements, whereas social classes were supposed to be formed by homogeneous experiences such as exploitation under supposedly similar conditions of production.

But what distinguished a cultural community from a nation? For Bauer the crucial factor was sentiment, a sense of the community's own shared destiny. For this reason Bauer spoke of nations as 'communities of fate' (*Schicksalsgemeinschaft*); here he revamped the unfortunate Hegelian phrase about peoples 'with' and 'without history' in order to underline the crucial role played by the memory of past historical struggles of wars, or formerly independent states, like Poland or Bohemia, whose memory could be invoked to arouse nationalist sentiment in the present.

In this emphasis on the central role of politics and nationalist sentiment, Bauer's theory of the nation strongly prefigured that of Max Weber. Five years after *Die Nationalitätenfrage* appeared and four years after Bauer had engaged in a high-profile debate with Karl Kautsky on the subject, Weber told the German Sociologists' Conference that a nation is a 'community of sentiment, which could find its adequate expression only in a state of its own, and which thus normally strives to create one'.[71] Just as Bauer contended that 'for me, history no longer represents the struggle of nations; instead the nation itself appears as the reflection of historical struggles',[72] so Weber too discarded those theories of the nation which made the *Volk* or *Volksgeist* the starting point of history instead of acknowledging its own historicity.[73] Most strikingly of all, Bauer and Weber both reworked Ferdinand Tönnies's dichotomy between *Gemeinschaft* and *Gesellschaft* in order to illustrate their ideal type of a national community. Tönnies had used the word *Gemeinschaft* to conjure up the image of an 'organic' medieval community in which trust and solidarity were natural and immediate in order to criticize the abstract, individualist and rational world of modernity.[74] Both Bauer and Weber applied this dichotomy to modernity in order to distinguish between those social identities which were spontaneous and pre-rational, like nations, and those which individuals could choose to join or withdraw from, like the institutions of state and civil society (parties, trade unions and cooperatives). For both Bauer and Weber the problem was to show by what contingent means national identity could aspire to the non-contingent status of a *Gemeinschaft*. Again both turned to the same mechanisms: politics, and the 'cultural work' of the ruling classes and state institutions provided the means for transmitting common values and language. And both also – unlike most Marxist theorists of their generation – considered that 'with the democratization of culture belief in the exclusiveness of their language community seizes the masses as well'.[75]

As a German nationalist, Max Weber might well complete this sentence with the rider that 'national conflicts become necessarily sharper, bound up as they are with the ideal and economic interests of mass communication in the individual languages'.[76] Otto Bauer's entire strategy was dedicated to preventing this extension of nationalist bigotry and to channelling conflicts of interest into other conduits. While it is clear that these motives exercised a powerful pull on Bauer's entire theory of the nation, it is difficult to evaluate the significance of that pull. After all, Karl Renner arrived at the same political conclusions without the aid of Bauer's theory. And Max Weber, who shared much the same theoretical framework as Bauer, could use it to justify a type of German *Machtstaat* and great power politics for which Bauer had little time. The main insight which the theory seems to have given Bauer over Renner was the conviction that state forms were extremely malleable. And that insight may go a long way to explaining their opposing attitudes towards the First World War and the Austrian state.[77] Perhaps the greatest accolade to Otto Bauer's theory of the nation – as well as the hardest to accept – was that it was sophisticated enough to explain the political failure of its own practical programme. In any case it marked the beginning of a tradition of theorizing and analysis so fruitfully continued in the present.

Of the 'successor states' set up at Brest-Litovsk and Versailles, only in Latvia and Estonia was the 'personality principle' applied after 1919 to endow minorities with national rights. The very word 'multinational state' was a response to the idea of the 'nation-state'. That this response proved so inadequate may have had many causes: the long period of 'slovenly autocracy' and the lack of democratic representation at the hub of the Austro-Hungarian empire may have meant that the centrifugal forces of integral nationalisms were already unstoppable by the time these complex federalist schemes were being proposed. A less pessimistic account might set the date later and emphasize the polarizing effects of the First World War: Austrian military rule and requisitioning especially in the Slav territories; the agitation of Czech, Polish, Croat and Slovene nationalist groups abroad and their encouragement by the *entente* powers; President Wilson's Fourteen Points; the enormous impact of the Russian revolution; and finally the military collapse of the Habsburg monarchy.[78]

Behind these contextual explanations it is also clear that any of the federal solutions on offer in Central Europe, Masaryk's and Beneš's federalism let alone Karl Renner's and Bauer's, could easily have unravelled in their own complexities. It is impossible to know whether they could have been made to stick even if they could have been effected in turn of the century Austria. Part of the irony of the situation was that the very conditions which made a multinational state the only equitable solution also militated against its success. Such federalism would have required a strong, efficient and impartial federal state authority and a considerable degree of social trust. Once the moment had passed, whenever that moment was, at which such authority and such trust were to be had, then the multinational programme was doomed. Only in Russia did that moment reappear, and then in the Hobbesian aftermath of a civil war whose victors imposed a far more centralist and less sensitive and less equitable nationalities policy. One of the reasons why that moment may have been lost relatively early and casually in Central Europe is because it was apparent only to a handful of humanist-minded intellectuals how great the social and political costs would be of fulfilling nineteenth-century liberal programmes and carving out homogeneous nation-states.

NOTES

1. Paper given at the Colloquium on Nations and the End of Empires, 28 May 1993, Centre for History and Economics, King's College, Cambridge.
2. W.J. Mommsen, *Max Weber and German Politics, 1890–1920* (Chicago, 1984), pp. 56–8; D. Beetham, *Max Weber and the Theory of Modern Politics* (Cambridge, 1985), p. 130.
3. Karl Renner, 'Was sind unsere Kronländer? Ein kritischer Beitrag zur Autonomie', *Der Kampf*, Jg. 1, 1.6.1908, p. 407; cited in R.J. Hoffmann, *T.G. Masaryk und die tschechische Frage, 1, Nationale Ideologie und politische Tätigkeit bis zum Scheitern des deutsch-tschechischen Ausgleichsversuchs vom Februar 1909* (Munich, 1988), p. 428.
4. J.P. Stern, *The Heart of Europe* (Oxford, 1992), p. 225.
5. G. Smith (ed.), *The Nationalities Question in the Soviet Union* (London, 1990), appendix 2, table 3, p. 365.
6. W. Connor, *The National Question in Marxist-Leninist Theory and Strategy* (Princeton, 1984), p. 315.
7. Connor, *The National Question*, pp. 28–50. For Lenin's polemic with Rosa Luxemburg in 1913–14, see V.I. Lenin, 'The right of nations to self-determination', *Selected Works*, 1 (Moscow, 1975), pp. 567–617; R. Luxemburg, *The National Question: Selected Writings by Rosa Luxemburg*, ed. H.B. Davis (New York, 1976).
8. J.V. Stalin, *Marxism and the National and Colonial Question* (New York, n.d.), p. 31.
9. Ibid., p. 85.
10. R.A. Kann, *The Multinational Empire: Nationalism and National Reform in the Habsburg Monarchy, 1848–1918*, 1 (New York, 1950), pp. 200–6; L. Brügel, *Geschichte der österreichischen Sozialdemokratie*, 4 (Vienna, 1923), pp. 318-43; H. Mommsen, *Die Sozialdemokratie und die Nationalitätenfrage im habsburgischen Vielvölkerstaat, 1. Das Ringen um die supranationale Integration der zisleithanischen Arbeiterbewegung (1867–1907)* (Vienna, 1963), pp. 266–94. Unfortunately, Mommsen never published the promised second volume of his work, which was meant to deal expressly with the ideas of Karl Renner and Otto Bauer and cover the period 1907–18.

11. H. Mommsen, *Die Sozialdemokratie und die Nationalitätenfrage*, pp. 155–80.
12. Kann, *The Multinational Empire*, 1, pp. 408–9; one of the first advocates of this German bilingual nationalism was Bismarck.
13. See Krapka's statement on behalf of the Czech executive at the *1900 Graz Parteitag*, p. 73; H. Mommsen, *Die Sozialdemokratie und die Nationalitätenfrage*, pp. 294–7.
14. K. Reinhold, *Die österrereichische Sozialdemokratie und der Nationalismus* (Vienna, 1910).
15. *1899 Brünner Parteitag*, p. 47; H. Mommsen, *Die Sozialdemokratie und die Nationalitätenfrage*, p. 298.
16. *Protokoll des internationalen Arbeiter-Congresses zu Paris* (Nuremberg, 1890), p. 43; J. Braunthal, *History of the International, 1864–1914* (London, 1966), p. 215.
17. Derived from the German *Zisleithania*, referring to the river Leitha; the official designation of Austria eschewed no name at all and referred simply to the 'lands represented in the Reichsrat'.
18. Hartmann (pseudonym 'Verus'), 'Die Nationalitäten in Österreich und die Sozialdemokratie', *Die neue Zeit*, 15.2, 1896–7, pp. 688ff. He was also one of the founders of the *Zeitschrift für Sozial- und Wirtschaftsgeschichte*, in 1893 with Carl Grünberg and Stephan Bauer; *Neue deutsche Biographie*, 7 (Berlin, 1965), p. 737; *Österreichisches biographisches Lexikon*, 2 (Graz, 1959), pp. 195–6. For references to Weber–Hartmann correspondence, see W.J. Mommsen, *Max Weber and German Politics*, especially the notes to chapters 7 and 9.
19. K. Kautsky, 'Der Kampf der Nationen und das Staatsrecht in Österreich', *Die neue Zeit*, 16.1, 1897–8.
20. Bernstein to Kautsky, 10.10.1898, Kautsky Nachlass, D IV, F. 461, International Institute of Social History; cited in H. Mommsen, *Die Sozialdemokratie und die Nationalitätenfrage*, p. 303.
21. *1899 Parteitag Brünn*, pp. 104ff. On the Austro-Marxist discussion of the national question see H. Mommsen, *Die Sozialdemokratie und die Nationalitätenfrage*; also Brügel, *Geschichte der österreichischen Sozialdemokratie*, 4, pp. 330–43; R. Schlesinger, *Federalism in Central Europe* (London, 1945), pp. 210–47; G. Kogan, 'The Social Democrats and the conflict of nationalities in the Habsburg Monarchy', *Journal of Modern History*, 21 (3), 1949, pp. 204–17; Kann, *The Multinational Empire*, 1, pp. 103–8, and 2, pp. 154–78; K. Deutsch, *Nationalism and Social Communication: An Enquiry into the Foundations of Nationality* (New York, 1953). Almost all of these accounts give a rather rosy picture of Social Democratic federalism to the exclusion of its elements of German nationalism and great power politics (discussed later in this chapter).
22. See J. Redlich, *Das österreichische Staats- und Verfassungsproblem*, 2 vols (Leipzig, 1920); Kann, *The Multinational Empire*; P. Geist-Lanyi, *Das Nationalitätenproblem auf dem Reichstag zu Kremsier 1848–49* (Munich, 1920).
23. O. Bauer, *Die österreichische Revolution* (Vienna, 1923), p. 61.
24. *1899 Parteitag Brünn*, pp. 80 and 91.
25. Ibid., pp. 78–9.
26. With typical Austro-Marxist tolerance, the Brno programme itself was not actually revoked until 1917 and then only to concede the inevitable break up of the Habsburg empire. Bauer, 'Erklärung der Linken', *Werkausgabe*, 5, ed. H. Pepper (Vienna, 1978), pp. 121–30.
27. Wilhelm Ellenbogen, *1899 Parteitag Brünn*, p. 85.
28. Synopticus, *Staat und Nation: Staatsrechtliche Untersuchungen über die möglichen Principien einer Lösung und die juristischen Voraussetzungen eines Nationalitätengesetzes* (Vienna, 1899); Rudolf Springer, *Der Kampf der österreichischen Nationen um den Staat: 1. Theil, Das nationale Problem als Verfassungs- und Verwaltungsfrage* (Vienna, 1902); Springer, *Die Krise*

des Dualismus und das Ende der Deakistischen Episode in der Geschichte der habsburgischen Monarchie (Vienna, 1904); and his last work published under the name Springer, *Grundlagen und Entwicklungsziele der österreichisch-ungarischen Monarchie* (Vienna, 1906).

29. See Karl Renner, *The Institutions of Private Law and their Public Functions*, ed. O. Kahn-Freund (London, 1949). On Renner's philosophy, see N. Leser, *Zwischen Reformismus und Bolschewismus: Der Austromarxismus als Theorie und Praxis* (Vienna 1968); for his biography, J. Hannak, *Karl Renner: Versuch einer Biographie* (Vienna, 1965).
30. Springer, *Der Kampf der österreichischen Nationen*, p. 147.
31. R. Springer, *Grundlagen*, p. 208.
32. Geist-Lanyi, *Das Nationalitätenproblem*; Kann, *The Multinational Empire*, 2, pp. 27–39.
33. K. Renner, 'Was sind unsere Kronländer?'; 'Das nationale Problem in der Verwaltung', *Der Kampf*, Jg. 1, 1.10.1907, pp. 23–30.
34. See especially R.J. Hoffmann, *T.G. Masaryk und die tschechische Frage*; also E. Schmidt-Hartmann, *Thomas G. Masaryk's Realism: Origins of a Czech Political Concept* (Munich, 1984); S.B. Winters (ed.), *T.G. Masaryk (1850–1937), 1, Thinker and Politician* (London, 1990).
35. See in particular E. Beneš, *Le problème autrichien et le problème tchèque* (Paris, 1908). There is some doubt whether Beneš, who was an impoverished student in Paris at the time, had actually read any of Renner's books; see Hoffmann, *T.G. Masaryk und die tschechische Frage*, p. 431.
36. Hoffmann, *T.G. Masaryk und die tschechische Frage*, pp. 425–6.
37. Beneš, *Le problème autrichien et le problème tchèque*, p. 258; also cited in Kann, *The Multinational Empire*, 1, p. 212.
38. K. Renner, *Das Selbstbestimmungsrecht der Nationen in besonderer Anwendung auf Österreich, 1. Teil, Nation und Staat* (Vienna, 1918); Victor Adler, who otherwise would have taken over the Chancellorship, had died the previous day. The author of the constitution of the first Republic would be a fellow neo-Kantian, Hans Kelsen, best known for his *Pure Theory of the Law* (Berkeley, 1967); but see also in this regard H. Kelsen (ed.), *Die Verfassungsgesetze der Republik Deutschösterreich* (Vienna, 1919).
39. J. Hannak, *Karl Renner*.
40. P. Crabitès, *Beneš: Statesman of Central Europe* (London, 1935).
41. As Nemec's intervention at Brno made clear this was also an objection of the Czech Social Democrats; see also A. Meissner, 'Löst die nationale Autonomie das nationale Problem?' *Der Kampf*, Jg. 1, 1.3.1908.
42. Proportional representation was supposed to protect minority rights here without recourse to any special quotas.
43. Masaryk, it is interesting to note, had used the same sort of metaphor in the 1890s when discussing thoroughly mixed areas: 'Zur deutsch-böhmischen Ausgleichsfrage', *Die Zeit*, 25.4.1896; cited in Hoffmann, *T.G. Masaryk und die tschechische Frage*, p. 425.
44. H. Mommsen, *Die Sozialdemokratie und die Nationalitätenfrage*, p. 276; on the different permutations of 'k. und k.' and 'k.-k.' see Robert Musil's novel *The Man without Qualities*, 1 (London, 1955), pp. 33–5.
45. O. Bauer, *The Austrian Revolution* (London, 1925), pp. 47–8.
46. *1904 Parteitag*, p. 164.
47. I would not like to push the analogy too far here. Weber's social reform proposals were, of course, also sharply critical of socialism: see W.J. Mommsen, *Max Weber and German Politics*, pp. 101–21 and 172–89.
48. V. Adler, *Aufsätze, Reden, Briefe*, ed. F. Adler, (Vienna, 1922–9), 6, intr. O. Bauer, p. xxxi.
49. R. Springer, *Der Kampf der Nationen*, p. 21.

50. Ibid., p. 18.
51. Ibid., pp. 16–18.
52. G. Stedman Jones, *Languages of Class* (London, 1983); A. Pzeworski, *Capitalism and Social Democracy* (Cambridge, 1985); I. Katznelson and A.R. Zolberg (eds), *Working-Class Formation* (Princeton, 1986); J. Lawrence and M. Taylor, 'The poverty of protest: Gareth Stedman Jones and the politics of language – a reply', *Social History*, 18 (7), 1993, pp. 1–15.
53. Springer, *Grundlagen*, pp. 56–7.
54. Beneš, *Le problème autrichien et le problème tchèque*, pp. 279ff; Kann, *The Multinational Empire*, 2, p. 214.
55. Bauer, *Die Nationalitätenfrage*, ch. 6; R. Luxemburg, *The National Question*. See also Bauer, *The Austrian Revolution*, pp. 276–7, including *inter alia* about the post-Versailles world, 'The antagonism between Jugo Slav and Great Serbian aspirations survives in the struggle over the constitution, in the resistance of the Croats and Slovenes to Great Serbian domination.'
56. R. Hilferding, *Finance Capital* (London, 1981). A careful reading of Weber's arguments in favour of imperialism and German *Weltpolitik* suggests that he actually based them on underconsumptionist Marxist theories, which Kautsky popularized in the 1890s and which Tugan Baranowsky, Böhm-Bawerk, Bauer, Hilferding and – in a different context – Weber himself criticized in the 1900s. For a resumé of Weber's arguments, see W.J. Mommsen, *Max Weber and German Politics*, ch. 4; for an introduction to the development of Marxist theories of imperialism at this time see R. Jacoby, 'The politics of crisis theory: Towards a critique of automatic Marxism II', *Telos*, 23, 1975, pp. 3–52.
57. Secret agreement was reached between the Austrian and German governments in March 1919 but vetoed in June at St Germain by the *entente* powers; Lewis Namier's verdict at the time is revealing: 'But ultimately the policy of German Austria will from the logic of fact have to go the way indicated by Bauer, i.e. towards closer union with Germany . . . Bauer out of office [he resigned over the allied veto] may become an even greater power than in office, & anyhow the cooperation between him & Renner is likely to continue – which is not a bad thing. Austria in the days of her greatness has never had such a decent government & able statesmen as she has got now.' Minute by L. Namier, 2.8.1919, FO 371, F. 3530, no. 110413; cited in F.L. Carsten, *The First Austrian Republic, 1918–1938* (Cambridge, 1986); see also O. Bauer, *The Austrian Revolution*, pp. 61ff.
58. Springer, *Der Kampf der Nationen*, p. 170; see also Springer, *Grundlagen*, p. 248.
59. On the programme see O. Bauer, 'Unser Nationalitätenprogramm und unsere Taktik', *Der Kampf*, Jg. 1, 1.2.1908, pp. 204–10, and *Die Nationalitätenfrage*, ch. 4; on great power politics, see Bauer, *Die Nationalitätenfrage*, 1907, p. 453. As Bauer knew, both Friedrich Engels and Karl Kautsky had asserted that the Austro-Hungarian empire would break up once the Russian revolution occurred: Engels to Bernstein, 22.2.1882, K. Marx and F. Engels, *Werke*, 35 (Berlin, 1967), p. 279; K. Kautsky, 'Der Kampf der Nationalitäten und das Staatsrecht', pp. 723ff; on German Social Democratic attitudes to great power politics under the impact of the 1905 revolution, see N. Stargardt, *The German Idea of Militarism: Radical and Socialist Critics, 1866–1914*, (Cambridge, forthcoming), ch. 6.
60. Ibid., ch. 2.
61. M. Weber, 'Deutschlands künftige Staatsform' (15.12.1918), *Politische Schriften*, p. 449; cited in W.J. Mommsen, *Max Weber and German Politics*, p. 50.
62. 'Deutschland unter den europäischen Weltmächten' (1916), *Politische Schriften*, p. 175.

In the midst of the world war and the Czech struggle for independence, Masaryk accused Renner (and Bauer) of accepting Friedrich Naumann's idea of a German-controlled Central Europe, but this assertion must be read in its context and does not do real justice to the pre-1914 political alignments; see Hoffmann, *T.G. Masaryk und die tschechische Frage*, p. 432; Kann, *The Multinational Empire*, 1, p. 214.
63. Renner, *Das Selbstbestimmungsrecht der Nationen*, p. 148; see also Springer, *Der Kampf der Nationen*, pp. 35–6.
64. Springer, *Der Kampf der Nationen*, pp. 6 and 21.
65. Kautsky, 'Die moderne Nationalität', *Die neue Zeit*, 5, 1887, pp. 404–5; V.I. Lenin, 'Right of nations to self-determination'; K. Marx and F. Engels, *Communist Manifesto* (Peking, 1965), p. 47.
66. E. Renan, *Qu'est-ce qu'une nation?*, 2nd edn (Paris, 1882), p. 10.
67. Bauer, *Die Nationalitätenfrage*, p. 6.
68. Ibid., p. 135. A striking example of this standardization of peasant dialects into a national language by urban intellectuals with nationalist aspirations is the work of the Slovak grammarian L'udevít Štúr: J.P. Stern, *The Heart of Europe*, p. 9.
69. *Die Nationalitätenfrage*, p. 531.
70. Ibid., p. 135.
71. M. Weber, *Gesammelte Aufsätze zur Soziologie und Sozialpolitik* (Tübingen, 1924), p. 484, and see p. 487. For Kautsky's critique of Bauer see K. Kautsky, 'Nationalität und Internationalität', *Neue Zeit*, Supplement 1, 1908. Bauer's reply is very important because it is the place where he first uses Tönnies's *Gemeinschaft–Gesellschaft* concept: O. Bauer, 'Bemerkungen zur Nationalitätenfrage', *Neue Zeit*, 26.1, 1907–8.
72. Bauer, *Die Nationalitätenfrage*, p. 138.
73. M. Weber, *Gesammelte Aufsätze zur Wissenschaftslehre*, (Tübingen, 1951), pp. 9–10. Weber's main reflections on nations are in *Economy and Society* (New York, 1968), pp. 395–8 and 921–6, and in his *Gesammelte Aufsätze zur Soziologie und Sozialpolitik*, pp. 456–62 and 484–91. See also the accounts by W.J. Mommsen, *Max Weber and German Politics*, ch. 3, and D. Beetham, *Max Weber and the Theory of Modern Politics*, ch. 5, on both of which I have drawn heavily here.
74. F. Tönnies, *Gemeinschaft und Gesellschaft: Abhandlung des Communismus und des Socialismus als empirischen Kulturformen* (Leipzig, 1887).
75. M. Weber, *Politische Schriften*, p. 234; D. Beetham, *Max Weber and the Theory of Modern Politics*, p. 123.
76. Weber, *Politische Schriften*, ibid.
77. Renner became the main leader of the party during the war and supported the government, while Otto Bauer was in the army, was taken prisoner by the Russians, and returned to lead the anti-war wing of the party, eventually winning support for the 'Programme of the Left' at the 1917 party congress.
78. Thus Bauer, *The Austrian Revolution*, pp. 11–52.

7

Intellectuals, Ethnic Groups and Nations: Two Late-twentieth-century Cases

Chris Hann

INTRODUCTION

The scholarly literature on nationalism has paid considerable attention to the role played by intellectuals in the establishment of national movements. Whether through linguistic purification, the forging of a new sense of the past, or the classification of folk dances and material culture, their cultural work has been indispensable. In a significant number of cases such intellectuals have also become political leaders, particularly in the early phases of national mobilization. I am in broad agreement with Ernest Gellner, who has consistently argued that intellectuals are the 'inventors' of nations (Gellner, 1964, 1983). The materials with which intellectuals work vary from one case to the next, and the extent of the invention may be reduced in cases of so-called 'historic nations'. But in essence Gellner is surely right to insist that, contrary to the metaphor of 'awakening' that they typically employ, the intellectuals are in fact constructing an entity that is quite new. Whether this construction requires literal forgery (e.g. of historical documents to prove the antiquity of a claim to territory) or only metaphorical fabrication (as in nationalist history generally, when the X are projected back into the distant past) is sociologically irrelevant.

These acts of construction raise important questions of ethical responsibility as well as scientific truth. In this paper I will focus on such issues of intellectual responsibility concerning the creation of new nations in the present day. It is obvious at once that such intellectuals operate in a climate of opinion quite different from the climate in which intellectuals created nations in Eastern Europe in the nineteenth century, or in various parts of the 'Third World' in the present century. The professionalization of academic life, and the connotations of such terms as 'tribalism' for larger audiences have forced most intellectuals to look critically at the consequences of their work. In the cases I consider here, it is not possible to invoke the sort of factors which, in Gellner's view, provide the true explanation for the emergence of nationalism. He argues that nationalism is tied to the requirements of a modern industrial society, which dictate a homogenizing of culture, mobility and efficient communication throughout the territory of the state. It is assumed that certain scale specifications must be met for such units to be viable. This approach may not provide a comprehensive general theory of nationalism (see Hall, chapter 2 of this volume) but it does undoubtedly capture features of central importance, as relevant to postcolonial states such as Indonesia as they are to both the historic and the new nations of Europe. But what are we to say about the role of intellectuals in contemporary contexts where they cannot be presented as the unwitting agents of modernizing processes, grounded in economic transformation, where it is plain that the goal of intellectual creativity is fundamentally at odds with the rational organization of economic life, not to mention inter-state relations and geopolitics? What difference does it make if the intellectual cannot present himself as one of 'the people', but is promoting their cause from the outside, with his legitimacy entirely grounded in his scholarship? The two cases that I wish to address in exploring these issues refer to peoples who have been profoundly affected by earlier national movements all around them. Through examining these late and peripheral examples of national identity, neither of which on present evidence seems likely to prove successful, I shall try to derive some more general conclusions concerning intellectual roles and responsibilities.

RUTHENIANS

The Carpathian lands that form the geographical centre of the European continent provide instructive examples of several varieties of nationalist experience. However, the people with whom I am concerned have not yet been definitively mobilized by any one of the available options. This has much to do with their relative isolation, economic backwardness and inadequate communications. Recently, however, fresh attempts have been made to forge a unity between people who undoubtedly still have much in common culturally, despite centuries of political division. Before I turn to the American intellectual who has been most instrumental in the revival of attempts to invent a Rusyn/Ruthenian nation, let me sketch the most essential background.

The main inhabitants of this mountain zone since at least the medieval period have been Eastern Slavs, that is speakers of an East Slav language/dialect and followers of the Orthodox or Byzantine liturgical tradition. Even this statement has been occasionally disputed, for example by Polish nationalist authors who have advanced alternative claims concerning the fraction of the population falling within Polish state borders (Pieradzka 1939); but the evidence seems overwhelming. These Eastern Slavs were also distinguished (though less sharply) from many of their neighbours by the economic practices associated with their upland environments: pastoral activities and forestry supplemented their inadequate agricultural endowments. Political frontiers in what Gellner terms the agrarian age seldom respected cultural criteria. Thus the border between the historic nations of Hungary and Poland was fixed from the middle of the fourteenth century to run along the ridge of the mountains, leaving substantial numbers of Eastern Slavs on both sides. When nationalism spread in the nineteenth century, this border marked the demarcation line between the Kingdom of Hungary and the Galician provinces administered by Austria. From 1867 these territories were linked by the Habsburg so-called 'Dual Monarchy', but the policies pursued in Budapest were quite different from those pursued in Vienna. In general, strong pressures to 'magyarize' the populations of Hungarian administered districts led many clergy, the main literate group in this society at the time, to adopt the (recently reformed) Hungarian language and to assimilate more or less fully into Hungarian society. In Galicia, on the other hand, the Austrian authorities, in part to counter the escalating demands of the Poles, were content to leave operating space for the emergent Ukrainian national movement. The Greek Catholic clergy formed the principal transmission mechanism of these new ideas in these remote regions (Himka, 1984).

During the period in which strong national movements developed in Central Europe, these isolated inhabitants of a mountainous environment were very difficult to mobilize for any national cause. People remained attached to their 'little community' and to their religion.

However, the seeds were sown for a three-way split as the age of agrarian empires drew to a close. One tendency was the Ukrainophile – commitment to the new nation invented by Shevchenko, Hrushevsky and other intellectuals in the nineteenth century. Another tendency emphasized the unity of all Eastern Slavs and looked to Moscow and the Romanov dynasty as its contemporary cultural and political centre; when the empires of the Habsburgs and Romanovs became enemies in the First World War, those sympathetic to this line (and many more innocents) paid a heavy price. The third tendency, which can be termed the Rusynophile, was to promote an autonomous national identity, one that would tie these people neither to Moscow nor to Kiev. It is this option that is being vigorously revived in the 1990s.

To complete this greatly simplified outline of a very complex narrative, the end of the First World War brought some major political changes. The Galicians were reincorporated into a state called Poland, dominated by nationalists and containing a large Ukrainian minority. (When the earlier Polish state was partitioned in the late eighteenth century no such nation existed.) The Polish authorities, supported by many scholars, did what they could to counter Ukrainophile tendencies, and in the remote areas of the mountains they enjoyed some success in the dissemination of alternative collective identities, including the Bojko, Hucul and Lemko 'ethnographic groups'. The new, shrunken Hungarian state was left with relatively few Eastern Slavs within its borders (it was to reincorporate some of them briefly in the course of the Second World War). The largest numbers of the Carpathian Eastern Slavs found themselves after 1919 inside the new state of Czechoslovakia. The invention of this state is still widely viewed as an instance of the Wilsonian principle of national self-determination and its Czech president, the distinguished truth-seeking intellectual Thomas Masaryk, continues to enjoy a high reputation as that rarity in this region, an enlightened liberal statesman. Nonetheless, the boundaries of this state were manipulated by Masaryk to include large numbers of people (almost one-third of the total population) who were neither Czech nor Slovak. The Carpathian Eastern Slavs tried but failed to establish themselves as the third nation within the new state and to win at least a substantial measure of administrative autonomy.

Debates about collective identity and forms of government effectively ceased during the Second World War and the socialist decades, but the problems did not go away. When the borders were redrawn once again in 1945, most of these people were incorporated into the Soviet Ukraine. Those who remained in Poland and Czechoslovakia were classified officially as a Ukrainian minority, but their fates have been very different. The 'Lemkos' of Poland were forcibly deported from their mountain homelands and dispersed across regions in the north and west previously belonging to Germany. They remain scattered and many have assimilated into Polish society, though significant numbers have found their way back to their native villages (Hann, 1985). The Ukrainians of the Prešov region of Eastern Slovakia have not been subject to such crude intervention, but here too assimilation has proceeded inexorably (Magocsi, 1983).

The most recent political developments, namely the collapse of communist power throughout the region, have brought about a situation in which the old issues of national identity can once again be freely aired. This is the stage on which Paul Robert Magocsi, Professor of Ukrainian Studies at the University of Toronto and prolific author on the history and culture of all these people, now makes his appearance.

Paul Robert Magocsi

Professor Magocsi is the American grandson of an East Slav immigrant born in the sub-Carpathian zone that before 1918 belonged to Hungary. His surname has a Hungarian root and conforms to the conventions of Hungarian orthography (rather than any of the several possible Slavic alternatives). Perhaps in some ways he fits the pattern of the third generation immigrant who needs to explore the family origins in the old continent, but it is not my purpose to speculate on motivations or personalities. In Magocsi's case we are certainly facing much more than a private quest for roots.[1] He has been extremely active for many years in promoting a particular view of 'Carpatho-Rusyn identity' for many years among the large North American diaspora communities. One of a number of publications (Magocsi, 1984) aimed at popular audiences is dedicated to his father, whose allegiance is said to have been to all the people of the Danubian region. This seems to be a code for dis-associating the Carpathian East Slavs from the main mass of Ukrainians, who have no such links to the Danube.

Magocsi's Rusynophile stance has also been developed in an impressive series of scholarly articles and monographs. His major work, *The Shaping of a National Identity: Sub-Carpathian Rus', 1848–1948* (1978), argues that the various identity options were all effectively open for the people of this region until Soviet military power led to its incorporation into the Ukraine in the aftermath of the Second World War. This book also includes short biographical notes on virtually all the intellectuals who contributed to the national debates during this period. Inevitably, however, Magocsi's work has been found wanting by those who do not share his commitment to the Rusyns' separate and distinct character. Perhaps the most significant criticism has been that he overlooks the evidence suggesting that the Rusyns were increasingly and inexorably adopting the Ukrainian orientation before Soviet interference, as a consequence of the political pressures to which they were subjected in the interwar decades (Rudnycky, 1987).

Clearly, then, Magocsi found himself, like his nineteenth-century predecessors, becoming embroiled in controversies that had repercussions well beyond the seminar rooms. His perceived pro-Rusyn standpoint upset the Ukrainian community in Toronto, the body that sponsors his Chair. But until the dramatic changes that transformed this part of Europe in 1989–90, even Magocsi must have doubted whether he would ever have the chance to deploy his talents and energies to take his message from the diaspora and Academia back to the Carpathian homelands. In recent years, he has seized his opportunity with characteristic vigour, proselytizing for the Rusyn cause in print and in person in all three of the states directly concerned: Ukraine, Slovakia and Poland (the numbers of Rusyns now left in eastern Hungary are minuscule). The first two of these represent new nations that have only now achieved full independent statehood. Magocsi has not argued explicitly for the creation of a new state; but he clearly does believe that, through forging a unified Rusyn culture, a new nation can be brought into existence. Thus he condemns what he terms the 'administrative imposition' of Ukrainian identity in the socialist period, and hails what he terms the 'Lemko national revival' in Poland. He applauds the role that activist intellectuals played in this revival long before the dramatic events of 1989:

> there does exist a group of Lemkos in Poland who have opted for an identity distinct from Ukrainians, and they have already embarked along the path of classic intelligentsia-inspired national movements, with the intent to produce literary works in the Lemko vernacular for use as a full-fledged literary language, to carry out historical research on Lemko topics,

and to sponsor annual festivals that encourage the masses to become aware and proud of their Lemko identity.(1990a: 208)

What are the prospects for Magocsi's programme on the ground? Everywhere in Eastern and Central Europe there is considerable uncertainty and instability. Some elements in Hungary talk openly about the need to amend frontiers. However, it is difficult to detect any general enthusiasm for Magocsi's ideals. To illustrate from the case I know best, let me probe further among the Polish Lemkos. They are not typical, because as noted above the Lemkos were subject to more extreme physical dislocation than East Slavs elsewhere in the mountains. Nevertheless, at least some elements of the Lemko case illustrate the difficulties facing Magocsi elsewhere in the region. We are fortunate in having a number of valuable studies of these people in earlier generations by Polish ethnographers, outstanding among whom is Roman Reinfuss. Travelling through the villages in the interwar period, Reinfuss found questions of identity to be complex (1948–9). People here did not even call themselves Rusyn, but used another expression from the same root, *Rusnak* (this was also the preferred version on the other side of the mountains in adjacent parts of Slovakia; all these terms of course refer back to the original unity of the Eastern Slavs in the polity of Kievan Rus', and not to modern Russia). But they did not use this term as an indication of national allegiance. Villagers seemed to lack this kind of identity, and preferred to describe themselves as 'the people from here', or to name their village or the local cluster of settlements in which they resided. There is little evidence in the work of the early Polish ethnographers that people used the term Lemko or had any collective consciousness of this kind. Yet Reinfuss and others used it to demarcate a distinct group, with precise contours and cultural contents. Later Polish ethnographers have accepted these basic assumptions, including some who now analyse sympathetically the prospects for a 'revival of Lemko ethnicity' (Nowak, 1993). What Reinfuss and others took pains to delineate as an 'ethnographic group' shortly before its physical disintegration is now regularly reified in the social science literature as an 'ethnic group' (for example Mucha, 1991).

Magocsi is therefore right to recognize the role of the intelligentsia in the production of ethnic and national movements. In the Lemko case this needs to be carefully explored over a long period. From obscure origins in the middle of the nineteenth century, when it was first applied to one cluster of East Slavs who used the word *lem* as a feature of their dialect, the word has come to refer to a bounded unit embracing perhaps 100,000 people in contemporary Poland. The difficulties have been very considerable, particularly in the Eastern Lemko districts where the inhabitants so labelled needed to be distinguished not from Poles but from other Eastern Slavs. Reinfuss and others devoted considerable scholarly effort to pinpointing the ethnographic boundary between Lemkos and Boikos, with reference to 'objective' ethnographic features (architecture, costume etc.). The futility of such cartographic exercises is obvious. Krystyna Pieradzka (1939) ignores the Eastern Lemko districts altogether (presumably because she was aware that their population was unsympathetic to her Polonizing aspirations). Magocsi, on the other hand, in his popular publications (1984), has located the Eastern Lemko boundary not in the valley of the Oslawa, where the 'experts' locate it, but considerably further east in the valley of the San. His justification is that the North American communities have applied the term Lemko in this way. Since the diaspora has undoubtedly played a major role in popularizing the term as well as in giving it scholarly legitimacy, this argument has some force.

In short, the term Lemko must be seen as part of the problem. It does not emerge 'naturally' from within the group so defined, but is an attempt to impose order and borders on a continuum of cultural variation. As a result of substantial investments by Polish intellectuals, later supported by activists from within the group and consolidated in a range of cultural products, including Lemko history books and dictionaries in preparation, it has come to be widely adopted. This affiliation was encouraged by the Polish authorities in the pre-socialist period to counter Ukrainian influence. In the socialist period the Lemkos, by now fragmented, were not officially distinguished from other Ukrainians in Poland. However, one page of the minority group's weekly newspaper was written in a version of the Lemko dialect, and many families were able to pass on a sense of being Lemko, sometimes as part of a larger Ukrainian nation, and sometimes as a distinct alternative to the Ukrainian identity. Increased tolerance of return migration to the Carpathian homelands and of small-scale cultural activities also contributed to the preservation of Lemko identity in the later decades of socialist rule.

Before turning to the present conjuncture it is essential to note that disagreements over secular identities have been accompanied by (but do not correspond exactly to) religious conflicts. The Eastern Slavs have remained clearly distinct from Poles and other Western neighbours, but ever since the Union of Brest of 1596 there have been serious divisions between the Orthodox and the Greek Catholics (also known as Uniates). The Lemkos became Greek Catholic following the political pressures of the Counter-Reformation, but this had little impact on their everyday religious practices. However, many converted to Orthodoxy in the twentieth century, on the grounds that this represented the original Church of the Eastern Slavs, even before the Greek Catholic Church was suppressed under socialism. The Greek Catholics have a very strong association with the national movement in Western Ukraine, and their re-emergence throughout Eastern and Central Europe following the events of 1989 has been one of the more remarkable results of the demise of the Soviet system. Greater religious freedom, however, risks opening up old conflicts throughout the Lemko region. It has already become apparent in a number of areas that the dominant Roman Catholic hierarchy is quite unsympathetic to a revival of Eastern rite Catholicism, and there have been major disputes over ecclesiastical property (for example in the city of Przemyśl).

In this situation the Lemkos, like other Ukrainians and other minority groups in Poland, harbour ambivalent feelings about post-socialist governments. Poland has been, since 1945, one of the more homogenous countries of the region; and the identity of Polishness with Roman Catholicism remains very strong. Some self-labelled Lemkos told me in 1980–1 of their fears of the consequences if the Solidarity movement were to come to power on a wave of Polish nationalism. After 1989, when the first non-socialist government had been formed, they remained apprehensive. They felt that a vulnerable minority might do better out of the 'divide and rule' strategies of a weak socialist government than it would from a freely elected but authoritarian nationalist government (cf. Mucha, 1992).

In the event, these fears seem to have been misplaced. Although the authorities have to tread a tightrope because of the conflicts between the Ukrainophile and Rusynophile orientations, Lemko cultural activities have been given more active official support than ever before. The authorities have not bestowed official recognition on the Lemkos, since this would of course antagonize other members of the Ukrainian minority, and perhaps jeopardize bilateral links with the new Ukrainian state. Limited plans to introduce teaching materials using the Lemko language/dialect for the first time are condemned by those who favour the Ukrainian orientation, who insist that only standard literary Ukrainian is suitable for educational purposes.

In any case, attempts to produce a Lemko dictionary and to standardize Lemko as a literary language will not necessarily help Magocsi in his general Rusyn programme, for the differences between this Lemko and the dialects spoken in adjacent Carpathian regions will remain significant. This is the central ambiguity in Magocsi's nation-building programme. When he discusses 'collecting, codifying and propagating the local culture' (1990a: 209) among the Lemkos of Poland, he believes the Lemkos to be not a nation in their own right, but part of a nation of Carpatho-Rusyns, with a larger component in Ukraine, a significant smaller one in Slovakia, and fragments elsewhere, in Hungary, Romania and former Yugoslavia, not to mention the North American communities. But how the Lemkos of Poland are to recognize this common identity is not specified. To me at least, on the basis of Polish fieldwork, it seems that the Carpathian East Slavs have become far too routinized into other states to be able to contemplate forging a new one of their own. Even the recognition of a common cultural base and the adoption of a standardized Rusyn language seem unattainable goals. So far, there has been little sign that anyone is seriously interested in breaking down these barriers.[2] The older activists are divided among themselves (for example, the major annual festival, the *Watra*, is now held on two separate occasions: once in the mountain homeland, where it attracts large numbers of Ukrainian performers and spectators, and once in western Poland, where it is organized on a smaller scale by those unsympathetic to the Ukrainophile orientation, who wish to emphasize the autonomy of Lemko culture). The new young Lemko intellectuals have good networks in cities such as Kraków and Warsaw, their kin are typically scattered throughout Poland, and they cannot conceive of a future outside the Polish state. As for the non-intellectuals, they remain extremely difficult to mobilize politically. The only organization that has had any success in galvanizing opinion is a group called *Krag Lemkow* (Lemko Circle), which campaigns for the restitution of economic resources, notably forests, to their original Lemko owners. If post-socialist states refuse to meet such demands and if the currently open cultural policies were to be curtailed, it is possible that Lemko opinion could harden against the Polish authorities. But at the time of writing (winter 1994) the prospects for Paul Robert Magocsi's Rusyn national movement seem gloomy. The successes of earlier generations of Polish intellectuals in patenting an ethnic group *within* Polish society are now impeding his own efforts to forge a nation.

LAZ

The second example I wish to present is that of the Laz, or Lazi as they describe themselves in a language, Lazuri, that is related to Georgian and very close to Mingrelian.[3] From the point of view of a Georgian nationalist the Lazi are essentially a Georgian people, in much the same way as the Lemkos are a Ukrainian people in the eyes of Ukrainian nationalists (cf. Vanilişi and Tandılava 1992). However, like the Lemkos, for many centuries before the rise of modern nationalism these people were remote and peripheral, inhabiting a different state from that of most of their closest linguistic relatives, and they appear not to have developed any strong sense of peoplehood in the modern (ethnonational) sense. Their state was the Ottoman Empire, and today the majority of Lazi are citizens of its successor in Anatolia, the Turkish nation-state. This modern republic has developed an effective nationalism of its own, and so the Lazi, like the Lemkos, have found themselves trapped between two powerful nationalist movements. Here too there has been significant external intellectual intervention; before examining this and the contemporary situation 'on the ground' it is important to explain a little more of the background.

Unlike the term Lemko, the use of the term Laz as an ethnonym is extremely ancient. However, it is difficult to identify precisely the populations to which it has been applied and their shifting locations. It was used some two millennia ago to describe the inhabitants of Colchis. More recently it has been applied to sections of the Greek-speaking population of the Pontos, and in contemporary Turkey it is commonly used to designate the entire population of the east Black Sea region. Only if we insist on applying the term in a modern nationalist way, as the label for a clearly bounded group, can we speak of inconsistencies or errors in such usage. From such a modern perspective, the Lazi–Turkish boundary has a precise location (at least in the twentieth century) in the valley of Melyat, near the small town of Pazar (formerly Atina). But although this boundary is recognized in the region it has virtually no significance other than linguistic (Hann, 1995). All other aspects of culture have long been freely exchanged and shared in this 'multi-ethnic' region. Many inhabitants of, say, Trabzon, some seventy miles to the west of the 'narrower' Lazi boundary, will in certain contexts describe themselves as Laz without being aware of the existence of a separate Laz language, related not to Turkish but to Georgian. The Laz in this regional sense are the subject of a certain stereotyping in the rest of Anatolia: not exactly flattering, but not entirely negative either, and this stereotype does not call into question their basic Turkishness (cf. Meeker, 1971).

Hence it is necessary to distinguish the Lazi region (defined by the linguistic frontier at Melyat) from a much larger Laz region (with boundaries imprecisely defined, perhaps stretching as far west as Samsun). To explain how such distinctions have evolved requires close attention to a wide range of geographical and historical factors. The mountains which separate the Lazi-speaking territory from the interior have always been a formidable natural barrier. But communications by land along the coast have been revolutionized by massive road building programmes in the second half of this century. The old steamer services have been replaced by the long-distance bus as the main vehicle for emigration: Istanbul and Izmir can be reached within 24 hours. The terrain would be still more favourable to external linkages in the east, where the railway network begins at the city of Batumi, just outside the Lazi region. In past centuries the Lazi did indeed travel widely to the cities of the Russian empire. However, from the end of the 1920s the coastal frontier was effectively closed, and political considerations dictated that it remained closed for the next half-century. This border followed a small stream that split the Lazi village of Sarp; the great majority of Lazi were left to the west of this line, within the Turkish state.

There is one further criterion of vital significance for understanding the identity of the modern Lazi. The spread of the Turkish language in this region after the Ottoman conquests was accompanied by the spread of Islam, and the predecessors of the modern Lazi were converted by the seventeenth century. Their descendants have no memory of an earlier Christian faith, nor is there any trace of Christian influence in their religious practices. The Laz, who established a reputation as soldiers and sailors in the Ottoman forces, also built up as reputation as devout and loyal Muslims.

Neither in Ottoman nor in republican times have the Lazi had recognition from the state as an ethnic group or a 'people'. They are split between the Provinces of Artvin and Rize, forming a minority within each. There is no education in Lazuri, and those who dare use it in public places are still liable to get into trouble. Their history, insofar as it has been tackled at all, is represented as part of Turkish history: the Lazi are presented as a people of true Turkish stock, who happened accidentally to acquire a number of superficial cultural traits in the course of their migrations (Kırzıoglu, 1972). The Lazi have no museums or festivals and the task of 'collecting, codifying and propagating the local culture' has barely begun. Unlike the Lemkos, many Lazi have become prosperous in recent decades without having to leave their native lands. This is largely thanks to the introduction of tea as a cash crop in the years after 1950 (Hann, 1990). All the same, emigration rates have been high throughout the century. Large Lazi communities exist in Ankara and Istanbul, though here again it is not open to them to organize cultural associations *as Lazi*.

Wolfgang Feurstein

A major influence behind recent efforts to promote the Lazi as a distinct people is the German scholar Wolfgang Feurstein. After visiting the region in the mid-1960s as a student, Feurstein later submitted a *Magisterarbeit* at the University of Freiburg on Lazi material culture (1983). Unlike Magocsi, he has no personal (family) links to his academic subjects. Nor does he have a permanent academic base from which to organize his activities: he works on the Lazi in his spare time and his published works are far fewer than those of Paul Robert Magocsi. Nevertheless, in a number of respects his efforts on behalf of the Lazi can be usefully compared with those of Magocsi on behalf of the Carpatho-Rusyns. Thus Feurstein attaches priority to promoting awareness of their culture and pride in their language among the Lazi themselves. To this end he has devised an alphabet for Lazuri, using the Latin letters with which all contemporary Turks are familiar (1984). Although he has not visited the region since the late 1970s, when he spent a short period in gaol following an alleged violation of frontier regulations, his pamphlets are sent by post and taken back from Germany by migrant workers. Other publications include more scholarly works, intended for academic audiences, and works aimed at a broad 'human rights' audience in the West, in which he has been severely critical of the Turkish government's policies towards minorities (for example Feurstein and Berdsena, 1987). One consequence of this activity is that Feurstein and his small group of associates (they include a few Lazi now domiciled in Germany) are almost certainly kept under surveillance by Turkish agents in Germany. He knows that, in the context of the 1990s, particularly the Kurdish problems, it would be risky for him to attempt to visit Turkey.

Feurstein has recently found a kindred spirit in the distinguished London-based Scots journalist Neal Ascherson, who has himself visited the region and found that the Lazi excited his general sympathy for small nations. Ascherson visited Feurstein at his home in the Black Forest in 1993, and published a very enthusiastic endorsement in his newspaper, the *Independent on Sunday*. Ascherson hailed the German explicitly in the mould of the nineteenth-century nation-builders:

> It was in the 1960s that Feurstein first went to the Lazi country, travelling among their villages and learning their language. What happened then to this mild, fair-bearded man was something like a religious revelation. It dawned on him that the Lazi were what Germans call a *Volk* – an authentic national group with a rich folk-identity, which was about to be lost forever. He resolved to save it. . . .
>
> What is so astounding about Wolfgang Feurstein's work for the Lazi is that he is repeating, step by step, the process of creating 'modern nations' out of folk-cultures which began in Central Europe almost 200 years ago. . . .
>
> . . . almost single-handed and quite unrewarded, Feurstein has set about nothing less than the foundation of a national culture. He has given the Lazi an alphabet, and prepared schoolbooks which are now beginning to circulate – clandestinely – in their villages. He and the small group of expatriates who form the 'Katchkar Working Group' (named after a mountain range) are working on the first dictionary and the first volumes of what is to be a source-book and bibliography of Lazi history. . . .
>
> To bring an alphabet to a people who have never written down their speech – that is something given to few human beings. . . . When I held in my hand Feurstein's Lazuri alphabet, done in Turkish Latin script for clarity with Georgian characters opposite, I felt a sense of awe. I was holding something like a seed, but also like a bomb. With an alphabet, a people – even a tiny one – sets out on a journey. These characters were seen last year on student placards in an Istanbul demonstration, which means that the journey has already begun. Ahead are novels and poems, handwritten family and love letters, perhaps one day newspapers and proclamations, perhaps even laws.

In contrast to his adulation for Feurstein, Ascherson refers in a dark aside to the research recently conducted by my wife and myself in the Lazi region:

> But there are other scholars who question the whole project. Why should a spoken language have to 'develop' into a written one? If the Lazi have chosen, with regret, the path of assimilation, into Turkishness, what right have outsiders to persuade them that this is the wrong path? For myself, I support Feurstein. A scientist is not just a camera. A scientist's duty to a vanishing culture is not just to record but to offer wisdom and say: 'This end is not inevitable. There is a way to survive, and I can point you towards it!'

I do not claim that the social scientist can be a camera, but I am uncomfortable with the vision and enthusiasm displayed by these intellectuals. Ascherson has barely the slightest acquaintance with them, and Feurstein, though he has devoted his life to their cause, has had no direct contact with the region for more than fifteen years. What, then, can I, as another foreign intellectual, say about the local response to this appeal? What are the self-identifications of the people recognized by Feurstein so clearly as a *Volk*?

Most Lazi are well aware of the linguistic border that distinguishes them from the Turkish population to the west ('Laz'). They know that the belt of Laz speakers stretches from Melyat to the state border and beyond. Within this region other groups are also recognized, notably the Hemşinli, mostly located further inland, with their own distinctive mode of subsistence. They are thought to be of Armenian origin, though many Hemşinli themselves do not acknowledge this link and all are quite certain that they are Turkish today. Just as there is no strong bond that links the eastern and western Hemşinli, who are geographically separated by several exclusively Lazi valleys, so there is no strong identity as Lazi that unites, say, a resident of Pazar, the first town of the region, with a resident of Hopa, the last small town before the state border. The Lazuri they speak is quite distinct, and there are further, less marked distinctions throughout the Lazi territory as one moves from one valley to the next. Depending on the context, some Lazi find it easier to use the medium of Turkish, even when talking to fellow Lazi from their own area. Quite apart from these dialect variations, which Feurstein is seeking to flatten with his language initiatives, there are also significant cultural differences between the eastern and western sections of the Lazi region. Levels of religious commitment are substantially higher in the west (Pazar and Ardeşen districts), which is also characterized by a more patriarchal pattern of gender relations (publicly visible in the high proportion of women who use a headscarf, for example, and confirmed in more private, domestic arrangements, such as control over household finances). It is therefore unsurprising that many residents of Fındıklı and Arhavi, where left-wing secularists have been stronger in local government, identify more strongly with remote urban centres rather than with putative co-ethnics to the west. Arhavi likes to present itself as 'Little Istanbul', particularly at the time of its annual Culture Festival, a series of events that draws crowds from a wide area, but in which there is no space whatever for any specifically Lazi culture.

It is in fact increasingly difficult to specify any distinctive features of Lazi culture. Even the language has been seriously weakened, especially among the small-town dwellers. It is no longer possible to record Lazi mythology (Feurstein was able to collect some rich narratives in the 1960s and 1970s), and although certain elements in wedding rituals may have distinctive origins, for the most part Lazi rituals and ceremonies, like their economic practices (dominated by tea), are now identical to those of their neighbours. Young people, despite their geographical remoteness from Ankara and Istanbul, seem fully integrated into the national society. Large numbers proceed to other parts of the country for higher education and employment (though few sever links permanently with the home, retaining a strong sense of belonging to the hamlet or small town where their tea gardens are located). They do their military service, read the popular fashion magazines, buy the latest Arabesk cassettes, etc. If there is one political issue that unites people here, it is their condemnation of the terrorist campaigns waged by the PKK (Kurdish People's Party).

The Lazi people are, then, like the Lemkos, divided internally at the same time as they are integrated *en masse* into the modern Turkish 'nation-state'. One further recent development that warrants attention is the influx of petty traders following the reopening of the road crossing into Georgia in 1988 (Hann and Hann, 1992). By the early 1990s, following the collapse of the Soviet Union, this part of Turkey was experiencing something of a cultural invasion. The feature consistently highlighted by local people and fanned in the media was a new pattern of prostitution (Bellér-Hann, forthcoming). There was some significant variation in attitudes towards these traders, and to the prostitutes too, with the inhabitants of the most easterly districts (those whose self-image tends towards the 'secular enlightened') more likely to show sympathy and an appreciation of the economic predicament of the visitors. But the key point is that this reopening, after half a century, to allow in the people who are the closest Caucasian neighbours of the Lazi, did not seem to inspire in the Lazi any feelings of ethnic or national solidarity. On the contrary, we received the strong impression that these renewed contacts reinforced a sense of difference and superiority – of professing a Turkish identity, with a more powerful economy (based on capitalism) and a more virtuous moral code (based on an Islam which ostensibly condemns that very capitalism).

Feurstein himself explains the absence of Lazi cultural activities in terms of the state's policies of assimilation. The implication is that the Lazi *would* spontaneously develop ethnic or national unity if state controls were relaxed and more information readily available. But in my view the present lack of interest cannot be attributed primarily to fear. The fact is that many Lazi, old as well as young, do not care about their Lazi identity as Feurstein would wish them to. Many do not even value their language. They value other identities more – they are supporters of one or other of the national political parties or of Galatasaray (one of the major Istanbul football teams), or they are members of a local women's association or a hunting club; they are more-or-less devout Muslims and more-or-less committed Turkish nationalists. These identities are not exclusive, and no doubt there is room for Lazi ethnic identity to be added to the list, to become a more powerful source of identity than it has been hitherto. But it is only the restrictive mindset of European nationalism that would expect this to become the most essential, fundamental aspect of personal and collective identity.

There are in fact a number of signs in the early 1990s that a Lazi cultural 'revival' may be imminent. A small museum is about to open (in 1994) in a disused primary school in the centre of the Lazi district, and a library has been founded in Arhavi. However, the more significant developments are being initiated not in the homeland but by elements of a secularized intelligentsia in the largest Lazi diaspora, in Istanbul. Here several issues of a new periodical *Ogni* (Hear!) were produced in 1993–4, written mostly in Turkish but also using Feurstein's alphabet to render short passages of Lazuri. Feurstein himself has supplied an article to this journal. It has been careful to promote only cultural issues, and to avoid any hint of separatist politics. Nevertheless, predictably, Kurdish groups and elements of the mass media have seized on this initiative to imply that the Lazi too have legitimate territorial claims. At the time of writing the editor of this new journal is facing charges of separatism in Istanbul, but its impact in the Lazi homeland has probably not been significant.

CONCLUSIONS

In this essay I have considered the efforts of two intellectuals to promote group identity in the late twentieth century. The groups in question can be seen as falling *between* two or more powerful established nationalisms: Ukrainian, Polish and others in the Lemko-Rusyn case, Georgian and Turkish in the Lazi case. In both examples it is clear that the demarcation of cultures through precise lines on a map, as required by nationalism, is an awkward if not impossible exercise. Europe, like other parts of the world, is full of borderlands, complex transition zones that inevitably pose problems for nationalist homogenizers.

Yet, rather than recognize culture as something that is continuously variable and blurred, with all attempts to impose boundaries that are 'fuzzy' at the edges, the intellectuals discussed here cling to the notion of the sharp boundary. They believe that the true, essential identity of a people has been violated by the political (or 'administrative') imposition of a foreign identity. Of course, the two cases differ greatly, not just in local detail but in certain structural respects as well. The Rusyns are split between several states. When he writes about the Lemkos, Paul Robert Magocsi is mainly concerned to protest against an oppressive identity imposed from *outside* the state in which they reside. For Feurstein, the threat to the Lazi comes from the Turkish state within which the great majority of them reside. Unlike the Central European states (at least in modern times), the Turkish government has not acknowledged any category of national minority or ethnic group. However, Lazi have not been subject to negative stereotyping by the majority in the way that Lemkos and other Ukrainians have been stigmatized in Poland.

In other respects there are close similarities: the numbers are comparable, as is the split between the territorially compact homeland and the influential diaspora groups; further common features include the absence of any large towns, the slow development of a standardized language, and a distinctive presentation of history. Of course, it is precisely because these latter needs have not been adequately met by locals that the Western intellectuals have been presented with an opportunity to offer a contribution of their own.

'Outsiders' have often been among the founders of national movements in the past, and yet the gulf between Toronto and the Lemko homeland is considerable, as is that between the Black Forest and the Lazi homeland. Respect for the intellectual sophistication of such an outsider can be tempered with ambivalence: he doesn't actually *live* with us, he can't appreciate our forests as we do, he can never really know our social world as an insider. Tensions that have little to do with the Lazi surface frequently in Turkish–German relations, and these have some impact on the readiness of Lazi to accept scholarly guidance from a German. Similarly, tensions in Polish–Ukrainian relations that have nothing to do with the Lemko-Rusyns may have an impact on the nation-building ambitions of Paul Robert Magocsi.

One factor above all others prevents either of these intellectuals from adopting a more active leadership role. The Lazi are overwhelmingly Muslim, and Feurstein is a *gâvur* (infidel). The Lemkos are, as we have seen, divided between Orthodoxy and Greek Catholicism. But Paul Robert Magocsi, in spite of his family links with the region, is basically a secular man who espouses the cosmopolitan or 'multi-cultural' values of North American society. This renders him well equipped to promote Lemko and Rusyn causes through a range of scholarly activities, but less well suited to a more active personal engagement.

Even if neither of these scholars is likely on present evidence to make the kind of contribution to the political sphere that was made by some of the nineteenth-century nation-builders, their activities still raise many questions of political and ethical responsibility. It is obvious that the general climate of opinion in at least some sections of Western Academia is now very different from what it was even two decades ago. Recently, I attended a large international conference entitled 'The Anthropology of Ethnicity: A Critical Review'. At a workshop that focused on language and religion, I discussed some of the problems concerning Lazi identity, and used the views of Ascherson and Feurstein, as summarized above, as a foil to present my own arguments about more complex, multiple identities in this region (Hann, 1995). The anthropological audience was basically sympathetic, but felt that I did not go far enough in my criticisms. For them, Lazi identity was obviously a quite artificial creation, the construction of someone who, if not necessarily a fascist reactionary, must be at best a crackpot or an amiable eccentric. As for

Ascherson's article (cited above), this was dismissed as *Realsatire*: a preposterous caricature of an 'essentialist' Herderian approach to identity that could not possibly be taken seriously by any contemporary anthropologist.

This sweeping dismissal made me uneasy. I have met both Feurstein and Ascherson, and although I have difficulty in accepting their presentation of the Lazi as a 'people', these intellectuals are liberal humanists rather than proto-fascists. I have formed very much the same impression in correspondence and in a (much briefer) meeting with Professor Magocsi. Their deep conviction that the collective rights of ethno-national groups should be observed is a conviction that demands respect. In contrast, what the anthropologists at this 'state of the art' conference had to offer was critical exposure of all such collective identities. Ethnicity was constructed, it was situational, it must always take its place alongside non-ethnic forms of identity, and at the end of the day no two individuals ever shared the same culture: consequently, to ground ethnic or national identity in culture could only lead to hopeless reifications. Despite the lacings of 'postmodernist' theory that he might not find congenial, this general position is consistent with Gellner's insistence on the 'invented' character of modern nations. And all this clearly has some affinity with my own general stance, as outlined above. But taken to this extreme, the critical deconstruction of ethnic and national loyalties is liable to blind anthropologists to an understanding of the force of these identities, and of the many ways in which they enrich the lives of group members. The efforts to promote Lazi or Lemko identity may not succeed, and the world might be a healthier place if all intellectuals committed themselves to more pluralist, deconstructivist approaches to society and culture. We – including I suspect you, the reader of this publication – may share a wide measure of agreement concerning the desirability of such a world (for which we have lots of new labels – mongrel hybridization, creole cosmopolitanism, etc., etc.). But the world outside Academia is a long way from such realization, and it behoves even those who recognize fuzziness and are prepared to expose construction and forgery to *understand* the very deep commitments to boundaries that exist in us all and acquire virulent forms in modern nationalism.

In terms of practical political strategies, my uncomfortable intermediate position leads me to argue that in many contemporary states it may be vital to recognize ethnic collectivities and to guarantee their collective rights, in spite of one's honest intellectual conviction that doing so only contributes further to the consolidation of a basically fictitious identity. This strategy is warranted because anything else would ignore the reality of other powerful fictions already well entrenched. In the Lemko case, the strong nationalisms of Poland and Ukraine are likely to go on making life uncomfortable in various ways for those who, however uncertain they may be of their collective identity, know and feel that they are different from the national majority, and who in Poland often receive frequent unpleasant reminders of the fact.[4] The Lazi case is a little more complex, since this 'ethnolinguistic minority' is not subject to such negative stereotypes by the dominant group and in some respects has done rather well out of the Turkish state (particularly through the subsidies poured into the tea industry since 1950). However, the situation in which Lazuri speakers have so far failed to develop any clear sense of identity as 'the Lazi' is also one in which the history of these people has been systematically falsified, in which no distinctive features of their culture, past or present, including the language, have any official recognition. Truth-seeking intellectuals who condemn such policies may respond by demanding recognition of the Lazi as an ethnic group. But such demands are better left to the people directly concerned; and it is rich indeed that the Turkish state should be condemned for infringing civilized norms of minority rights by a Central European.

NOTES

1. Without relating his discussion to his personal background, Magocsi has himself commented on the 'roots' phenomenon in 1970s American culture in a paper in which he traces some of the close links between the diaspora identity debates and the identities of the homelands (Magocsi, 1990b).
2. For example, at the elections in spring 1994 there was lower than expected support for proposals to increase the regional autonomy of the Transcarpathian district of Ukraine, in spite of endemic political and economic instability in the new republic. Similarly, the flurry of organizational activity among the Rusyn-Ukrainians of the Prešov region of Slovakia has not been sustained, and, although the University of Prešov contains a group of committed cultural activists, they are by no means united in political strategy.
3. Research on the Lazi has been carried out jointly with Dr I. Bellér-Hann, with the support of an ESRC Research Grant (*Culture and Economy Among the Laz*, 1991–3, R 000 23 3208), which is gratefully acknowledged. For further discussion of the Laz(i), see Hann, 1995; Andrews, 1989.
4. For an expanded version of this argument in the case of the Lemkos, see Hann, forthcoming.

REFERENCES

Andrews, P.A. (ed.), 1989 *Ethnic Groups in the Republic of Turkey* (Wiesbaden: Otto Harassowitz).
Ascherson, N. 1993 'Journey to the end of an alphabet', *Independent on Sunday*, London, 7 November 1993.
Bellér-Hann, I., forthcoming, 'Prostitution and its effects in North East Turkey', *Feminist Review*.
Feurstein, W. 1983 'Untersuchungen zur materiellen Kultur der Lazen', Magisterarbeit, Albert-Ludwigs Universität, Freiburg.
Feurstein, W. 1984 *Lazuri Alfabe; lazca alfabe; Entwurf eines lazischen Alphabetes*, Parpali 1 (Gundelfingen: Lazebura).
Feurstein, W. and Berdsena, T. 1987 'Die Lazen; eine südkaukasische Minderheit in der Türkei', *Pogrom*, 129, pp. 36–9.
Gellner, E. 1964 *Thought and Change* (London: Weidenfeld & Nicolson).
Gellner, E. 1983 *Nations and Nationalism* (Oxford: Basil Blackwell).
Hann, C.M. 1985 *A Village Without Solidarity; Polish peasants in years of crisis* (New Haven: Yale University Press).
Hann, C.M. 1990 *Tea and the Domestication of the Turkish State* (Huntingdon: Eothen Press).
Hann, C.M. 1995 'Ethnicity, language and politics in northeast Turkey', in C. Govers and J. Fox (eds), *The Politics of Ethnicity* (Amsterdam).
Hann, C.M., forthcoming, 'Ethnicity in the new civil society: Lemko-Ukrainians in Poland', in L. Kürti and J. Fox (eds), *Beyond Borders: Remaking Eastern European Identities in the 1990s* (Columbia University Press).
Hann, C. and Hann, I. 1992 'Samovars and sex on Turkey's Russian markets', *Anthropology Today*, 8 (4), pp. 3–6.
Himka, J.-P. 1984 'The Greek-Catholic Church and nation-building in Galicia, 1772–1918', *Harvard Ukrainian Studies*, 8, pp. 426–52.
Kırzıoglu, M.F. 1972 'Lazlar/Canarlar', *Türk Tarih Kongresi VII*, 1, pp. 420–45.
Magocsi, P.R. 1978 *The Shaping of a National Identity: Sub-Carpathian Rus', 1848–1948* (Cambridge, MA.: Harvard University Press).
Magocsi, P.R. 1983 *The Rusyn-Ukrainians of Czechoslovakia: An Historical Survey* (Vienna: Wilhelm Braumüller).
Magocsi, P.R. 1984 *Our People: Carpatho-Rusyns and their Descendants in North America* (Toronto: The Multicultural History Society of Ontario).
Magocsi, P.R. 1990a 'Nation-building or nation-destroying? Lemkos, Poles and Ukrainians in contemporary Poland', *Polish Review*, 35 (3), pp. 197–209.
Magocsi, P.R. 1990b 'Made or re-made in America? Nationality and identity formation among Carpatho-Rusyn immigrants and their descendants'. Paper presented at panel, 'The persistence of regional cultures: Rusyn-Ukrainians in the Carpathians and abroad', IV World Congress for Soviet and East European Studies, Harrogate, July 1990.
Meeker, M.E. 1971 'The Black Sea Turks: Some aspects of their ethnic and cultural background', *International Journal of Middle Eastern Studies*, 2 (4), pp. 318–45.
Mucha, J. 1991 'Ethnic composition of the Polish part of the Carpathian region', *Ethnologia Polona*, 15 (6), pp. 33–59.
Mucha, J. 1992 'Democratization and cultural minorities: The Polish case of the 1980s/90s', *East European Quarterly*, 25 (4), pp. 463–82.
Nowak, J. 1993 'Reconstruction of ethnic identity vs. inequalities: Lemkos in Poland',

Paper presented at the conference, 'The Anthropology of Ethnicity: A Critical Review', Amsterdam, December 1993.

Pieradzka, K. 1939 *Na Szlakach Łemkowszczyzny* (Kraków: Nakladem do spraw szlachty zagrodowej na wschodzie Polski).

Reinfuss, R. 1949–9 *Łemkowie jako grupa etnograficzna*, Prace i Materialy Etnograficzne, Vol. 7, pp. 77–210 (Lublin: wyd. Polskiego Towarzystwa Ludoznawczego).

Rudnycky, I.L. 1987 'Carpatho-Ukraine: A people in search of their identity', in I. L. Rudnycky, *Essays in Modern Ukrainian History* (Edmonton: Canadian Institute of Ukrainian Studies), pp. 353–74.

Vanilişi, A. and Tandılava, M. 1992 *Lazlar'ın Tarihi* (Istanbul: Ant Yayınları).

8

Breaking the Mould?
Quebec Independence and Secession in the Developed West

Hudson Meadwell

INTRODUCTION

Quebec today stands poised on the brink of a peaceful transition to independence.[1] Will it jump? Will it be pushed? Will it pull back? The ultimate answers to these questions are of some interest for a broader class of cases for which Quebec is often taken to be a critical case. These are the movements for independence that have developed in the liberal democratic, advanced capitalist world. Quebec appears to be the case in this broader class that is the most likely candidate for a democratic transition to independence. If Quebec cannot win through to independence, can we expect other cases in the developed West to achieve this goal? If its movement for independence is successful, Quebec will break the historical mould, for there is no case of secession in the liberal, advanced capitalist world. For this reason, Quebec will be the fulcrum of the analysis in this chapter. This focus will allow a look backwards at earlier cases of secession and a comparison with contemporaneous cases in the developed West. Moreover, in examining the special features of the nationalist movement that have brought Quebec, in the eyes of many observers, to the brink of independence, I will also be examining this broader question: Why no successful secession in the developed West?[2] This question, however, is felicitously posed only if it admits variation within the developed West. The problem with the argument that Quebec will reproduce a broader historical pattern within the West is that it cannot account for why and how the option of independence has progressed as far as it has in Quebec. The argument does not recognize what is distinctive about state- and regime-formation in Canada. What is needed is an argument that accounts for Quebec while preserving a larger argument about the developed West.

Thus this chapter has two purposes: to account for the absence of secession in this part of the international system while, at the same time, to explain why one of the cases in this class of cases appears to be poised for a peaceful transition to independence. It is this combination of purposes that produces the logic of comparison in this chapter, which combines diachronic and synchronic analysis. In looking backwards at earlier cases, I will contrast Quebec with Ireland and the American South. In looking at other cases in the advanced West, I will compare Quebec with Scotland and Catalonia. This design will support two conclusions. First, the 'long peace' in the developed West has not produced an independence movement that has shown the same mobilizational capacity as the movements for secession in the American South or Ireland. This leads to the conclusion that the causal conditions that produced Irish independence and the secession of the American South have not been reproduced, and cannot be reproduced, in the world of liberal democratic, advanced capitalism; and that this difference across time accounts both for the absence of secession in the developed West and for these two cases in earlier periods. Second, neither of the movements for independence in Scotland and Catalonia has been able to mobilize as much of local society to support independence as the movement in Quebec. I argue that the distinctive institutional profile of Quebec accounts for the differences among these cases in the advanced West. The question is whether what distinguishes Quebec from other contemporary cases is enough to compensate for those forces that produced powerful secessionist movements in Ireland and the American South and that appear to be absent in the Quebec case.

An explanation for the absence of secession in the developed West might well include, in specifying those features that distinguish the West, the political benefits of liberal institutions and the economic costs of exit. In order to provide such an account for the former, I will draw out some of the implications of Allen Buchanan's normative analysis of secession.[3] My comments on the costs of exit will be much briefer since I have discussed this issue elsewhere,[4] and because my research design allows me to suggest that one important set of structures and institutions that affect the costs of exit, namely the international political economy, enters explanation only after domestic contexts and institutions have been specified.

I have argued in other works that the international economy of the long peace has made secession easier because it has lowered the costs of transition and the economic risks of independence. But I have also argued that these effects are sequenced after a prior process of institution-building and identity-formation. The design of this chapter allows this argument to be extended for two reasons. One is that I can show that interdependence and international regimes are features of the environment of the entire class of cases of independence movements in the developed West, yet only one of them, Quebec, plausibly can be said to be poised to initiate a transition to independence. Moreover, secession was successful, either in terms of mobilizing local society and/or changing the territorial structure of the international state system in the cases of the American South or Ireland in international economic contexts that were very different from the long peace. Thus the international political economy of the long peace is a problematic explanation for the politics of secession in the developed West. It accounts for neither variation within or across international political economic regimes with regard to the presence or absence of, and support for, secession.

The rest of this chapter proceeds in seven sections. In the next two sections, I examine some relevant features of state- and regime-formation in the Canadian case. Once the distinctive institutional design of the Canadian state is identified, I go on in the next section to discuss its constituent features: consociation and federation. In the two sections that then follow, I place Quebec in comparative context, and only in the last two sections of the chapter paper do I summarize some of the micro-processes of mobilization that occurred in Quebec within the opportunity structures produced by this institutional design. My major concern is to identify the institutional design of state and regime in Canada and to discuss its effects. Historical origins are of lesser importance in this chapter and will be discussed in more detail on a later occasion.

LIBERALISM AND SECESSION

The empirical question 'Why no secession in the developed West?' can be given a normative answer that carries empirical implications –

liberalism constitutes the best possible political regime. While the status of this claim within normative theory can be bracketed for the purposes of this chapter, liberalism may well have recognizable empirical consequences. These can be addressed within positive theory without directly addressing normative issues. Yet if a liberal regime, which I will understand here as combining competitive elections and inclusion, has consequences, something like the following must be true.

The virtues of a liberal regime will usually in the end be apparent to its citizens. Political rationality will counsel continued support for, and participation in, the regime. Liberal polities, further, are often flexible enough to hold out some promise that they can be improved from within and inclusion and recognition can be gained for excluded groups. As a consequence, a liberal regime should make exit (secession) less likely.

Leaders of nationalist movements in the developed West therefore should have difficulty in translating nationalism into independence. Movements for independence in the developed West have failed, this line of argument would suggest, because enough individuals in the relevant groups are liberals before they are nationalists so that procedures of collective decision-making, such as referenda, cannot produce sufficient support for secession to initiate a peaceful transition to independence.

A different explanation for the absence of secession, as already noted, emphasizes the issue of the costs of exit. Procedural barriers, while only the first step in the process of separation, are the essential starting-point for a democratic transition to independence. The *real* barrier to crossing this threshold, however, and thus the reason why movements for independence have not been able to transform nationalism into independence, is the difficulty of convincing the public that the costs of the transition to independence are bearable and that independence is economically viable. In other words, this explanation emphasizes the importance of the economic barriers to exit, and how changes to these barriers affect the relationship between nationalism and secession. Economic constraints make it difficult, even given a favourable political conjuncture, to transform nationalism into support for independence.

Whichever of these accounts we want to emphasize – the politics of inclusion or the economics of exit – or however we decide to combine them, they offer a plausible explanation, once appropriately filled out, for the absence of secession in the developed West and, by extension, a prognosis on the case of Quebec. Thus it should immediately follow as a conclusion that Quebec will not break the historical mould.

This explanation, moreover, has clear comparative implications. According to this logic, the absence of liberalism and capitalism should create predisposing conditions for secession. This expectation is broadly consonant with the experience of the developing world and with the breakup of the Soviet Union. It is also consistent with the recent separation of Slovakia and the Czech Republic, a political divorce which would not have occurred, according to many observers, if it had been decided democratically through referenda, and a divorce that may have been motivated in part in the Czech lands by a desire within the political elite to quicken and entrench the transition to a capitalist economy.

In this chapter, I want to assess some features of this explanation of the failure of secession in the West, particularly its first part – the extension of Buchanan's analysis of secession. Against an argument that shows how the Canadian case is like others in the West and hence likely to reproduce its patterns, I show how it is distinctive. These differences, I will argue, have made secession a more important expression of nationalism in Quebec than other cases of local nationalism in the postwar liberal, advanced capitalist world.

Perhaps the best place to begin in addressing this broader question, and within it the status of the Quebec case, is with the distinctive institutional features of the Canadian state. In its origins as a Dominion in the British Commonwealth, it was both consociational and federal.[5] On both counts, the Canadian state was, from the start, differently designed from the states of Western Europe.

STATES IN THE WEST

Historical sociologists, and realists, have argued that the absence of central authority in the emergent European state system after the Peace of Westphalia was conducive to war, and that modern warfare, in turn, contributed to the emergence of unitary states, indirectly to liberal institutions and to nationalism. Unitary states were efficient solutions to the problem of self-help under anarchy because they supplied the infrastructure for the extraction of resources.[6] Liberal institutions were an historic achievement within this world, as limits to the legitimate authority of the state, and were made possible by the unique combination of war, commerce and constitutionalism.[7] National identities were forged in inter-state conflict and, once formed, they provided another mechanism to mobilize society.[8] Only in the twentieth century, under security regimes that have lowered the costs of decentralization and changed the military economies of scale, have federal and consociational practices had any prominence.[9]

The evolutionary logic of this argument about war and state-making is mirrored in a rival interpretation of nationalism, rooted not in the imperatives of inter-state war but in the requisites of industrial society.[10] Both produce a similar expectation: nations mobilized around states. In short, the solution to these twin imperatives of modernity, war and industry was the nation-state. This argument has been made by Jack Snyder, for example, who, in refusing to choose between the warfare thesis and the industrialization thesis, combines them in his interpretation of nationalism.[11]

An explanation for the institutional features of the Canadian case is then straightforward. The emergent nineteenth-century Canadian state escaped these acute security dilemmas. State-formation in North America did not occur in the same sort of anarchy as original state-making in Europe. There was some room for variation from the canonical form of state predicted by this literature on state-making. In other words, its developmental path to democratic, advanced capitalism was distinctive, and was shaped by its history as a settler society in this regional subsystem. Quebec did not choose to go it alone during the debate about Confederation: its leaders preferred accommodation with English-Canadians within federal arrangements.[12] The Canadian state, as a consequence, was consociational and federal. Thus Canada (and Quebec), while cases in this class of the 'developed West', simultaneously stand outside it in important ways that, I will argue, have worked to make secession a prominent possible solution to contemporary constitutional impasse and a more likely outcome than in other cases in the developed West.

The literature built around the distinctiveness of the West suggests that consociationalism and federalism were selected out through the sorting effects of inter-state war and industrialization. They were not constitutive features of the experience of the West. Consequently, they have been relatively neglected topics of study in this literature. In the next section, therefore, I will discuss some of the more important features of both consociation and federation.

CONSOCIATION AND FEDERATION

Consociation and federation are institutional principles that operate at different levels. Consociation provides a description of state–society relations.[13] As political practice, it is designed to regulate a distinctive political and social problem, namely relations between deeply divided subcultures, usually defined along religious, ethnic or linguistic lines. There is no presumption in consociation and consociationalism, as a theoretical model or political practice, that these groups are also divided along territorial lines. Before I go on to discuss some of their differences, however, let me point to the similar morphologies of the two institutional principles.

The normative justification for consociationalism is that its practices provide a second-best form of governance when liberal principles and institutions are infeasible because of subcultural cleavages. When the cleavage structures that underpin pluralism are not present, the consociational form of politics is an alternative to instability, even civil war.[14]

Interpretations of federalism, on the other hand, tend to have a shared feature because they treat federation as a solution to two-dimensional problems in territorial organization. Hence the most general explanation of a federation, namely that it reconciles unity and diversity. A different argument suggests that federalism satisfies the dual desiderata of size and smallness.[15] Another interpretation, which shares this same structure, sees federalism as emergent when territorial expansion is desired but conquest is infeasible. In this case, federalism is an alternative to empire.[16] In all cases, the claim is that a federation emerges when the achievement of some goal or desired state is costly because there is some other goal or desire, equally important, that would not be satisfied. Federalism emerges, then, as a second-best alternative to a unitary state when this principle is infeasible, whether because of diversity, size or the infeasibility of conquest.

In this specific sense, these two principles thus do share a structure. Each of the literatures built around these principles, to draw out just one implication, presupposes that the first-best form of governance is a liberal, unitary state, thus confirming in an indirect way the centrality of this form of state in Western experience. Yet, at the same time, this exercise suggests that it is not as clear whether the centrality of this form of state is as an historical form, as the historical sociologists have suggested, or whether the liberal, unitary state is important, not as a dominant historically present form, but rather as a critical ideal. In this regard, it is significant that the literatures on consociations and federations both suggest as a necessary condition for these political and territorial forms the presence of some external military-diplomatic threat which, at least roughly speaking, historical sociologists and realists have argued is conducive to unitary and to liberal states. Apparently, roughly the same conditions that produced unitary states can also contribute to the formation of federations and consociations. This point would support two different conclusions. If, indeed, unitary, liberal states were dominant, some other cause was at work to produce them; or, alternatively, this form of state was not dominant, in which case the Western commitment is to the unitary, liberal state as a critical ideal. The literatures on federation and consociation do suggest that the unitary, liberal state does not arise directly out of anarchy but varies with other factors as well. These two features (particularly the unitary principle) emerge when territories are not too large, not too diverse and not too costly to conquer.

There is another similarity between consociation and federation when juxtaposed to this model of the liberal, unitary state. In the politics of consociation, relations between autonomous subcultures often resemble relations between states. Conflict regulation through elite accommodation is therefore analogous to international diplomacy among sovereign states. As a consequence, there is not as sharp a difference between domestic and international politics in the model of consociation as there is in the model of the unitary, liberal state, which is built on the presupposition that the domestic sphere is characterized by the rule of law and the international sphere by anarchy. By contrast, the model of consociation could be drawn out so that it describes a set of homologous principles that structure, though to varying degrees, both spheres. The same could be said for the principle of federation, which has been used to describe both domestic politics and a normative model of international relations that is a rival to realist models.

Perhaps at this point the morphological similarity ends. In the case of federations, it is the combination of valued desiderata that makes a unitary state infeasible. In the case of consociations, it appears that it is not a combination of characteristics but the mere presence of subcultural segmentation that makes liberalism a non-starter. We can say, in other words, that a unitary state is consistent with smallness, unity or empire, and inconsistent with size, diversity or costly territorial expansion. We can say, as well, that liberalism can be consistent with weak subcultural segmentation, but not consistent with deep subcultural segmentation[17]. The difference is that, in the latter case, there is one yardstick, one metric at work: the degree of segmentation. In the case of the federal principle, a federation allows the reconciliation of independently valued desiderata. A federation, according to Forsyth, provides the advantages of size and the benefits of smallness, and this argument, for example, must presuppose that alternative states of affairs are located along two dimensions.

This point can be developed further so as to illustrate more fully how the principles of consociation and federation differ. As a principle of institutional design, federalism implies greater degrees of political freedom than consociationalism. Subcultural segmentation makes liberalism impossible, so it is argued; but, of course, it does not automatically produce consociational politics. Subcultural segmentation is still a constraint that must be escaped if a consociation is to emerge. Consociation is uniquely linked to these particular problems of cleavage. Group leaders must have enough room to manoeuvre: they must have enough autonomy so that they will not be punished (replaced) if they pursue moderation for this problem of cleavage to be resolved. As a consequence of this constraint, elite accommodation in consociational politics tends to be secret. When negotiations between group leaders are secret, they can present public and private faces. When negotiations are transparent, the politics of representing the rank and file of the group intrude directly into intergroup bargaining because leaders have to weigh the intragroup costs of pursuing intergroup accommodation. Secrecy allows leaders to separate their activity in negotiations from their functional position as representatives of their rank and files. Agreements thus must be satisfactory to all parties, otherwise they are unlikely to be self-enforcing; dissatisfied parties will have incentives to undermine negotiations, not necessarily by being obstructive, but through breaking the convention of secrecy by leaking the negotiating positions of others to their constituencies.

Federalism operates at a different level. It is, first of all, a formal description of a type of territorial division of power.[18] It cannot be linked uniquely to a particular kind of political problem for which it acts as a possible regulatory device. I say this in part because of the various interpretations of the rationale for, and the origins of, federation outlined earlier. Interpretations of the origins of federations, it seems to me, are either contested or vacuous. That they are contested is precisely a result of the formal characteristics of the federal principle. I suspect that there is no free-standing political theory of federalism; a political theory of federalism is always dependent on a theory of something else. So, too, for federalism as practice. The practical rationales for federalism vary because federalism can be used for different sorts of situations and problems. Empirically speaking, this means that when looking at moments of institutional design, it is useful to ask what the formative political question was and, if federalism was part of the design, what role it played. The corollary is not to mistake the effects of federalism for the effects of something else.

This is particularly important for the two institutional principles that I am discussing here because federalism can be a consociational device when subcultural segmentation has a territorial dimension. Canada, for example, has been called the first case in which the decision to form a federal rather than a unitary state was determined by the desire to accomplish ethnic accommodation.[19] There is thus nothing in the principle of consociation that links it exclusively to a unitary state, such that a consociation is a consociation if and only if the state is unitary.

It is clear, however, that federalism has a life independent of ethnic accommodation, even if it can be a consociational device. We need look no further than to the other case of federalism in North America. American federalism also illustrates an earlier argument about the relation of federalism to formative political projects. In the US the central political problem was how to reconcile republicanism with modernity.[20] Federalism entered the picture as a contribution to this project.[21]

The Canadian case is quite different, although my main point is not just that this case is different from US federalism. What more sharply distinguishes the two cases is the difference between consociationalism and pluralism. I do not want to be misunderstood here, however. It is consequential that consociation in Canada was organized within a federal framework. My point is that the animating issue in the origins of Canadian state and society, however, was accommodation between French and English; this kind of problem can be understood quite independently of federalism and the way to understand it is through consociation. To do so requires some attempt to distinguish the effects of these two institutional principles in a case such as this where they are joined. This is the purpose of the remainder of this section.

Consociation is a difference-preserving form of political regime and strategy of ethnic conflict regulation.[22] When its principles are built into the institutional design of a state, it maintains, indeed depends on, segmental or group boundaries. This system of accommodation is extremely sensitive to the behaviour of group elites and must be so constructed that those elites who prefer accommodation cannot be replaced, nor have incentives to change their preference for accommodation, once such a preference has formed. The incentive structure must also be durable enough that the intergenerational replacement of group elites preserves intergroup accommodation.

Consociational institutions are not particularly robust. A consociational system of institutions is a delicately balanced creation, dependent on an original moment of institutional design. This original moment is typically formed in a particular conjuncture and, thereafter, consociational systems are sensitive to changes in the original conjunctural conditions that made consociationalism possible. A consociational system is peculiarly vulnerable because, in its institutional design, too many conditions must be held constant for it to be stably reproduced over time. The range of normal politics defined by its design is narrow and, consequently, its foundational principles are too easily threatened in political action. This political problem of consociationalism is also mirrored in its social structure which, in its segmentation, depends on social entropy and which sets an upper limit on mobility.

Consociationalism is successful when group differences are maintained and intergroup accommodation achieved. Politically and socially, it is built on stasis. It is reproduced over time through the replication of the original moment of institutional design. Static rather than dynamic, this form of state and society leaves as its legacy, when accommodation does break down, organized and relatively disciplined corporate groups.

Consociation thus also is transformed not only when accommodation breaks down, but when group differences are effaced over time. When group boundaries no longer encapsulate self-contained subcultures, consociational politics is no longer needed and indeed cannot be practised. Our interest in consociationalism still lies, however, in the possibility of intergroup accommodation, even in the face of group differences. When these differences decline or disappear, the problem that consociational politics can be said to be designed to manage also declines and, obviously, consociationalism can be abandoned as a model of state–society relations in such a case. While there still may be traces of consociational politics, consociation is no longer a thoroughgoing description of society and politics. Political accommodation may still be required, but it is no longer strictly an issue of relations between internally stratified subcultures. This could be said for the contemporary Netherlands,[23] the classic site of consociational politics.

Federalism need not be a consociational device, but when consociationalism is present and groups are geographically segmented, there will be a tendency towards federalism, when federalism is not part of the original moment of institutional design (witness Belgium). Where consociationalism and federalism overlay one another, moreover, the continuity of the latter depends on the stability of consociationalism. If consociationalism breaks down, the federal status quo is likely to be immediately challenged because, with this combination of institutional principles, territorial arrangements are politicized in a way that would not occur if federalism was joined to liberal, rather that consociational, principles. When consociationalism and federalism are joined, much of the infrastructural capacity of the group can depend on the powers delegated to the territorial subunits; thus demands for changes to the federal status quo can be used to challenge consociational principles and the practices of power-sharing. While federalism can be, and has been, a consociational device, it still contributes to intergroup relations independently of consociationalism. The difference between Canada and Belgium illustrates this effect. In both cases, elements of consociational power-sharing have been present since their formation, probably more prominently and centrally in the case of Belgium. When consociational arrangements broke down in the two cases, it was Canada, where consociation was joined to a federal state, that experienced the more important secessionist challenge. For some time in Belgium, where consociationalism was linked to a unitary state, the major intergroup political issue was the status of Brussels.[24]

In distinguishing the effects of consociationalism and federalism, to summarize, consociationalism, as principle, legitimates organized and disciplined corporate groups and, as practice, contributes to their preservation over time. Federalism, in principle, provides a separate domain of power that, in practice, can supply local political institutions for the group. Federalism also implies a written constitution and this is another of its effects: when consociationalism breaks down in a federal system, the focus of debate will be the constitutional division of powers, and the redesign of intergroup accommodation will be, at the same time, the redesign of the territorial state.

Constitutional debate is so important a process because it creates openings for institutional re-creation and political entrepreneurship. Constitutional reform in liberal democracies is an expression of a peaceful commitment to possible changes in the rules of the game and the identities of the players. At the same time, the stakes of constitutional negotiations can be quite high. They are debates about entrenching enduring rules in written documents, and are often dependent on amendment procedures that are devised so that the agreement needed to change the constitution is difficult to achieve. Thus this expression of democratic governance can have the unintended effect of crystallizing and hardening positions.

For the most part, my reference point for this stage has been the democratic, advanced capitalist world and I will continue to use this perspective. To recapitulate my major argument: the strength of the independence option in Quebec, distinctively strong in this context of the developed West, is rooted in the institutional characteristics of consociation and federation. In the next two sections, I will examine in more detail how consociation and federation provided an institutional basis for separatism, by briefly contrasting Quebec with contemporaneous and earlier cases. A summary of some of the micro-processes of mobilization that developed within these opportunity structures will be presented in the final two sections.

QUEBEC IN COMPARATIVE PERSPECTIVE

The combination of consociation and federation in the institutional design of the Canadian state has meant that nationalist entrepreneurs in Quebec have been able to entrench nationalism and to translate it into support for independence. By contrast, in Scotland the Scottish National Party (SNP), while it has come to use as a mobilizing trope the idea of an independent Scotland in the European Community (after earlier resistance to integration largely on economic grounds), cannot build on the same institutional capacity as the movement in Quebec. Judging by the results of the last UK general election, this political strategy of linking Scottish independence to Europe, while it has modified the structure of public opinion with regard to autonomy, has made little practical difference in the electoral representation of the SNP. Politically speaking, institutional arrangements and the tradition of parliamentary supremacy direct all attention to the British House of Commons and it is no surprise that the core organization of Scottish nationalism is organized around competition in this arena.

The institutional infrastructure that Scotland maintained after the Act of Union (1707), though substantial in a comparative context, illustrates, through its absence, the importance of a local legislature with separate powers from the national legislature. The Union signalled Scottish agreement to the Hanoverian succession and to legislative unity. For English governments, these concerns went hand in hand since it was feared that a rebellious Scots parliament would alter the succession settlement so that the next monarch of England would not succeed to the Scottish throne.[25] Hence, an incorporation of parliaments was the English demand; the Scottish demanded freedom of trade.[26] The Union thus entrenched the principle of parliamentary supremacy in a unitary form (a federal form was not seriously considered by the English), and the political mould of Scottish–British relations was set.

This constitutional framework has made it difficult to translate popular support for decentralization into political pressure. The institutional problems of a nationalist movement rooted in a party without a local legislature may come eventually to produce a different sort of movement organized more explicitly around the issue of representation and perhaps mobilized more outside the party system. It is only very recently, however, that the hegemony of the SNP within nationalist politics has been challenged by the Constitutional Convention, and then only partially. Parliamentary supremacy, majoritarian electoral institutions and an unwritten constitution have combined to produce a durable political system that has made both partisan party competition, and this alternative to it, weak mechanisms for renegotiating the constitutional status of Scotland.

The Catalan case points to a different feature of Quebec – its distinctive pattern of liberalization in the postwar period. Liberalization in Quebec, known metaphorically as the 'Quiet Revolution', produced a move to redesign the earlier institutional arrangements of confederation. The pact-making of the democratic transition in Spain is structurally analogous to the first moment of state-formation in the Canadian case rather than this second period of renegotiation that followed change in Quebec. The availability of liberal capitalism through continued participation in the Canadian state was never in doubt as Quebec began to modernize politically and economically in the 1950s and 1960s. This process of liberalization was purely a local affair, and assumed the continuity and stability of the Canadian political regime. By contrast, in Catalonia the question of regime and the national question had to be bargained for simultaneously in the 1970s. Liberalization was a society-wide process. The power-sharing arrangements that local elites have achieved in Catalonia, which have provided an important degree of institutional capacity including an autonomous parliament, therefore are set within a different constitutional context than in Quebec.

In supporting Spanish liberal democracy in the territorial form in which it was bargained for, Catalan political elites to an important extent bought into the territorial status quo. Inclusion in the Spanish state was accepted by the Catalan political elite because support for the territorial integrity of the state would make a stable liberal transformation more likely. The commitment to liberal democracy, and participation in pact-making, trumped the commitment to Catalan nationalism and moderated demands. In the Catalan case, the democratic transition actually limited the nationalist posture of the Catalan political elite; it did not open the door to extreme nationalist demands and secession, though if the transition had failed, the history of other cases suggests that the likelihood of territorial fragmentation would have increased. The differences between the Quebec and Catalan cases are strongly related to the different constitutional histories and institutional makeup of the Canadian and Spanish states. The one state has an uninterrupted history of liberal democracy; the other has only recently become liberal democratic. The result has been that, in Quebec, nationalists have been able to push faster and further for increased local powers and a renegotiated status within Canada. They have had more to build on – consociation and federation were legitimate features of Canadian and Quebec political institutions from confederation. Elites in Catalonia could not bargain for so much after the death of Franco because of the priority given in the constitutional debates to entrenching liberal democracy after a long period of authoritarian rule.

Although these cases are different, because liberalization was a local affair in one instance but not in the other, they are also similar in an important sense. In neither case did liberalization immediately yield regions mobilized for independence.[27] The separatist movement in Quebec did not become a political force until the 1970s and, when it became important, it was much changed as a result of the disciplining effects of democratic institutions, even in its commitment to independence, couched for partisan political reasons in the language of 'sovereignty-association'.[28] The process of mobilization in support of independence is ongoing in the Quebec case and, in Catalonia, is far weaker in terms of popular support or organized political party activity.[29]

ILLIBERAL SOCIETIES AND SECESSION

Before moving on to discuss how the principles of consociation and federation shaped political mobilization in Quebec, I should point to the theoretical importance of secession (the Civil War) in the United States and in the unitary state of the United Kingdom (Irish independence). These cases have dropped out of my discussion simply because of my focus on late-twentieth-century politics, but they are obviously relevant for the more general thrust of my argument. Each points to a potential problem in my argument about consociation and federation.

The US case illustrates that federalism without consociationalism can contribute to secession, thus suggesting that the causal combination of consociation and federation and their joint effects on secession in Canada are case-specific. In fact, the United States is a useful counter-case because the episode of the Civil War is quite consistent with the logic of consociational politics. The Civil War was the result of the refusal of the North to accept a form of power-sharing to be entrenched in the doctrine and practice of states' rights – a form of illiberal consociation that would have had built into its design subcultural segmentation and subcultural autonomy that would have reproduced intolerably illiberal practices. When the demand for consociation was rejected, the South moved towards secession. Just as consociational theory suggests, the failure of consociation increased the likelihood of civil war.

The Irish case demonstrates that secession from a state unified in a single legislature can be successful. The run-up to Irish independence thus indirectly confirms my earlier conjecture that it is not federalism *per se* that is the leading edge of change, but rather the form of state–society relations. The Irish case thus allows my conjecture to be extended: like its federal alternative, the unitary principle is, on its own, no explanation for the presence or absence, success or failure, of secession. The Irish case is interesting because of Ireland's peculiar status as both a part of the British metropole and a colony of the British empire, an arrangement that gave it representation in the House of Commons while maintaining an essentially colonial economic relationship more characteristic of Britain's economic relations with its overseas colonies than with the rest of its metropole. In the end, Irish independence was imaginable to the British precisely because Ireland could be seen as a colony, rather than as a constitutive part of the metropole,[30] and because it was an alien presence, a Catholic society, in Protestant Britain.

These are the two most important cases of secession in the modern West.[31] It is therefore important to note that they share an important feature: they were expressions of illiberal and, to some extent, pre-modern societies. Each, in different ways and to varying extents, drew on republican traditions to justify their practices and their plans for change, and to distinguish their societies from the larger societies of which they were a part. Classical Athens, which was claimed as an illustration of the compatibility of democracy and slavery, was the favoured republican archetype in the South,[32] and a common argument for slavery was that it was needed to maintain a republican form of government.[33] In Ireland at the end of the eighteenth century, republicanism replaced monarchism as the source of resistance to Britain. The Irish had traditionally looked to France for support for the exiled Stuarts; nationalist republicans replaced the Bourbons with the Jacobins.[34] In this process of differentiation from the enemy, Ireland would not only be Catholic, it also would not be monarchist.

I therefore take these two cases as further support for my argument that the effects of federation are often confused with the effects of other institutional principles. The oft-noted Janus-face of federalism as both a solution to, and a cause of, ethnic conflict may be an artefact of the fact that federalism is not a foundational principle, working as it always does in conjunction with other principles.

Having now satisfied one of the purposes of introducing these two countercases, that is to address one kind of potential challenge to my arguments, let me now turn to another reason for discussing them. These three cases – Quebec, the American South and Ireland – can be usefully compared. The formative events of Canadian confederation, the Civil War and Irish independence all preserved illiberal local societies. If we follow these cases through time, moreover, they all begin to change at roughly the same point, about the 1960s. In Ireland, the role of the

Church in local society was beginning to change; there was growing interest in an economic opening, especially towards the rest of Europe; and Catholics began civil rights demonstrations in the North. The American South began to be desegregated at about the same time. Consociational arrangements in Canada had held back liberalization in Quebec. They provided the means by which a very conservatively orientated Catholic Church and local notables controlled politics. In Quebec, the Catholic Church's relation to state and society was transformed, and the cultural division of labour began to change in the same period – the 1950s and 1960s.

Whereas in the American South and in Ireland, the changes of the 1960s were fundamentally forms of liberalization, the changes in Quebec were liberal but also nationalist, and support for secession became an important form of nationalism. Nothing in the history of Quebec had foreclosed the possibility of secession, as the American Civil War had for the South. When the movement for independence did emerge and gained ground in the 1970s it was in a very different context than turn of the century Ireland, where Catholicism thoroughly structured society and politics, and where the economy provided fertile ground for popular mobilization that could be turned to nationalist ends. In the cases of the South and Ireland, moreover, there was little pretence that liberalism was to be of any importance in the societies to be created through secession. Their forms of republicanism were thoroughly illiberal and the illiberalism of these societies was a powerful motivational force in their movements for independence.

What is different about Quebec, when set against the backdrop of these other cases, is that secession is not connected to deeply entrenched illiberalism as it was in the American South and Ireland. 'Can secession be achieved after liberalization has occurred?' is the question that the case of Quebec raises. The project of *indépendantiste* political entrepreneurs in Quebec has been to construct a nationalism in which secession after liberalization was possible. They have opted for a form of civic nationalism organized around linguistic hegemony, thus trying to strike a balance between their commitments to French-Canadian Québécois and to Quebeckers who are not French-Canadian. The political regime that might be anticipated in Quebec after independence, if it were to be achieved, would be designed differently from the Canadian state. The drive for territorial consolidation and linguistic and cultural hegemony in an independent Quebec would be inconsistent with consociation or federation, despite the fact that the regime would confront well-organized aboriginal, allophone and anglophone communities.

It remains to discuss how mobilization around the option of independence developed in Quebec from the 1960s onwards. This is the goal of the last two sections of this chapter. In the next section, I very briefly establish as an historical baseline the pattern of incorporation of French-Canadians in confederation, and then examine how the accommodation that was built into this pattern was changed by the Quiet Revolution of the 1950s and 1960s, and opened up a prolonged and still unfinished process of constitutional negotiation.

POLITICAL MOBILIZATION IN QUEBEC

There were three central elements to the pattern of incorporation of French-Canadians in the Canadian state in confederation. The Canadian state was built on the earlier military conquest of the French in the colonial wars between France and Britain. The accommodation that was reached at the time of confederation was federalist, and, finally, confederation also established a tacit concordat between the Canadian state and the French-Canadian Catholic Church. The Church preserved its organizational structure and its place in French-Canadian society, and became a key institutional support for conservative governments in Quebec and for French-Canadian nationalism. From confederation until the 1950s, then, consociational arrangements preserved central illiberal elements in Quebec society and politics, and the fundamental constitutional expression of consociation was federal.

Since this devolution of power was embedded in a federal state, political power located in the provincial state became in the 1950s the locus of activity for a modernizing coalition of intellectuals, trade unionists, lower clergy and white-collar professionals. This new political class contested the local power of the Church and of the traditional political elite, as well as the power-sharing arrangements underlying confederation.[35]

Their political critique took up two lines of attack. One was basically liberal and hostile to traditional French-Canadian nationalism, but equally opposed to more secular forms of nationalism in Quebec. The other strand sought to disengage nationalism from the control of the Church and the traditional political elite, not in order to destroy nationalism, but to reconstitute it on other foundations so that it might be compatible with modernity.

Now the older version of nationalism had always had contained in it a vision of an independent Quebec, separated from the profane world of liberal capitalism, but this had existed, sociologically speaking, as a millenarian myth rather than a social or political project. This myth was the other side of *la survivance*; it expressed the wish that was intertwined with the fear of cultural (and, for some, racial) extinction. In this vision, Quebec was already separate because it had been invested with a divine mission: to constitute a centre of Catholicism in North America. 'To be ourselves, absolutely ourselves, to constitute as Providence intends, an independent French state, such must be, from now on, the hope that guides our efforts, the flame that never dies.'[36] This was the eschatological side of French-Canadian Catholicism, the mystical expression of mission that, at root, rejected the bargain of confederation because it was beneath the nation that had been given this glorious civilizing mission by God. French-Canadian nationalism thus already had available to it the rejection of union. This counterpoint to the accommodation of the consociational bargain was thoroughly religious and, more specifically, tied to an otherworldly, apolitical form of Catholicism. It had no political agents that could carry it forward as a political project.

For those nationalists in the 1960s who supported independence, the problem was how to bring this vision of separation down to earth. The opening-up of Quebec, marked in 1959 by the death of Maurice Duplessis, constrained their politics in three relevant ways as they began to organize themselves. They had to mobilize support without the institutional or symbolic resources of the Church. They had to build an *indépendantiste* coalition in a society that was modernizing economically. And they had to confront a competing political programme that could also claim to be nationalist. Within these constraints, *indépendantistes*, however, could build on the continuing effects of consociational power-sharing and the institutional arrangements of federalism. Consociation had preserved the boundaries of the ethnic group and this provided a resource for mobilization in the first stages of organization. Federalism provided direct political mechanisms that could be built into a strategy of mobilization.

Consociation thus had the consequence of determining that post-Quiet-Revolution politics in Quebec would be nationalist. Power-sharing had preserved the boundaries of the group, though religious markers had become much less important in defining them. The process of liberalization, moreover, was also shaped by the trace effects of consociation. Liberalism in Quebec did include a discourse of rights, but that discourse included a central place for group rights. At the same time, however, the effects of consociation were limited by liberalization. While group rights were important in the politics of nationalism, they were important because they ranged over individuals, protecting the value that individuals found in group membership. (This was not the only version of the importance of communal goods among nationalists; there were other more group-centred interpretations that did not justify these goods in terms of the individual.) These consequences of liberalism for nationalism are probably also a consequence of capitalist development in the province. To put it very simply, Québécois are by and large satisfied with capitalism and what they enjoy are the individual opportunities it provides. The statist approach to modernization at the provincial level, characteristic of all governments from the 1960s onward, took this into account and was designed to distribute opportunities to francophones that were not available earlier.

The interpretation here can be made in the language of the previous discussion. Consociation was transformed in two contradictory ways. A leadership emerged that rejected the power-sharing arrangements of the confederation bargain. Their goal was to replace the local elites that had continued to accept the terms of the bargain and, simultaneously, to challenge the bargain directly. At the same time, the very transformations, capitalism and liberalism, that made this challenge possible and opened the door to a political form of *indépendantisme* also changed the corporate boundaries of the group. This was the dilemma of the *indépendantistes*.

In very broad strokes, this was the political field in which *indépendantistes* had to mobilize support. Despite the strength of the independence option in Quebec in the late 1980s and early 1990s, this process of popular mobilization was not easy. The strategy that was eventually settled on was to use federalism against itself, taking advantage of federal institutions to build a coalition of support. This move addressed their dilemma: the infrastructure of federalism provided a substitute for the institutional capacity of the Catholic Church. Nationalism, understood as the principle that nation and state should be congruent, supplied a substitute for the symbolic resources of Catholicism. In linking their fortunes to participation in federal institutions at the provincial level, they took advantage of the formal characteristics of the federal principle, which was compatible with capitalism, liberalism and nationalism.

The breakdown of consociation, however, had also produced a rival version of nationalism under which the principle of congruence between nation and state did not entail independence, but instead the strengthening of the Quebec state vis-à-vis the Canadian state. The salience of independence as a political option was thus not written into the transformation of consociation; it was the work of political entrepreneurs. Their first stage of mobilization was ethnic and economic in orientation and tied to a political rhetoric of ethnic class. This ideological position was inspired by the movements for liberation in the developing world and attempted to take political advantage of the economic transition in Quebec.

This political strategy had to be abandoned, essentially because it was anti-capitalist, or independence itself given up as a political project. The mobilizing rhetoric of *indépendantistes* has changed dramatically since those early years of the movement in the 1960s. The leading organizational edge of the movement, the Parti québecois (PQ), has increasingly moved away from an ethnic to a civic definition of the nation (though their linguistic and cultural demands resonate much more deeply with ethnic francophones – French-Canadian Québécois), and from economic grievances towards a rhetoric that stresses the political, emphasizing that the Québécois are second-class citizens of Canada and that the constitutional framework of Canada does not allow them to be a part of Canada as Québécois. The symbolism of these politics draws on the collective identity of francophone Quebeckers and downplays the significance of economic class as a source of grievance. The constitutional debate in Canada lends itself naturally to this rhetoric. Indeed, this language is an integral part of the debate. It focuses attention on shared attributes and concerns among francophones in Quebec. As a consequence, the nationalist movement, in this rhetorical emphasis, was less likely to be fragmented by the kinds of division which a rhetorical strategy tied to class would produce.

The constitutional debate about the status of Quebec is now thirty years old. It produced a referendum in Quebec in 1980 on the issue of separation, and a national referendum in 1992 on a broader package of constitutional reforms. This long period of constitutional debate, which has provided a focus and forum for the articulation of a distinctive

Québécois identity, appears to be a contributing cause of political mobilization in Quebec. Moreover, it gives the case of Quebec a distinctive political profile within the developed West. Aside from the debates of the democratic transition in the peripheries of Spain, only Belgium has gone through a similarly prolonged debate about a written constitution.

THE POLITICS OF CONSTITUTIONAL REFORM

The current state of constitutional debate in Quebec and Canada is a result of the failure to ratify the Meech Lake Accord. This agreement was signed by the First Ministers (the Canadian prime minister and provincial premiers) in June 1987. Its ratification required legislative approval in all provincial legislatures and the federal parliament within three years. The Accord was not ratified by the provincial legislature of Manitoba (and ratification by the legislature of Newfoundland was rescinded when Clyde Wells became premier) by June 1990, and the agreement became null and void. This failure had momentous consequences in Quebec. It strengthened the political position of *indépendantistes*, and weakened the position of Quebec federalists.

The origins of the Meech Lake Accord, however, lie in the constitutional negotiations which led to the Constitution Act of 1982; and this Act, in turn, has at least its proximate roots in the period leading up to the earlier Quebec referendum on sovereignty-association in 1980. The referendum asked voters to give the provincial government 'the mandate to negotiate' a proposed agreement between Quebec and Canada which 'would enable Quebec to acquire the exclusive power to make its laws, administer its taxes and establish relations abroad – in other words, sovereignty – and, at the same time, to maintain with Canada an economic association including a common currency. Any change in political status resulting from these negotiations will be submitted to the people through a referendum.' While there has been considerable rhetorical manoeuvring around the meaning of this arrangement, it has two core components. The first is the political independence of Quebec. This has meant, minimally, no directly elected national parliament with powers to tax and regulate. The second component is a continued economic relationship between Quebec and Canada. Exactly what this relationship would be, and how it might be negotiated, are key issues in Quebec–Ottawa gamesmanship.

In a speech four days before the referendum in Montreal, Canadian Prime Minister Pierre Trudeau promised 'renewed federalism' if the referendum was defeated. This promise occurred against the backdrop of constitutional negotiations in the late 1970s in which the federal agenda for constitutional change emphasized patriation and an amending formula. (The formal power of constitutional amendment still resided in the British parliament.) The division of powers in social policy, communication and immigration was to be settled later through federal–provincial agreements rather than through formal constitutional reform. The Parti québécois, in power in Quebec in 1976, opposed this sequential approach because they hoped to trade support for patriation for concessions on division of powers. Agreement to patriation, on the promise of later concessions, was not acceptable. Their decision to hold a referendum was designed to demonstrate popular support in Quebec for fundamental constitutional change, a demonstration that could be used in later negotiations. While a calculated gamble, a referendum was a less risky way to mobilize support than an election. The referendum was defeated (60% voted against, and it did not receive majority support among francophones).

After the referendum, Trudeau began the 'patriation round' of constitutional talks. He initially threatened unilateral repatriation after discussion with provincial premiers ended without agreement in September 1980. This initiative was challenged in the courts by Manitoba, Quebec and Newfoundland. In September 1981, the Supreme Court held that there was a constitutional convention requiring 'a substantial degree of provincial consent' in the patriation of the constitution, but that observance of the convention was not 'legally required'. This mixed decision created incentives for both the federal and provincial governments to reopen discussion. Debate developed around two proposals. The proposal of the central government (also supported by Ontario and New Brunswick), described by one observer as a 'nation-building offensive', sought to include a Charter of Rights and Freedoms in the patriated constitution. The principle of the Charter was, and is, anti-federal and non-territorial. Its language recognizes individual rights and social pluralism, and this discourse runs counter to the Canadian federal tradition in which provincial governments represent territorial identities. The other proposal, supported by the remaining provinces ('the Gang of Eight'), sought to maintain provincial power by eliminating the Charter and through an amending formula which provided for provincial withdrawal, with financial compensation, from transfers of power to the federal government.

Rene Lévesque, the Premier of Quebec and leader of the Parti québécois, came to the bargaining table weakened by the result of the referendum, and the common front he formed with the other provinces included several concessions on his part. He consented to patriation with an amending formula, without a concomitant agreement on the division of powers. He also dropped his demand for a Quebec veto on constitutional amendments. Quebec, however, had a distinctive preference with regard to constitutional change. If both proposals failed, Lévesque could return to Quebec and claim that no agreement with the federal government or the other provinces was possible. But for the other provinces in the Gang of Eight, patriation was preferred to the status quo. Their sticking-point was the Charter. However, they were under a great deal of pressure to accept a Charter. Trudeau had managed to present the federal proposal as the 'peoples' package', which left the premiers in an awkward political position. Their rejection of the Charter might have appeared as a rejection of popular principles. There was also the possibility that Trudeau might still proceed on a unilateral basis, despite the political cost, leaving them with no influence in the patriation package. When they were offered a 'notwithstanding clause' (legislative review of judicial review), which provided a legislative override with respect to certain provisions of the Charter, the common front fell apart. The result was that the Constitution Act of 1982 was not signed by Quebec, though it was legally binding within the province. This set the stage for the Quebec round to 'bring Quebec back in'.

Two features of the Act profoundly affected the ability to include Quebec. The first was the entrenchment of the Charter of Rights and Freedoms. This embedded a non-territorial principle in constitutional politics. At the time of signing, the political consequences of entrenching this principle were largely unanticipated. The second was the amending formula, which required (depending on the amendment) the consent of seven or ten provinces, ratification by legislatures, provincial and federal, and which established a three-year time limit for ratification of certain amendments.

The Quebec round really began after changes in government at the federal level and in Quebec. The Liberals and Trudeau were replaced federally by the Conservatives and Mulroney in 1984; the Parti québécois was defeated by the provincial Liberal party and Bourassa in

1985. Bourassa's room for manoeuvre was very limited, once he took office in Quebec. No Quebec government could sign the Act as it stood and maintain popular support. Yet a constitution without Quebec's consent was also unacceptable, at least in part because amendments to it, especially with regard to aboriginal issues, were close to impossible without Quebec's participation. Liberal participation in negotiations, at the same time, was risky. If negotiations failed because the demands of Quebec were not accepted by Ottawa or the provinces, the arguments of *indépendantistes* – that no agreement was possible – would be reinforced. If negotiations succeeded because of concessions by the Quebec Liberal government, the provincial Liberals would have great difficulty selling an agreement in Quebec. The Liberals opened in 1986 by presenting a list of minimum conditions, which were consistently described by Liberal leaders as a final, rather than a negotiating, position.

The Meech Lake Accord of 1987 provided Quebec with constitutional recognition as a 'distinct society', control over candidates for the Supreme Court and Senate, the right to opt out of national shared-cost programmes, constitutional recognition of bilateral Quebec–Ottawa agreements on immigration, and a limited veto over constitutional amendments. However, it was not ratified within the three-year time limit. The Accord foundered on three kinds of opposition in Canada, all of which had developed a political allergy to activity organized around French–English lines: supporters of provincial equality, interests institutionalized in the Charter since 1982, and aboriginal peoples.

The failure of Meech Lake had dramatic consequences in Quebec. The upsurge in support for sovereignty after Meech Lake was driven by the sense that political recognition and inclusion had not been achieved in constitutional reform. This sensibility does not appear to have been engineered; it was a fairly spontaneous reaction, though *indépendantiste* leaders were quick to take advantage of it. In hindsight, if a referendum, worded much like the earlier resolution of 1980, had been held at this point, it might well have passed.

Polls and surveys after the failure of the Meech Lake Accord showed both an increase in support for independence and sovereignty-association, and a continuing gap between the two. In June 1990, 57% of Quebec residents (63% of francophones) were somewhat or very favourable to Quebec sovereignty; 40% were somewhat/very favourable to Quebec separation.[37] In mid-November, 66% had similar attitudes towards sovereignty; 58% supported Quebec independence.[38] Another survey indicated that 52% of Quebec residents (61% of francophones) supported sovereignty even without a political association; 64% (71% of francophones) supported sovereignty-association.[39]

The PQ was able to mobilize new support among *indépendantistes* who were not politically active or sympathizers who were previously held back by risk-averse attitudes with regard to independence, and among federalists who took a more radical position after Meech Lake. The changes in attitudes, which moved public opinion towards the position of the PQ, obviously left the party in a much stronger position. They gained support without any modification to their programme of sovereignty-association. At the same time, the party maintained its organizational capacity and activist base because the party depended less on recruitment outside its constituency of sovereignists, and thus avoided the organizational costs (factionalism and resignations) associated with such recruitment.

Instead, it was the provincial Liberal party which experienced factionalism. The changes in public opinion weakened the position of the provincial Liberal party. They provided incentives for the party to move away from a federalist position and created party factions. Bourassa tried to placate activists dissatisfied with federalism by providing them with a party forum – the Allaire committee (and subsequent report). He also tried to satisfy federalists in the party by delaying the referendum on sovereignty. Thus, there was a narrow range of manoeuvrability available to Bourassa within his party, and his organizational dilemma mirrored his broader dilemma in negotiations with the federal government. Concessions that he might extract from the central government also had to be accepted in Canada. If they were not, his position in Quebec would be greatly weakened. Concessions had to be substantial enough that a federal offer could be sold in Quebec, but not so substantial that the federal package could not be sold in Canada. Much of the jostling for position by the PQ and the provincial Liberals in the immediate aftermath of the failure of Meech Lake was premised on the fear or hope that the changes in public opinion were temporary. The goal of the Parti québécois and the Bloc québécois was to transform this conjunctural change into an enduring advantage. They argued for an early referendum on independence, threatening to force the government's hand by mobilizing protest demonstrations in the early spring and summer of 1991 in support of a 1991 referendum. They could do little more, since they were the opposition in the province of Quebec. The ultimate decision to call a referendum remained with the provincial premier. Bourassa attempted to buy time, expecting that public support for independence would decline to a level which made some form of renewed federalism a politically feasible Liberal policy.[40]

The state of public opinion in Canada also constrained the provincial Liberals and federalists in Quebec because it signalled an unwillingness in Canada to accept a distinct constitutional status for Quebec. At the same time, the process of constitutional negotiation had become more open in Canada, and more complex: the Quebec question was only one of several issues and constituencies which are now a part of constitutional change. Elites were much less insulated from their mass publics and had less freedom to make deals at the elite level.[41] Attitudes in Canada and the declining degree of elite autonomy thus contributed to the local dilemma of the Liberals in Quebec and strengthened the position of the PQ. That constitutional discussions after the failure of Meech Lake were broadened to include issues other than Quebec was not simply a result of political pressure from groups in civil society; the federal government feared that the Quebec problem could not be resolved as a single issue, and attempted to provide the basis for logrolling among groups across issues.

The basic dilemma of Bourassa and the provincial Liberals continued to constrain their constitutional politics in the run-up to the October 1992 national referendum on constitutional reform. Concessions to Quebec in constitutional negotiations have to be substantial enough to appeal to nationalist Quebeckers but not so substantial that they cannot be sold in Canada. This is a delicate balancing act that may be maintained only if federalists present different private and public faces, so that mutually exclusive constituencies are satisfied. One strategy in this context is to make concessions in private negotiations and claim publicly that nothing meaningful was conceded. This depends, however, on maintaining control over private information: parties to the private negotiations who prefer to renegotiate their settlements have an incentive in making public the negotiating stance of the federalists. The set of potential defectors includes nationalists who believe that federalists negotiating for Quebec gave up too much, and parties from outside the province who have to convince their own constituencies that they bargained hard.

This is precisely what happened to Robert Bourassa after the private negotiations leading up to the 1992 constitutional referendum and it contributed to the failure of the referendum in Quebec. (The referendum also failed in Canada as a whole.) When he returned to Quebec to sell the Accord, he was undercut by leaks from his own negotiating team and by a member of the team that represented the province of British Columbia.

CONCLUSION

In this chapter I have wanted to show why secession is a more prominent expression of nationalism in Quebec than in other cases in the developed West. My approach has been institutional in focus, because I have located the answer in the combination of consociation and federation in the formation of the Canadian state; the continuing effects of the former, even as it has been transformed, and the institutional features of the latter.

I claim that there is no more effective combination in the developed West for the maintenance and extension of group infrastructure than consociation joined to federation. The capacity to protect group infrastructure in the liberal, capitalist context of the developed West is, I also have implied, the fundamental foundation for nationalism and hence for secession. In the first instance, the possibility of secession in the developed West has not been constrained by the international economy, and the problems of transition costs and future economic viability, but by the fact that local nationalism loses its primordial base, and corporate groups are the exception rather than the norm within liberal capitalism.

This is the reason why successful secession has been absent in the liberal, advanced capitalist world; thus these effects of the international economy are sequenced only after the effects of those forces that work on group infrastructure. More specifically, interdependence in a liberal capitalist political economy can work to weaken the likelihood of secession because actors do not have to support secession to gain freer trade; it is already available. This is the dilemma that nationalist entrepreneurs who support secession confront. They must establish a motivational set within their potential constituency such that independence is independently valued for reasons other than access to freer and institutionalized international trade, since the latter is, as I say, already available. Here, too, lies a related problem: entrepreneurs must convince nationalists that they can only fulfil their national goals if they constitute a sovereign state. But if the agents in the potential constituency were thoroughgoing nationalists, they should not be affected at the margin by the issues of transition costs and economic viability. When they are affected at the margin, so that changes in the international economy have potential effects, they are not nationalist all the way down; liberal capitalism has already wrought its effects. These effects on the corporate boundaries and carrying capacities of groups weaken the prior conditions that must be present for the effects of changes in the international political economy to operate.

Finally, this analysis thus suggests that Quebec has come as far as it has down the road to independence because of the politicizing effects of constitutional negotiations, a process that, once set in motion, has an institutional logic and dynamic of its own that open up otherwise unavailable opportunities to nationalist entrepreneurs.

NOTES

1. I would like to thank John A. Hall, Siobhan Harty, Michael Keating, Michael Lusztig and the members of the Nationalism Seminar, Central European University, for comments on an earlier draft. Research for this chapter was supported by SSHRC, Canada.
2. See John A. Hall (ed.), *The State*, vol. 2 (London: Routledge, 1994), p. 6.
3. Allen Buchanan, *Secession* (Boulder, CO, and London: Westview Press, 1991).
4. See Hudson Meadwell, 'The politics of nationalism in Quebec', *World Politics*, 45 (1993), pp. 203–41, and Meadwell, 'Transitions to independence and ethnic nationalist mobilization', in William James Booth, Patrick James and Hudson Meadwell (eds), *Politics and Rationality* (Cambridge and New York: Cambridge University Press, 1993), pp. 191–213.
5. For a useful recent account, see S.J.R. Noel, 'Canadian responses to ethnic conflict', in John McGarry and Brendan O'Leary (eds), *The Politics of Ethnic Conflict Regulation* (London: Routledge, 1993), pp. 41–61. See also S.J.R. Noel, 'Consociational democracy and Canadian federalism', *Canadian Journal of Political Science*, 4 (1971), pp. 15–18; Arend Lijphart, 'Consociation and federation: Conceptual and empirical links', *Canadian Journal of Political Science*, 12 (1979), pp. 499–515.
6. See, for example, Charles Tilly (ed.), *The Formation of National States in Western Europe* (Princeton, NJ: Princeton University Press, 1975); Theda Skocpol, *States and Social Revolutions* (Cambridge and New York: Cambridge University Press, 1979); John A. Hall, 'War and the rise of the West', in Colin Creighton and Martin Shaw (eds), *The Sociology of War and Peace* (London: Macmillan, 1987), pp. 37–53; Michael Mann, *States, War and Capitalism* (Oxford and New York: Basil Blackwell, 1988).
7. John A. Hall, *Powers and Liberties* (Oxford and New York: Basil Blackwell, 1985); Brian M. Downing, 'Constitutionalism, warfare and political change in early modern Europe', *Theory and Society*, 17 (1988), pp. 7–56; H.G. Koenigsberger, 'Monarchies and parliaments in early modern Europe – *Dominium Regale* or *Dominium Politicum et Regale*', *Theory and Society*, 5 (1978), pp. 191–217.

8. See the discussion of the British case in Linda Colley, *Britons* (New Haven, CT: Yale University Press, 1992); and more generally, Michael Mann, 'The emergence of modern European nationalism', in John A. Hall and I.C. Jarvie (eds), *Transitions to Modernity* (Cambridge: Cambridge University Press, 1992), pp. 137–65, and Barry R. Posen, 'Nationalism, the mass army and military power', *International Security*, 18 (1993), pp. 80–124.
9. See John A. Hall, 'Nationalisms, classified and explained', *Daedalus*, 12 (1993), reprinted as chapter 2 of this volume.
10. Ernest Gellner, *Nations and Nationalism* (Ithaca, NY: Cornell University Press, 1983).
11. Jack Snyder, 'Nationalism and the crisis of the post-Soviet state', in Michael E. Brown (ed.), *Ethnic Conflict and International Security* (Princeton, NJ: Princeton University Press, 1993), pp. 79–102.
12. The fear in Quebec was not so much military conquest by the Americans, despite the discussion of annexation, but of gradual absorption by the United States. By the mid-1850s, French-Canadian migration to the northeast United States was a political problem. Confederation appeared to offer an alternative to the economic and political dependence on the United States that was feared if French-Canadians opted for an independent state. For a discussion of the political dimensions of migration and attempts to deal with it after confederation, see Hudson Meadwell, 'Forms of cultural mobilization, Quebec and Brittany, 1870–1914', *Comparative Politics*, 15 (July, 1983), pp. 401–17.
13. The classic source on consociational politics is Arend Lijphart, *The Politics of Accommodation* (Berkeley and Los Angeles: University of California Press, 1968). For innovative recent work, see George Tsebelis, *Nested Games* (Berkeley and Los Angeles: University of California Press, 1990), ch. 6; and Brendan O'Leary, 'The limits to coercive consociationalism in Northern Ireland', *Political Studies*, 37 (1989), pp. 562–88.
14. See Arend Lijphart, *Democracy in Plural Societies* (New Haven, CT: Yale University Press, 1977).
15. Murray Forsyth, 'Introduction', in Murray Forsyth (ed.), *Federalism and Nationalism* (Leicester and London: Leicester University Press, 1989), pp. 1–7.
16. William A. Riker, *Federalism* (Boston: Little Brown, 1964). This explanation could contradict the second explanation since the latter implies that, past some threshold of size, empires would be federal. Since Riker argues that federation and empire are competing alternatives, he assumes that an empire must not be too large.
17. There is more to be said about the relationship between liberalism and groups, and about liberalism and consociationalism, but I leave these issues to one side for this chapter, save for the following comment. Consociational democracies in the developed West are mixed regimes of individual and collective rights, and they presuppose a liberal background. This was evident even in Lijphart's discussion of the conditions conducive to consociation. Two of the conditions, roughly speaking, were a prior tradition of compromise, and the presence of an overarching loyalty to the state among the subcultures. Of course, if these conditions were present, one wonders (as Hans Daalder did) how deep were the divisions in the Netherlands, for example, or in any other of the successful cases of consociational accommodation. What seems to be presupposed – basically civil society – is often absent in other cases of subculturally divided societies.
18. Occasionally there is discussion of non-territorial federalism. See Alain Gagnon,

'The political uses of federalism', in Michael Burgess and Alain G. Gagnon (eds), *Comparative Federalism and Federation* (Toronto: University of Toronto Press, 1993), p. 43, note 57.
19. Forsyth, 'Introduction' to *Federalism and Nationalism*, p. 3.
20. See Forrest McDonald, *Novus Ordo Seclorum: The Intellectual Origins of the Constitution* (Lawrence, KS: University Press of Kansas, 1985); Carl J. Richard, *The Founders and the Classics* (Cambridge, MA: Harvard University Press, 1994); Vincent Ostrom, *The Political Theory of a Compound Republic*, second edn (Lincoln, NE, and London: University of Nebraska Press, 1987).
21. See Samuel H. Beer, *To Make a Nation* (Cambridge, MA: Harvard University Press, 1993).
22. See John McGarry and Brendan O'Leary, 'Introduction: The macro-political regulation of ethnic conflict', in McGarry and O'Leary (eds), *The Politics of Ethnic Conflict Regulation*, pp. 1–40.
23. See Herman Bakvis, *Catholic Power in the Netherlands* (Montreal: McGill-Queens University Press, 1981), and the special issue of 'Politics in the Netherlands: How much change?', *West European Politics*, v.12 (1989), pp. 1–210.
24. See Aristide R. Zolberg, 'Splitting the difference: Federalization without federalism in Belgium', in Milton J. Esman (ed.), *Ethnic Conflict in the Western World* (Ithaca, NY: Cornell University Press, 1977); Lisbeth Hooghe, *A Leap in the Dark: Nationalist Conflict and Federal Reform in Belgium* (Cornell University Western Studies Program 1992, #27).
25. Alexander Murdoch, *'The People Above': Politics and Administration in Mid-Eighteenth-Century Scotland* (Edinburgh: John Donald Publishers), p. 2.
26. Rosalind Mitchison, *Lordship to Patronage: Scotland 1603–1745* (London: Edward Arnold, 1983), p. 131. See also for a discussion of the economic background, Christopher A. Whatley, 'Economic causes and consequences of the Act of Union of 1707: A survey', *Scottish Historical Review*, 186 (October, 1989), pp. 150–81. Whatley correctly notes that it was not so much free trade that was demanded, but protected trade, and an end to English threats to Scottish trade (the Alien Act of 1705): Whatley, 'Bought and sold for English gold', *Studies in Scottish Economic and Social History*, 4 (1994). The politics of this exchange that resulted in Union requires more detailed treatment than I can give it here.
27. This shared feature is especially prominent when we compare these two cases to other cases from other contexts. Thus, in the Soviet Union, liberalization immediately yielded regions mobilized for independence; the question of the form of regime could not be separated from the territorial structure of the state. In Pakistan, in a different set of local conditions, the process of transition from an authoritarian regime, essentially the election of 1970, set in motion the events that produced the formation of Bangladesh.
28. See the analysis in Hudson Meadwell, 'The politics of nationalism in Quebec'.
29. See Michael Keating, 'Spain: Peripheral nationalism and state response', in McGarry and O'Leary (eds), *The Politics of Ethnic Conflict Regulation*, pp. 221ff.
30. Ian S. Lustick, *Unsettled States, Disputed Lands* (Ithaca, NY: Cornell University Press, 1993).
31. I do not discuss the case of Norway in this chapter.
32. See Jennifer Tolbert Roberts, *Athens on Trial* (Princeton, NJ: Princeton University Press, 1994), pp. 263–5.
33. Lacey K. Ford Jr., *Origins of Southern Radicalism: The Southern Carolina Upcountry 1800–1860* (New York: Oxford University Press, 1988), p. 351.

34. See Daniel Szechi, *The Jacobites* (Manchester and New York: Manchester University Press, 1994), pp. 133–4.
35. My account of the importance of the Quiet Revolution is necessarily brief. For more detailed analysis, see Kenneth McRoberts and Denis Posgate, *Quebec: Social Change and Political Crisis*, 2nd edn (Toronto: McClelland & Stewart, 1980); Michael D. Behiels, *Prelude to Quebec's Quiet Revolution* (Montreal: McGill-Queens University Press, 1985).
36. Lionel Groulx, 'Notre avenir politique' (1922), in Susan Mann Trofimenkoff (ed.), *Abbé Groulx: Variations on a Nationalist Theme* (Toronto: Copp-Clark Publishing, 1973), p. 182.
37. *La Presse*, 21 June 1990, pp. A1–A2.
38. *La Presse*, 26 November 1990, pp. A1–A2.
39. *Le Devoir*, 6 April 1991.
40. However, as the recession deepened after the failure of Meech Lake, Parizeau acknowledged that he would prefer a referendum 'in a year or two' (mid-1992 or 1993), because he expected the Quebec economy to be in an upturn by that time. He was confident enough, however, to have supported the circulation of a province-wide petition demanding a referendum as scheduled for the fall of 1992, as a means of continuing to pressure Bourassa. There was therefore an interesting dilemma built into the time horizons of federalists and *indépendantistes* as they considered the joint effects of the failure of Meech Lake and the economic recession, because each of these factors pushed them in different directions. For the federalists, an ideal time for a referendum would have been long enough after Meech Lake so that the symbolic effects of Meech were weaker, but not so late that the referendum was held in a period of economic expansion.
41. Alan C. Cairns, 'The Charter, interest groups, executive federalism and constitutional reform' in David E. Smith, Peter MacKinnon and James C. Courtney, *After Meech Lake: Lessons for the Future* (Saskatoon, Sask: Fifth House Publishers, 1991), and Alan C. Cairns, 'Political science, ethnicity and the constitution', in David P. Shugarman and Reg Whitaker (eds), *Federalism and Political Community* (Peterborough, Ontario: Broadview Press, 1989).

9

Institutional Plurality: Problem or Solution for the Multi-ethnic State?

Hans van Amersfoort

INTRODUCTION

Hardly a day goes by in which we do not read about ethnic conflicts in our newspapers or watch outbursts of ethnic violence on our televisions. These conflicts occur in all parts of the world, in very different societies, and in the context of various political constellations. Ethnic conflicts seem ubiquitous and it is not surprising that several theories have been put forward to describe and analyse them. In a previous paper I described these theoretical approaches to the problem of the multi-ethnic state and formulated a preliminary step towards a theory of ethnicity in the modern state (van Amersfoort, 1991). In this chapter I will repeat part of the general argument of the 1991 paper but I primarily concentrate on one particular issue in the entire field of ethnicity. This chapter is focused on the role of 'ethnic institutions'. I want to explore how far institutional plurality can provide a solution to the problems of the multi-ethnic state. I will first give some definitions. I will then sketch the historical background of perspectives on the relation between 'state' and 'people'. In the third section I will discuss the reactions of states to ethnic diversity in their populations. One of these reactions, the acceptance of institutional plurality, is singled out and discussed in greater detail in the concluding sections.

Ethnic groups and nationalities

To have conflicts there must be parties. We call some of these parties ethnic groups, and when these ethnic groups make specific territorial claims we call them *nationalities*. When ethnic groups are parties engaged in a process of interaction, we do not have *one* ethnic group. We need at least a bipartite differentiation in order to be able to recognize ethnic groups. I define such parties as *ethnic groups* when the membership is ascribed, when they are thought to derive from persons of common descent, possessing essential means of communication as language, belief systems and norms, in short 'culture'.

On close inspection the borders of ethnic groups are never so totally closed that the only way to become a member is to be born into the group. But it is fair to say that the normal way to enter an ethnic group is by birth and upbringing. Ethnic groups defined in this way generally have a bond with a territory, but this is not necessarily so. Ethnic groups can live in dispersed territories, and sometimes they live in complicated territorial patterns with other ethnic groups. In Northern Africa, for instance, we see (or saw until recently) very complicated patterns in which nomadic or semi-nomadic groups had specific rights on territories that were inhabited by other sedentary groups. To the modern European mind this is at first sight difficult to understand, until we remember that it is also not unknown within Europe that the right to fish in a river or to hunt on land may not rest with the owner of the river or the land. Needless to say, this kind of arrangement may easily be a source of conflict and requires some form of regulation.

In modern societies (and this chapter is restricted to the ethnic phenomenon in modern societies) there are two particular characteristics that make 'ethnic groups' different from all other social groups or categories. In the first place, ethnic groups are intergenerational. In the second place, the ethnic form of categorization takes priority over all other forms of social categorization such as age, sex, economic interests etc. When one of these two characteristics does not (any longer) hold, the ethnic group ceases (gradually) to exist.

Ways and modes of inclusion

In the previous pages I have argued that ethnic groups are parties that are in interaction and that are, therefore, in one way or another part of a political arrangement. In modern societies this means that they are inhabitants of the same state. The historical processes that have led to the sharing of government are complicated but two ways and two modes of inclusion need to be analytically distinguished, since these ways and modes of inclusion have a bearing on the nature of ethnic contacts and consequently on eventual conflicts.

The first way is the extension of government over territories which were previously outside the realm. The first mode in which this inclusion can be realized is hierarchical. This occurs when a ruling class succeeds in extending its rule over new territories, and subjects its inhabitants to the status of a 'lower class'. This results in ethnic stratification and the cultural division of labour. This mode of inclusion is common to all sorts of colonialism. It forms the starting point of Hechter's theory of internal colonialism (Hechter, 1975; Hechter and Levi, 1979). The second mode of inclusion may also be a consequence of conquest but it is one in which indigenous institutions are to a certain extent left untouched. The government accommodates itself to pre-existing institutions, which results in a 'parallel inclusion'. The extension of British rule over Ireland and Scotland are, respectively, examples of these different modes of inclusion. Parallel inclusion leads to ethnic specialization in the occupational structure. It leads to a vertical division of labour which is more complicated than a simple division into higher and lower classes.

But conquest is not the only way in which ethnic groups come into being. Yet another way is through migration. Some form of migration has occurred in all societies. Immigrants may be brought in by a patrimonial ruler to colonize virgin lands in his territory. They may have been imported as slaves or may have come on their own initiative in smaller or greater numbers. They may have become included in a hierarchical way after their migration, like the African slaves brought over to the New World. Or they may have become totally absorbed in the new society, losing their ethnic characteristics. There are also forms of inclusion resulting from migration which can be considered as belonging to the parallel mode of inclusion. The migrants are recognizable, different in some cultural characteristics, and often concentrated in specific occupations, but they cannot simply be classified as high or low. An example of this form of inclusion is represented by those groups in the United States who are generally described as 'white ethnics'.

Ways and modes of inclusion form the historical background of the existence of ethnic groups and determine the character of ethnic conflicts in specific societies. To describe actual configurations and to identify the relevant variables for the development of inter-ethnic relations within these configurations is beyond the scope of this chapter. Valuable contributions to the empirical analysis of various configurations have been made by the late Stein Rokkan and recently by Mikesell and Murphy (Rokkan and Urwin, 1983; Mikesell and Murphy, 1991).

GOVERNMENT, PEOPLE AND TERRITORY

In the European context, ethnic conflict is related to the rise of the modern state. The complicated process by which people, government and territory became amalgamated was set into motion by patrimonial rulers and the bureaucracies they created to govern their realms. (For descriptions and interpretations, see for instance Smith, 1973, 1986, 1988, 1989; Gellner, 1983; Zubaida, 1989). Especially in France, the ruling kings were so successful in furthering this process that they brought about their own downfall. Once the amalgamation of territory, government and people was sufficiently advanced, the idea arose that sovereignty rested not in the rulers, but in the entity itself which we call the 'sovereign state'. The emphasis shifted from the rulers to the ruled and the legitimation of the political arrangement was no longer based on the 'will of the king' but in the 'nation' itself.

As Anthony D. Smith has argued, the nation as fountainhead of legitimate rule, as source of the 'common will' based on its history and destiny, is undoubtedly a modern construct, a 'myth', but it was not constructed out of thin air (Smith, 1988: 3). The myth of the nation supposes its unity to be a primordial given, whereas in fact it was a creation of government. But it is also undeniable that the construct, in some places at least, has become, to some extent, a reality. The question is not so much, as Walker Connor has argued, what a nation is, as when a population has become sufficiently 'assimilated' (to use the classical term of Karl Deutsch) and defined by the territory of a state to be called a nation (Connor, 1990). An important experience endowing the myth with persuasive power may have been the occurrence of wars, especially when wars came to be fought by conscript armies and were no longer the business of an unattached class of professional soldiers. Perhaps even more importantly, albeit less dramatically, people and territory were welded together by the growth of communication through a state-controlled infrastructure (roads, railways and canals) and enculturation in a common culture by a state-controlled school system and 'national' mass media.

The legitimation of government over a territory, based on the will of the people living in it, gave birth to the twin concept of the 'nation-state'. At the same time, however, a fundamentally different concept was born, that of 'citizenship'. As with most concepts, the roots of the concept of citizenship reach well into the past. In the Roman Empire there was already a similar idea of citizenship. But the concept became articulated and salient in political thought with the rise of the modern state. At first sight, the difference between conceptions of a people as a 'nation' or as a collectivity of citizens may not seem fundamental. Citizenship appears only to be the legal form in which nationality is expressed. But this is not so. Citizenship is not a primordial given, and it is not self-evident; it can be acquired, and it can be lost. A basic property of a citizen is that he takes part in the process of government. Not all members of 'the nation' need therefore to be citizens. Citizenship refers to a community that is created not by history and nature but by a social contract. This can be seen very clearly in the case of nations that are made up of immigrants, as in the United States. Where the nation-state is not a model but a reality, the difference between nationality and citizenship does not exist. But such a difference does exist and forms a source of conflict when ethnic groups that belong to the nation feel that they are excluded from (full) citizenship. The concept of citizenship contains a notion of fundamental equality that runs counter to the experience of ethnic groups that are hierarchically included in the nation (Marshall, 1964: 71–3). This is the most common source of ethnic conflicts in the modern state. This kind of conflict may take the form of a separatist movement. Such a group may claim to be a separate nation entitled to its own territory, or its aim may be to belong to another nation that has already realized its own state. But this is not necessarily so. The aim of groups who feel excluded may also be to achieve full citizenship in the existing nation. This has been, for instance, the main reaction of the black population in the United States.

When ethnic groups have acquired citizenship and can take part in the political life of the state, political parties based on ethnic criteria may arise. The sheer existence of ethnic parties is in itself often seen, particularly by American political scientists, as a source of unresolvable conflicts (Rabushka and Shepsle, 1972). Political systems based on ethnic parties should lack the capacities for negotiation and compromise between the loyalties of diverse interests that secure the democratic process. This is a convincing logical deduction. But in reality ethnic parties do not always disrupt democratic stability. Governments based on a system with ethnic parties may not correspond to the Westminster or Washington two-party model, but they can produce stable, democratic systems (Lijphart, 1977). Party systems based on ethnic cleavages are no more prone to degenerate into political violence than systems based on other cleavages (van Amersfoort and van der Wusten, 1981). Rabushka and Shepsle may have been a bit too hasty in their conclusions, but we will come back to their book, which contains important theoretical findings. Ethnic groups do not always need to form separate parties to enter the political arena. A different way in which they can take part in the process of political decision making is to operate as a 'bloc' within a larger party, as has been traditional for white ethnic groups in the United States.

Summarizing the previous argument, we can state that there are two different ways to conceptualize ethnic conflicts. The first approach uses the nation-state model. The descriptive value of this model is limited. The nation, as an entity antedating the state and in fact giving rise to it, is seen as a myth by most modern historians. But the prescriptive side of the model has great impact on the perception of ethnic strife and violence. In terms of this model, the problem is defined as an imbalance between national boundaries and state frontiers. A solution to ethnic conflict is sought in ways to redress this imbalance.

The second form of conceptualization concentrates on the concept of citizenship, whereby the state is seen as founded on the political will of its citizens. Especially in states where immigration has been the great formative factor of the population, where the nation is formed out of different peoples acquiring citizenship, this model seems to have more descriptive value. Breton has analysed how the vision of the nation as a given entity is giving way in French Canada to the idea of the nation as based on citizenship. This is an interesting case where both concepts are entering the perception of public opinion at the same time (Breton, 1988). But as with the first model, the more important part of this construct is its prescriptive side. In this approach, ethnic violence is seen as an expression of social injustice and oppression. Attention is focused on social reform and on ensuring full citizenship for all ethnic groups, and not on the reformulation of political borders.

Precisely because both models are more prescriptive than descriptive, they exert great influence on the way people approach conflicts between ethnic groups. Whereas such conflicts in the first half of the twentieth century were predominantly perceived as a 'nationality question', attention after the Second World War has been focused on the question of 'full citizenship' for different ethnic components of national populations. It is only in the last few years that the crisis in the Soviet Union and its satellites has reopened the debate on the relation between cultural divisions and political borders. At the same time, the growing numbers of immigrants and the institutionalization of immigrant cultures in Western Europe has led to the mobilization of xenophobic groups who use the nation-state model not to redefine political borders but to formulate a policy with regard to immigration and immigrants.

STATES AND ETHNIC DIVERSITY

States in action

With the rise of the state and the increasing interference of the state in the everyday life of its population, a certain level of homogeneity became a prerequisite for the functioning of society. Although the state was in theory based on the nation, all nineteenth-century European states followed an active policy of 'nation-building'. National feelings were created and promoted, and other identities had to be made secondary to them. This process of unification has been described well for the Netherlands by Knippenberg and de Pater (1988). The ways in which states have tried to further homogenization and to cope with cultural divides can be summarized in the following three reactions.

Elimination

The state can try to suppress certain cultural properties through the use of violence or through a persistent policy of 'reculturation' to try to change people's religion, language, or whatever. An example of a language-based policy is the rigorous policy of the French state towards non-French-speaking populations included in its territory, be it the Dutch speakers of French Flanders, or the Occitan, Catalan or Basque speakers of the south. The ultimate form of elimination is, of course, genocide, which is also a solution of some kind.

The conflict need not always be started by the central government. It can also be pursued by ethnic groups who classify themselves as belonging to a separate nation or to a nation belonging to a different state. Separatism and irredentism are manifestations of this type of conflict. In different ways all these reactions seek the outcome of a homogeneous state population, through the elimination of cultural diversity within the state population.

Marginalization

In this kind of policy, cultural characteristics are not so much forbidden or suppressed but, rather, it is denied that they have any bearing on public life and policymaking. For instance, the French state has not so much eliminated as marginalized the ancient regional cultures of France through its strongly centralized educational system. The geography book *Le tour de France par deux enfants*, by G. Bruno, once widely used in French schools, is an excellent example of this policy.

In general, the secular state has succeeded in this way to eliminate 'religion' as an important source of social conduct. We see the same process of marginalization occurring in many immigrant groups over the course of generations. What were vital cultural properties for their grandparents have become folkloristic leisure activities for the grandchildren.

Some cultural elements are easier to marginalize than others. For instance, it is easier to marginalize religion, by supposing that the state is a non-moral and neutral agency, than it is to marginalize language, because every government must express itself in a language or an agreed set of languages.

Institutional plurality

The third reaction seeks to neutralize the disruptive effects of ethnic diversity by forms of institutionalization. Marginalization can only occur in the long run and in the absence of open conflicts. When elimination of the dissident cultures is not an option there seems to be no other way than to accept them to a certain extent. Institutional plurality occurs in many states and in many forms. Countries with a great regional variety often have a form of 'federalism' in their constitutional makeup. The problem then is to find a balance between central authority and regional autonomy. Belgium has tried to keep the peace between the Flemish- and Walloon-speaking sections of its population by rebuilding the unitary Belgian state into a federation. In the Netherlands, pillarization is (or was?) a good example of institutional plurality as a response to religious diversity. We will look into the phenomenon of institutional plurality more closely in the next sections of this chapter.

It is not my intention to suggest that these reactions are always consciously planned by a 'sovereign mastermind'. Although there are certainly examples in which one of these three reactions can be described as a conscious policy of a government or ruling elite, in other cases they are the outcome of an interplay between several social forces. Regardless of the conscious or more-or-less accidental nature of these reactions, ethnic diversity is seen in each form of reaction as a potentially dangerous and disruptive force.

States in crisis

However, there are also cases in which ethnic conflicts do not seem to be so much the cause as rather the consequence of political instability. When a state loses its legitimacy and can no longer maintain political and economic order, political dissent will seek a channel through which to articulate protest and it will look for principles upon which a new order can be based. Examples of such sequences are not difficult to find. The present-day rise in ethnic sentiments in Eastern Europe has followed the demise of communist one-party rule. The collapse of the Habsburg and Ottoman empires at the end of the First World War was also followed by a wave of ethnic and nationalistic conflicts.

In such crises there is often no other base for political orientation than ethnic characteristics transmitted over generations. Especially after dictatorial rule there is no political tradition, nor are there parties, trade unions or independent mass media that can articulate a new political order. Moreover, ethnic movements have at first sight a simple and ready-made answer to the uncertainty of the crisis. Only when they really come to power is their answer soon found in most cases to be too simplistic to form a basis for government. The unity of an ethnic movement always runs the danger of melting away when there is no longer a clear enemy and internal divisions of interest become visible.

THE MODERN STATE AND INSTITUTIONAL PLURALITY

Immigration and institutional plurality

We have seen that immigration is one of the ways in which ethnic groups may come into being. As this experience is most recent in Western Europe, I will start this discussion of institutional pluralism with the situation of immigrants who move into already established states.

Peoples have always moved and this has always been a source of contact and conflict. The size of population movements and the impact of migration on the life of individuals and the fate of societies in the past must not be underestimated. But with the stabilization of state power and the success of the nation-state ideology, people who move became the object of state regulations. We now distinguish almost automatically between international migration and migration within states, assuming the former to be more problematic than the latter. But even 'internal migration' is regulated by many states. Indeed, many states are so large and/or ethnically heterogeneous that there is no reason to assume that the crossing of the state border in itself makes a difference to the social effects of migration. However, as all states make the differentiation, there is a juridical distinction between immigrants and 'people who have moved', and this juridical distinction has, or can have, social effects.

Whatever the importance of migration may have been in previous periods, it is fair to say that the absolute number of people that migrate in the present time to other state-territories and inside their own country is larger than ever. And contrary to the ideology of the nation-state and the right it asserts to control entry to the country, this migration process proves difficult – if at all possible – to control through state regulation.

In this way, immigration confronts all developed – and many undeveloped – states with a certain level of ethnic mobilization. The immigrants become aware of their own culture. If they arrive in sufficient numbers they also have a mobilizing effect on the host society, leading to a growing awareness of its own culture and possibly even to the rise of xenophobic feelings. The process of ethnic mobilization makes the discussion of citizenship inevitable. Immigrants clearly do not belong to the nation, but can they become citizens, and in what length of time and on what conditions?

Immigration leads, albeit with different levels of scope and intensity, to the institutionalization of immigrant cultures. Clubs, newspapers, churches, mosques, special language classes for children, all kinds of common activities must ensure the continuity of the most valued aspects of the home culture. These forms of institutionalization are especially interesting when they are not only maintained by the immigrants but also recognized by the host society as important elements of social life. At a time when the state has to a large extent monopolized the institutional framework of society, ethnic groups try to become recognized by the state in order to have their institutions subsidized in one form or another. This leads to a discussion about the positive and negative aspects of 'institutional plurality' in public life.

Immigrant institutions generally have a conservative function when they come into being. They are, in McKay's terms, 'traditionalist' in character (McKay, 1982). They try to avoid contacts with the host society as much as possible. But, on the other hand, immigrant institutions also want, in most cases, to help their countrymen to improve their chances in the new surroundings. Immigrant institutions characteristically develop an ideology in which they see themselves as forming a bridge between the individual immigrant and the host society. There is an inherent tension between the conservation of the ethnic culture and adaptation to the host culture. It is characteristic of the role of immigrant leaders that they must master this tension.

Institutional plurality may regulate contact between groups and prevent conflicts. In the period during which the modern state arose, it is already possible to find instances of 'institutional plurality'. For instance, many pre-industrial cities had populations that were institutionally segregated into 'ethnic neighbourhoods' with a certain level of autonomy in cultural and legal affairs. The best known form of these communities is, of course, the Jewish ghetto, but this kind of institutional plurality has been quite common in pre-industrial cities all over the world.

Institutional plurality provides an answer to cultural diversity, but it also perpetuates ethnic cleavages. The evaluation of ethnic institutions depends on the value one wishes to attach to the preservation of the immigrant culture, on the one hand, and to the participation of individuals in the larger society, on the other hand.

For groups that put a high priority on preserving their own culture, institutional plurality is an attractive policy to pursue. When some groups succeed in this, other groups are also stimulated to follow this route. The relatively new phenomenon of mass immigration in European societies has in this way changed the definition of the situation for autochthonous minorities or 'nationality groups'. This is especially visible in France, which has always had a strongly assimilationist approach towards both indigenous regional groups such as Basques, Bretons and the Flemish, and towards immigrants.

The failure of the assimilationist approach with regard to the new immigrants, especially the Arabic-speaking North Africans, and the institutionalization of new immigrant cultures has had a revivalist effect on the indigenous minorities in France. In another setting, the same sort of thing has happened in Canada where the rise of the Parti québécois has stimulated native Indian and Inuit peoples to put forward their cultural and territorial claims.

Institutional plurality may result from the need to cope with mass immigration. But it can also be the consequence of incorporating different ethnic communities in the state. The Netherlands and Belgium are historically characterized by a high degree of institutional plurality. In such cases, immigrants will look upon this plurality as providing them with the possibility to maintain their culture. The founding of Islamic elementary schools in the Netherlands is impossible to understand without taking into account the country's tradition of organizing educational services along religious divisions.

The level of traditional acceptance of institutional pluralism is an important context variable for the emergence and continuation of immigrant ethnic groups. An interesting and somewhat disquieting feature of institutional pluralism is that it tends to result in fragmentation. Once the ideology of the equality of cultures is accepted, it is very difficult to find a rationale for the limitation of groups with cultural rights. Why should we respect a language spoken by millions but not one spoken by only a few thousand persons? Why should not all peoples, however small, be entitled to some exclusive territorial rights? Especially when the issue is put forward in absolute terms in the course of the debate, it is impossible to redress it with practical and materialistic considerations. We have in fact witnessed the same development in the process of decolonization, when the claims of ever smaller territorial units to become states and full members of the United Nations became recognized.

Nationalities and institutional pluralism

Most of what has been said about institutional pluralism as a response to the ethnic diversity which results from immigration is also valid in the case of nationalities. In fact we have already touched upon feedback processes in their respective situations. However, there are also some important differences. Nationalities generally result from the first way of inclusion identified earlier, the inclusion of new peoples and territories in an expanding political unit. They have, therefore, a more-or-less concentrated form of settlement in geographical terms, and a historical relation to a territory or 'homeland'. Their demand for institutional plurality therefore more often takes the specific form of a quest for local autonomy of one sort or the other. The classical response to this kind of situation is the federalized structure of the state, as in Switzerland and the former Soviet Union. This solution is in reality often more complicated than it looks in theory. The population of territories is rarely as homogeneous as the theory or the ideology of nationalism supposes it to be. The economic costs of federalization, or in more extreme cases even separatism, are easily disregarded in political debates, but not in everyday life when it comes to practical matters. The history of the Balkan area after the First World War has shown how difficult it is to translate cultural divides into political borders, let alone state frontiers. But, in principle, forms of institutional plurality founded on a territorial basis are possible, as concrete examples prove. (The question of South Tirol, for instance, has lost its violent character through the working of an arrangement of institutional plurality for that specific province.)

The disadvantages that were mentioned in the previous section also apply in this case. Institutional pluralism does diminish the chances of conflicts but it also poses a barrier to individual interaction. For instance, it ties populations much more strongly to a geographically limited labour market than a mono-institutional system.

INSTITUTIONAL PLURALITY: PROBLEM OR SOLUTION?

In the previous section, institutional plurality was described as a more-or-less spontaneous response to ethnic diversity in society. This description already hinted at some possible positive and negative aspects of this response. In this section I will try to formulate a clearer view on the advantages and disadvantages of institutional plurality and to find an answer to the problem that this chapter addresses.

In order to analyse the advantages and disadvantages of institutional plurality, it is necessary to specify the kind of institutions in which we are interested and to be more precise with regard to the level of analysis. It must be pointed out that the institutional plurality relevant to the present discussion must apply to the public domain. We are not, at this moment, interested in institutions that are not directed at the production and/or distribution of public goods. Granted that it is not always possible to draw a sharp line between public and private, and that the two may interact, it is useful to make this distinction analytically. The modern state has regulated political participation and the education of children, has made legislation about labour contracts and health care, and is involved in the construction and distribution of houses. When we are discussing institutional plurality we are looking for institutions that perform functions that are also provided by 'general' or 'state' institutions and which offer an alternative to these general 'public' institutions. A special instance of these institutions is the political party, which, of course, does not itself perform these functions but which allows the protagonists of ethnic institutions to be represented in the political arena.

The nature of the ethnic institutions so defined must be looked at in relation to the mode of inclusion of the population in the state system. We have distinguished between hierarchical and parallel inclusion. Pure forms of hierarchical institutional plurality, like in the classical 'Deep South' of the United States, do not need to be further discussed in this chapter. These are better regarded as forms of oppression than institutional plurality because they are inherently instable when not constantly enforced by the politically dominant group. More interesting are the institutions that are parallel, or which at least aim to be or to become parallel institutions. In the case of nationalities this claim can be realized in the form of federalization or regional autonomy. In the case of ethnic groups the parallel institutions divide only a social field and do not form or aim at separate geographical units. An important point for the evolution of institutional plurality is the time perspective that leaders and followers have. The remark that these institutions seek to become parallel implies that they may start as institutions of a disadvantaged ethnic group. The Dutch pillar system (*verzuiling*), which is a good example of parallel institutional plurality, originated in the quest for emancipation of the Roman Catholics and orthodox Protestants. When these institutions first took shape they could hardly be described as parallel, but their aim was to become a fully developed alternative to public institutions.

The functions of ethnic institutions are, of course, not exactly the same for all members of the ethnic community. Leaders may gain prestige and political power from their roles in the institutions, whereas ordinary members of the group do not reap such direct benefits. In the present discussion we will restrict ourselves to the aggregate level of analysis and only consider the general effects of institutional plurality.

The advocates of institutional plurality see it as the ideal solution for the multi-ethnic state. They see it as an arrangement which makes it possible to avoid open conflicts and which at the same time gives each group the possibility of transmitting its cultural values to the next generation. Their opponents consider structural plurality to be a problem. They see it as an inherently conservative arrangement which leads to a continuation and even a strengthening of ethnic divisions, which excludes a rational presentation of interests and the solution of societal problems through negotiation and compromise.

These two opposite evaluations both point to empirical examples that support their position. It is always difficult in the social sciences to resolve this kind of debate by empirical investigations. It is not that data are scarce, for history provides us with a wealth of material, but the relevant information is rarely collected systematically and is almost always open to more than one interpretation.

The positions *pro* and *contra* institutional plurality are therefore not only grounded in empirical data. They are also connected with wider political and philosophical orientations. Adherents of the idea that the state is the expression of the 'will of the nation' (even when they admit that this is the outcome of historical developments which are to some extent accidental) stress the inevitable necessity of structuring society around deeply rooted loyalties. They tend to see individuals primarily as formed by, and belonging to, a group. Those who are more orientated to universalistic values tend to see the state as a historical construct which is based on interests and which finds its legitimacy in the consent of 'free citizens'. Their orientation is more towards individual rights than to cultural traditions. Whereas the first party values tradition and stability, the second tends to value change and modernity.

These two factors, the great variety in historical cases, and the link with the general *Weltanschauung* make it difficult to come to a final evaluation of structural plurality. But a first step towards such an evaluation may be to get a clearer idea of *under what circumstances* the advantages and disadvantages of institutional plurality obtain.

The disadvantages are consistently spelled out by Rabushka and Shepsle in their analysis of the political process in multi-ethnic states. They formulate a theory of the working of ethnic parties once ethnicity has become salient; that is to say, once ethnic categorization has gained priority over any other form of social categorization. They are not able to explain why ethnicity becomes salient, for the genesis of the problem is simply not part of their theory (Rabushka and Shepsle, 1972: 62–5).

From this starting point they develop a theory, based on general game theory reasoning, which concludes that such societies, whatever the configuration of the ethnic groups, will automatically turn to 'authoritarian rule' or outright civil war. They illustrate this theory with a number of case studies which are in themselves quite convincing. Their pessimistic view of the situation in Yugoslavia was certainly not generally accepted at the time their book appeared but has been confirmed by the developments of recent years (Rabushka and Shepsle, 1972: 183–9). Their analysis shows that ethnic parties tend to define politics as a game, in which parties have downright contradictory interests. An interesting point in their book is that they do not consider institutionalization in the forms of 'federalization' or non-territorial 'parallelism' to be fundamentally different. Both forms of institutionalization (as, for instance, in Yugoslavia and in Lebanon) are considered to be equally prone to lead to instability and open conflicts. Generally, studies of 'ethnicity' tend to treat either 'nationalities' or 'ethnic groups', and few studies regard them as being manifestations of basically the same problem.

Rabushka and Shepsle are aware of some rival theories, but they do not regard them as valid alternatives. The best known of these other theories is Lijphart's theory of 'consociational democracy'. They have three objections towards Lijphart's theory. In the first place, they think that the notional role of an elite working out deals in 'secrecy' is not really democratic. Secondly, they have the idea that sooner or later these 'democracies' like Belgium and Lebanon may also develop instability. And thirdly, they point to the high costs of institutional plurality. The first and third arguments are difficult to contradict as no comparison is made with 'secrecy' in the functioning of non-ethnic parties, as for instance in the United States; nor is a systematic comparison made with the costs of democracies of a different type. (The American electoral system, for instance, looks very expensive to European eyes.) The second argument is difficult to contradict as long as no time horizon is specified. As long as it has not happened, we can of course still expect a civil war to break out sometime in any country. Rabushka and Shepsle seem to be so much under the spell of their theory that they do not regard alternatives seriously. This has induced van Amersfoort and van der Wusten to make a study of the outbreak of political violence in general and to try to assess the importance of the ethnic factor in these outbreaks. Since Rabushka and Shepsle had only studied societies in which the ethnic factor was relevant, this was a better test of their theory. Van Amersfoort and van der Wusten found as many outbreaks of violence in societies where the ethnic factor was present as where it was absent or irrelevant to the conflict. They identified four important variables predicting the outbreak of violence: the sudden creation of a mass electorate; the birth of democracy under violent circumstances; unrealistic expectations concerning the state's capacity to promote economic growth; and the existence of an established state bureaucracy prior to the introduction of universal franchise (van Amersfoort and van der Wusten, 1981: 467–85). There may still be a connection between the existence of ethnic parties and democratic instability as there is also a correlation between the existence of ethnic parties and the sudden creation of a mass electorate, but this relation is interpreted as indirect. Van Amersfoort and van der Wusten tend to see ethnic conflicts more as a consequence of political instability than as a cause. This is not to say that the work of Rabushka and Shepsle is not of great value for the understanding of the dynamics of ethnic conflicts once they have come into being.

In the same way as the antagonists of institutional plurality tend to concentrate on the disadvantages of institutional plurality and to point to cases where it has hampered peaceful development, the advocates tend to point to situations where institutional plurality has proved to be a workable response to ethnic divisions. Switzerland and the Netherlands as examples of, respectively, a 'territorial' and a 'parallel' form of successful institutional plurality seem to prove the point that institutional plurality provides a solution for the ethnically divided state. Such arguments also take into account a question that Rabushka and Shepsle neglect: 'What makes the salience of the ethnic factor fluctuate in time?' For we know that there are ethnic divides that were once vehement but that have lost their violent nature over the course of history. Lijphart has described the working of societies that have succeeded in overcoming such divides through institutional plurality. It is no accident that it was a Dutch political scientist who addressed this question and coined the term 'consociational democracy'. The Dutch 'pillarized system', which allowed for the peaceful emancipation of Roman Catholics and the general working together of groups deeply divided along religious and secular ideologies, is perhaps the best example of a consciously created system of institutional plurality. But institutional plurality has played a role everywhere in Western Europe in overcoming the religious antagonisms of the sixteenth and seventeenth centuries. The only notable exception, of course, is Northern Ireland, which shows a development fully in line with the argument of Rabushka and Shepsle. This brings us back to the circumstances which allow a system of institutional plurality to work. When we combine the analytical insights put forward by Lijphart and by van Amersfoort and van der Wusten in their analyses, three conditions can be spelled out.

In the first place, gradual political and economical development seems a prerequisite. Even when such a system is the outcome of a conscious political process, it is not an 'instant creation'. A second condition is that the members of the ethnic group must have, or can realistically aspire to, the status of 'citizenship'. A legal construct of equal participation must be accepted at least in theory. When one or more 'ethnics' are excluded from participation, they do not have a stake in society. Only when people have something to lose can their primordial orientation become combined with other considerations. In such a case, institutional plurality makes them part of the whole fabric of society. For the leaders of these institutions, the functioning of the total fabric will in these circumstances become an asset that makes it worthwhile to subjugate expressive needs to the negotiation of package deals in the political field. To fulfil its role the leadership must be strong enough, on the one hand, to ensure the goals of their group, but also, on the other hand, to have an 'educational hold' on their followers. Only when they succeed in educating their followers in the rules of the political setup of a 'consociational democracy' can they avoid demagogic processes of outbidding.

Only in these rather precarious circumstances can institutional plurality offer a solution to the problem of ethnic diversity in the modern state. The remarkable point in the development of the Dutch pillarized state was that it did not crumble away in the severe crisis of the Second World War. On the contrary, it provided the framework for rebuilding Dutch society in the ten very difficult years after the war. It is one of the ironies of history that after this success the old religious and secular ideologies lost much of their hold and became marginalized. The pillarized society lost much of its legitimacy in the 1960s, especially for younger people.

CONCLUSION

It is not possible to say simply whether institutional plurality is to be considered a solution or a problem for the multi-ethnic state. In this chapter I have tried to point out that the role of institutional plurality in the total political process varies considerably with the context. In the context of 'a state in crisis', institutional plurality offers a direct framework for the articulation of ethnic demands and the build-up of tensions. The way in which the crisis in the (former) communist states of Eastern Europe has been translated into ethnic conflicts illustrates this point. However, it must be realized that whereas some of these states (the Soviet Union, Yugoslavia) were indeed constructed on the basis of the existence of 'nationalities', others had institutionalized the ethnic factor to a far lesser extent or had even tried to suppress it (Hungary, Romania).

In periods of great political turmoil, xenophobic feelings seem to be there, ready for exploitation, regardless of whether ethnicity was institutionalized or not, and whether the ethnic factor was in any concrete way related to the political crisis. The rise of antisemitism in Germany after the First World War should remind us that agitation does not need to have 'real' content to be effective in mobilizing violence.

It seems that only in the context of relatively long periods of gradual political and economic development does institutional plurality contribute to the solution of ethnic antagonisms in the state population. However, the prerequisites for making institutional plurality successful seem to be rare in the present-day world and can hardly be consciously created.

I would conclude that it is too optimistic to state that institutional plurality offers *the* solution to the problems of the multi-ethnic state, but too pessimistic to deny that it may form part of the solution.

REFERENCES

Breton, Raymond 1988 'From ethnic to civic nationalism: English Canada and Quebec', *Ethnic and Racial Studies*, 11, pp. 85–102.
Connor, Walker 1990 'When is a nation?' *Ethnic and Racial Studies*, 13. pp. 92–103.
Francis, E.K. 1976 *Interethnic Relations: An Essay in Sociological Theory* (New York, etc.: Elsevier).
Gellner, E. 1983 *Nations and Nationalism* (Oxford: Basil Blackwell).
Hechter, Michael 1975 *Internal Colonialism: The Celtic Fringe in British National Development* (London: Routledge).
Hechter, M. and Levi, Margaret 1979 'The comparative analysis of ethnoregional movements', *Ethnic and Racial Studies*, 2, pp. 260–74.
Knippenberg, Hans and de Pater, Ben 1988 *De Eenwording van Nederland* (Nijmegen: SUN).

Lijphart, A. 1977 *Democracy in Plural Societies: A Comparative Exploration* (New Haven, CT: Yale University Press).

McKay, James 1982 'An exploratory synthesis of primordial and mobilizationist approaches to ethnic phenomena', *Ethnic and Racial Studies*, 5, pp. 395–420.

Marshall, T.H. 1964 *Class, Citizenship and Social Development* (New York: Doubleday).

Mikesell, Marvin and Murphy, Alexander B. 1991 'A framework for the comparative study of minority-group aspirations', *Annals of the Association of American Geographers*, 81, pp. 581–604.

Rabushka, Alwin and Shepsle, Kenneth A. 1972 *Politics in Plural Societies: A Theory of Democratic Instability* (Columbus, OH: Merrill).

Rokkan, Stein and Urwin, Derek W. 1983 *Economy, Territory and Identity: Politics of West European Territory* (London: Sage).

Schermerhorn, R.A. 1970 *Comparative Ethnic Relations* (New York: Random House).

Smith, Anthony D. 1973 *Nationalism: A Trend Report and Annotated Bibliography*, Current Sociology, 21, Paris and The Hague.

Smith, Anthony D. 1979 'Towards a theory of ethnic separatism', *Ethnic and Racial Studies*, 2, pp. 21–35.

Smith, Anthony D. 1986 *The Ethnic Origins of Nations* (Oxford: Basil Blackwell).

Smith, Anthony D. 1988 'The myth of the modern nation and the myths of nations', *Ethnic and Racial Studies*, 11, pp. 1–26.

Smith, Anthony D. 1989 'The origins of nations', *Ethnic and Racial Studies*, 12, pp. 340–67.

van Amersfoort, Hans 1991 'Nationalities, citizens and ethnic conflicts: Towards a theory of ethnicity in the modern state', in Hans van Amersfoort and Hans Knippenberg (eds), *States and Nations: The Rebirth of the 'Nationalities Question' in Europe* (Amsterdam: Instituut voor Sociale Geografie), pp. 12–19.

van Amersfoort, Hans and van der Wusten, Herman 1981 'Democratic stability and ethnic parties', *Ethnic and Racial Studies*, 4, pp. 476–85.

Zubaida, Sam, 1989 'Nations old and new', *Ethnic and Racial Studies*, 12, pp. 329–39.

10

Nations, Nationalism and European Citizens

John Keane

EARLY MODERN ORIGINS

What is a nation? Do nations have a right to self-determination? If so, does that mean that the national identity of citizens is best guaranteed by a system of democratic government, in which power is subject to open disputation and to the consent of the governed living within a carefully defined territory? And what of nationalism? Does it differ from national identity? Is it compatible with democracy? If not, can its growth be prevented, or at least controlled, so as to guarantee the survival or growth of democracy?

These questions, pressingly familiar in contemporary politics though strangely neglected in contemporary political theory, have their roots in early modern Europe. With the decline of the Carolingian empire, a new sense of collective identity, national awareness, began to emerge as a powerful social force. This process of nation-building was championed initially by sections of the nobility and the clergy, who used derivatives of the old Latin term *natio* to highlight their dependence upon a common language and common historical experiences.[1] The 'nation' did not refer to the whole population of a region, but only to those classes which had developed a sense of identity based upon language and history and had begun to act upon it. Nations in this sense were seen as distinctive products of their own peculiar histories.

From the fifteenth century onwards, the term 'nation' was employed increasingly for political purposes. According to the classic definition of

Diderot, a *nation* is 'une quantité considérable de peuple qui habite une certaine étendue de pays, renfermée dans de certaines limites, et qui obéit au même gouvernement'.² Here 'nation' described a people who shared certain common laws and political institutions of a given territory. This political conception of 'the nation' defined and included the *societas civilis* – those citizens who were entitled to participate in politics and to share in the exercise of sovereignty – and it had fundamental implications for the process of state-building. Struggles for participation in the state assumed the form of confrontations between the monarch and the privileged classes, which were often organized in a parliament. These classes frequently designated themselves as advocates of 'the nation' in the political sense of the term. They insisted, in opposition to their monarch, that they were the representatives and defenders of 'national liberties' and 'national rights'.³ If the sovereign monarch came from a different nation – as in the Netherlands during the war against Habsburg Spain – then such claims were sharpened by another dimension: the struggle for privileged liberties was transformed into a movement for national emancipation from foreign tyranny.⁴

During the eighteenth century, the struggle for national identity was broadened and deepened to include the non-privileged classes. Self-educated middle classes, artisans, rural and urban labourers, and other social groups demanded inclusion in 'the nation', and this necessarily had anti-aristocratic and anti-monarchic implications. From here on, in principle, the nation included everybody, not just the privileged classes; 'the people' and 'the nation' were supposed to be identical. Thomas Paine's *Rights of Man* (1791–2) was the most influential European attempt to 'democratize' the theory of national identity.⁵ *Rights of Man* sparked bitter public controversies about the merits of monarchies and republics, forced Paine into permanent exile from his native England, hunted by death threats, and led to a general crackdown against 'Paineites', all for suggesting that each nation is entitled to its own system of representative government.

Paine had first proposed this thesis during the American revolution and several of his eighteenth-century contemporaries – Vattel and Sieyés for example – had explored, or were exploring, the same theme. But *Rights of Man* examined the political dimensions of national identity with unprecedented intellectual fire. Paine's prose burned with the drama of the French revolution. Its bristling optimism also reflected the breakthroughs of the American revolution: the declaration of the natural and civil rights of the sovereign people of a nation, including the right to resist unlawful government, and the establishment of a republican democracy on a wholly new federal basis. Paine spat at the court and government of George III and warned all other monarchic rulers that the outbreak of revolution in Europe heralded a new dawn for democratic principles. 'Monarchy is all a bubble, a mere court artifice to procure money', he wrote, though he admitted that the pompous power and money-grubbing of monarchy still trapped the world in a cage of war and rumours of war. 'There are men in all countries', he continued, 'who get their living by war and by keeping up the quarrels of nations.' He nevertheless insisted, in the face of this trend, that citizens of all nations, united in their love of republican democracy, had a duty to expose the taxing hypocrisy, fraud and gun-running of monarchic despotisms, understood as aggressive governments accountable only to themselves. And he concluded that the struggle for representative government – for periodic elections, fixed-term legislatures, a universal franchise, and freedom of assembly, the press and other civil liberties – required recognition of the right of each nation to determine its own destiny. 'What is government more than the management of the affairs of a nation?', he asked. 'It is not', he answered. 'Sovereignty as a matter of right, appertains to the nation only, and not to any individual; and a nation has at all times an inherent indefeasible right to abolish any form of government it finds inconvenient, and establish such as accords with its interest, disposition and happiness.'[6]

Paine's thesis that the nation and democratic government constitute an indivisible unity subsequently enjoyed a long and healthy life. Nineteenth-century Europe saw the emergence of two great powers (Germany and Italy) based on the principle of national self-determination; the effective partition of a third (Austria-Hungary after the Compromise of 1867) on identical grounds; two revolts of the Poles in support of their reconstitution as a nation-state; and the formal recognition of a chain of lesser independent states claiming to represent their sovereign nations, from Luxembourg and Belgium in the west to the Ottoman successor states in southeastern Europe (Bulgaria, Serbia, Greece, Romania). During the twentieth century, especially after the First World War, the principle of 'the right to national self-determination' enjoyed considerable popularity among international lawyers, political philosophers, governments and their opponents, who supposed that if the individual members of a nation so will it, they are entitled to freedom from domination by other nations, and can therefore legitimately establish a sovereign state covering the territory in which they live, and where they constitute a majority of the population. From this perspective, the principle that citizens should govern themselves was identified with the principle that nations should determine their own destiny, and this in turn produced a convergence of meaning of the terms 'state' and 'nation'. 'State' and 'nation' came to be used interchangeably, as in such official expressions as 'League of Nations', the 'law of nations' or 'nation-state', and in the commonplace English language usage of the term 'national' to designate anything run or regulated by the state, such as national service, national health insurance or national debt. Such expressions reinforce the assumption, traceable to the eighteenth century, that there is no other way of defining the word 'nation' than as a territorial aggregate whose various parts recognize the authority of the same state, an assumption captured in Karl Deutsch's famous definition of a nation as 'a people who have hold of a state'.[7]

The principle that nations should be represented within a territorially defined state echoes into our times. In the European region – to mention several examples – the birth of Solidarność and the defeat of martial law in Poland, the dramatic velvet revolution in Czechoslovakia, the collapse of the Berlin Wall to the trumpet sounds of 'Wir sind ein Volk', and the successful struggle of the Demos government and its supporters to achieve Slovenian independence simply cannot be understood without reference to this equation. The same powerful dynamic worked to secure the collapse of the Soviet empire. The Soviet Union was an empire comprising a diversity of nationalities all subject to the political dominance of a Russian-dominated Communist party that ensured for seven decades that the federal units of the Union had no meaningful political autonomy and that demands for 'national communism' would trigger a political crackdown backed if necessary by military force.

This multinational empire harboured a self-paralysing contradiction. The party insisted on subjects' conformity to its Russified definition of policies for securing 'socialism', all the while governing through national cadres, promoting national cultures, encouraging education in the local language and even talking of eventual rapprochement (*sblizhenie*) and assimilation of nations (*slyanie*). From the Khrushchev period onwards, this contradiction fostered not only the growth of national *nomenklatura* who ran the republics, particularly in Transcaucasia and Central Asia, as fiefdoms controlled by Party 'mafias' rooted in circles of friends, kinship networks and local and regional systems of patronage. It also stimulated the growth of civil societies expressing themselves in a national idiom, protesting against Russification and ecology-damaging enforced industrialization, and demanding 'democracy' and 'independence', thereby lunging with a dagger at the heart of the imperial system structured by the leading role of the Russian-centred party.[8]

NATIONAL IDENTITY AND CITIZENSHIP

The collapse of the Soviet empire under pressure from struggles for national self-determination adds weight to the thesis that a shared sense of national identity, in Hungary and Russia no less than in Scotland and Slovenia, is a basic precondition of the creation and strengthening of citizenship and democracy. Understood in ideal-typical terms, national identity is a particular form of collective identity in which, despite their routine lack of physical contact, people consider themselves bound together because they speak a language or a dialect of a common language; inhabit or are closely familiar with a defined territory, and experience its ecosystem with some affection; and because they share a variety of customs, including a measure of memories of the historical past, which is consequently experienced in the present tense as pride in the nation's achievements and, where necessary, an obligation to feel ashamed of the nation's failings.[9]

National identity so defined is a specifically modern European invention and its political importance is that it infuses citizens with a sense of purposefulness, confidence and dignity by encouraging them to feel 'at home'. It enables them to decipher the signs of institutional and everyday life. The activity of others – the food they prepare, the products they manufacture, the songs they sing, the jokes they tell, the clothes they wear, the looks on their faces, the words they speak – can be recognized. That familiarity in turn endows each individual with a measure of confidence to speak and to act. Consequently, whatever is strange is not automatically feared; whatever diversity exists within the nation is more or less accepted as one of its constitutive features. The borders between a national identity and its 'neighbouring' identities (of class, gender, religion and race, for example) are vaguely defined, and its security police and border guards are unreliable and tolerant.[10] There is even some acceptance of the fact that members of the same nation can legitimately disagree about the meaning and extent of their nationhood. This tolerance of difference is possible precisely because nationhood equips members of a nation with a sense of belonging and a security in themselves and in each other: they can say 'we' and 'you' without feeling that their 'I', their sense of self, is slipping from their possession.

Whenever they are denied access to a shared sense of nationhood, citizens tend to experience the world as unfriendly and alien – in the extreme case of enforced exile they experience the nasty, gnawing, self-pitying and self-destructive *Hauptweh* described by Thomas Mann and others – and this renders them less capable of living democratically. After all, democratic regimes are the most demanding of political systems. In contrast to all forms of heteronomous government, democracy comprises procedures for arriving at collective decisions through public controversies and compromises, based on the fullest possible and qualitatively best participation of interested parties.[11] At a minimum, democratic procedures include equal and universal adult suffrage within constituencies of various scope and size; majority rule and guarantees of minority rights, which ensure that collective decisions are approved by a substantial number of those expected to make them; freedom from arbitrary arrest, and respect for the rule of law among citizens and their representatives; constitutional guarantees of freedom of assembly and expression, and other civil and political liberties, which help ensure that those expected to decide or to elect those who decide can choose among real alternatives; and various social policies (in fields such as health, education, child care and basic income provision) which prevent market exchanges from becoming dominant and thereby ensure that citizens can live as free equals by enjoying their basic political and civil entitlements. Expressed differently, democracy requires the institutional division between a certain form of state and civil society. A democracy is an openly structured system of institutions which facilitate the flexible control of the exercise of power. It is a multi-layered political and social mosaic in which political decision-makers at the local, regional, national and supranational levels are assigned the job of serving the *res publica*; while, for their part, citizens living within the nooks and crannies of civil society are obliged to exercise vigilance in preventing each other and their rulers from abusing their powers and violating the spirit of the commonwealth.

Although democracy in this sense does not require citizens to play the role of full-time political animals – too much democracy can kill off democracy – it is always difficult to generate or to sustain its momentum. That task is rendered even more arduous in contexts lacking traditions which are home to the virtues of democratic citizenship: prudence, common sense, self-reliance, courage, sensitivity to power, the knack of making and defending judgments in public, the ability to (self-)criticize and to accept criticism from others in turn, and the capacity to join with others in dignity and solidarity to resist the enervating miasma of fear. The last-mentioned quality is especially important in the democratic transformation of despotic regimes, when fear of power corrupts those who are subject to it and fear of losing power corrupts those who exercise it.

Shaking off fear is always a basic condition of democracy and it is normally assisted by citizens' shared sense of belonging to one or more ethical identities, national identity being among the most potent of these. Fearlessness is not a naturally occurring substance. It is a form of courage or 'grace under pressure' (Aung San Suu Kyi) developed wherever victims of political lies, bullying and violence make a personal effort to throw off personal corruption and to draw on their inner and outer resources to nurture the habit of refusing to let fear dictate their actions. Grace under pressure normally precedes and underpins attempts to institutionalize democracy. To be effective, it must be practised in small daily acts of resistance that in turn feed upon citizens' sense that they speak a common language, and share a natural habitat, a variety of customs and historical experiences.

Consider Poland. The experience of more than a century of foreign domination after the partitions of 1772, 1793 and 1795, by which Poland was carved up by the Russian empire, the Habsburg monarchy and the kingdom of Prussia, nurtured a distinctive national consciousness among the nobility (*szlachta*) of that country. During the nineteenth century, these Poles considered themselves (and were widely regarded) to be fighters for the freedom of humanity, a nation martyred in the cause of democratic liberty. Their shared sense of nationhood merged with the ability to act gracefully under pressure; to be Polish meant the refusal to be bullied and intimidated by power. The leader of the revolt of 1794, Tadeusz Kościuszko, a friend of Thomas Paine's, was a hero to all European democrats, and his name was celebrated in America and even in Australia, whose highest mountain is named after him. The Polish legions organized by Henryk Dabrowski took as their slogan 'for our liberty and yours' (*za nasza i wasza wolność*) and Polish patriots played a prominent part in the 1848 revolutions in Hungary, Germany and Italy. Today, the national identity crystallized in such experiences surprises and even perplexes many people who are not Polish. The Poles are sometimes seen as brash and crafty anarchists who have a deeply romantic soul traceable to poets such as Adam Mickiewicz, who viewed Poland as the Christ of Nations, crucified so that it could be resurrected and all other nations could be redeemed. Traces of such arrogance are indeed still evident in various parts of today's political spectrum in Poland, especially in the call for a 'Catholic State of the Polish Nation'. But, overall, the messianic fervour with which certain nineteenth-century Poles reacted to misfortune and oppression has receded. A striking feature of contemporary Polish national identity is its embrace of the language of democratic freedom; as Adam Michnik remarked in the mid-1980s, the Polish struggle for freedom against military dictatorship and communist empire was simultaneously a struggle for the freedom of humanity.[12]

THE RISE OF NATIONALISM

The preceding analysis appears to confirm the eighteenth-century doctrine of national self-determination. It implies that Paine and others were correct in thinking that the defence of 'the nation' and the struggle for democracy against political despotism are identical, that when the winds of national feeling blow, the people, like beautiful birds, grow wings and fly their way to a land of independence. And yet the experience of the French revolution, which inspired Paine's *Rights of Man*, casts doubt upon any such conclusion. For a time, the rise of Louis Napoleon seemed to reveal a political weakness specific to the French. Paine drew this conclusion and returned to America, wings under his arms. Only in our time, after the logic of the French revolution has been broadly repeated in so many countries, has it become possible to discern the operation of a new aspect of modernity, the unfolding of a process in which the French revolution proved to be a fundamental watershed. The revolution destroyed for ever the faith in the divine and un-challengeable right of monarchs to govern and it sparked a struggle against the privileged classes in the name of a sovereign nation of free and equal individuals. Those acting in the name of the sovereign nation were ever more tempted to emphasize faithfulness to *la patrie* – that is, citizens' obligations to their state, itself the guarantor of the nation, itself said to be 'one and indivisible'. The motto of the *ancien régime*, 'Un roi, une foi, une loi' ('One king, one faith, one law') was replaced by 'La Nation, la loi, le roi' ('The Nation, the law, the king'). Thenceforward the nation made the law, which the king was responsible for implementing. And when the monarchy was abolished in August 1792, the nation became the titular source of sovereignty. 'Vive la Nation!' cried the French soldiers one month later at Valmy, as they flung themselves into battle against the Prussian army. Everything which had been royal had now become national. The nation even had its own emblem, the tricoloured national flag, which replaced the white flag of the house of Bourbon. The new spirit of *nationalism* had surfaced, bringing with it a lust for the power and glory of the nation-state which finally overwhelmed the democratic potential of the revolution. The first nationalist dictatorship of the modern world had been born.

The formation of a despotic regime sustained by nationalist appeals to the nation was an utterly novel development – Europe's Greek gift to itself and to the rest of the world.[13] Since that time, and despite its extraordinary global impact, the eighteenth-century doctrine of national self-determination has been subject to a smouldering crisis, whose contemporary resolution necessitates a fundamental rethinking of that doctrine, a more complex understanding of the relationship between national identity and nationalism, and greater clarity about the nature of democratic procedures.

Max Weber once defined democracy for the benefit of General Ludendorff, and with his approval, as a political system in which the people choose a leader who then says, 'Now shut your mouths and obey me'.[14] The impatience with ongoing public clashes of opinion and disagreement implied in this definition of democracy misses one of its quintessential features. Democratic procedures tend to maximize the level of reversibility or 'biodegradability' of decision-making. They invite dispute and encourage public dissatisfaction with currently existing conditions, from time to time even stirring up citizens to anger and direct action. Under enduring despotisms – Salazar's Portugal or Brezhnev's Russia – things are otherwise. Time appears to stand still. Individuals continue to be born, to mature, to work, to love, to play, to quarrel, to have children and to die, and yet everything around them becomes motionless, petrified and repetitious. Political life becomes utterly boring.

In fully democratic systems, by contrast, everything is in perpetual motion. Endowed with liberties to criticize and to transform the distribution of power within state and civil institutions, citizens are catapulted into a state of permanent unease which they can cope with, grumble about, turn their backs on, but never fully escape. The unity of purpose and sense of community of pre-democratic societies snaps. There is difference, openness and constant competition among a plurality of power groups to produce and to control the definition of reality. Hence there are public scandals which unfold when publics learn about events which had been kept secret because if they had been made public ahead of time they could not have been carried out without public outcries. Under democratic conditions the world feels as if it is gripped by capaciousness and uncertainty about who does and should govern. Existing relations of power are treated (and understood) as contingent, as lacking transcendental guarantees of absolute certainty and hierarchical order, as a product of institutionally situated actors exercising power within and over their respective milieus.

It is this self-questioning, self-destabilizing quality of democratic regimes which not only provides opportunities for the advocates of national identity to take their case to a wider public. It also increases the magnetism of anti-democratic ideologies such as nationalism. Democratic conditions can severely test citizens' shared sense of the unreality of reality and chronic instability of their regimes, to the point where they may crave for the restoration of certainty about 'reality' by suppressing diversity, complexity and openness within and between the state and civil society. Democracies never reach a point of homeostatic equilibrium. They are dogged permanently by public disagreements about means and ends, by uncertainties, confusions and gaps within political programmes, and by hidden and open conflicts, and all this makes them prey to forms of post-prison psychosis (Havel), morbid attempts to simplify matters, to put a stop to pluralism and to foist Unity and Order onto everybody and everything.

The events of the French revolution revealed this dynamic for the first time, confirming the rule that whenever believers in a nation assemble they risk being seduced by the language and power fantasies of nationalism. The distinction between national identity and nationalism – overlooked by many commentaries on the subject, including Eric Hobsbawm's *Nations and Nationalism since 1780*[15] – is fundamental in this context. Nationalism is the child of democratic pluralism – both in the sense that the existence of open state institutions and a minimum of civil liberties enables nationalists to organize and to propagate their nationalism, but also in the less obvious sense that democracy breeds insecurity about power, sometimes fear and panic, and, hence, the yearning of some citizens to take refuge in sealed forms of life.

In the European region, nationalism is at present among the most virile and magnetic of these closed systems of life, or what I prefer to call ideologies.[16] Like other ideologies, nationalism is an upwardly mobile, power-hungry and potentially dominating form of language game which makes falsely universal claims. It supposes that it is part of the natural order of things and that the nation is a biological fact, all the while hiding its own particularity by masking its own conditions of production, and by attempting to stifle the plurality of non-national and subnational language games within the established civil society and state in which it thrives.

Nationalism is a scavenger. It feeds upon the pre-existing sense of nationhood within a given territory, transforming that shared national identity into a bizarre parody of its former self. Nationalism is a pathological form of national identity which tends (as Milorad Pavić points out in *Dictionary of the Khazars*) to destroy its heterogeneity by squeezing the nation into the nation. Nationalism also takes advantage of any democratizing trends by roaming hungrily through civil society and the state, harassing other particular language games, viewing them as competitors and enemies to be banished or terrorized, injured or eaten alive, pretending all the while that it is a universal language game whose validity is publicly unquestionable, and which therefore views itself as freed from the contingencies of historical time and space.

Nationalism has a fanatical core. Its boundaries are dotted with border posts and border police charged with the task of monitoring the domestic and foreign enemies of the nation. In contrast to national identity, whose boundaries are not fixed and whose tolerance of difference and openness to other forms of life is qualitatively greater, nationalism requires its adherents to believe in themselves and to believe in the belief itself, to believe that they are not alone, that they are members of a community of believers known as the nation, through which they can achieve immortality. Nationalism requires them and their leader-representatives (as Ernest Renan put it in *Qu'est-ce qu'une nation?*) to participate in 'un plebiscite de tous les jours'. This level of ideological commitment ensures that nationalism is driven by a bovine will to simplify things – by the kind of instruction issued by Bismarck: 'Germans! Think with your blood!'

If democracy is a continuous struggle against simplification of the world, then nationalism is a continuous struggle to undo complexity, a will not to know certain matters, a chosen ignorance, not the ignorance of innocence. It thereby has a tendency to crash into the world, crushing or throttling everything that crosses its path, to defend or to claim territory, and to think of land as power and its native inhabitants as a 'single fist' (Ayaz Mutalibov). Nationalism has nothing of the humility of national identity. It feels no shame about the past or the present, for it supposes that only foreigners and 'enemies of the nation' are guilty. It revels in macho glory and fills the national memory with stories of noble ancestors, heroism and bravery in defeat. It feels itself invincible, waves the flag and, if necessary, eagerly bloodies its hands on its enemies.

At the heart of nationalism – and among the most peculiar features of its 'grammar' – is its simultaneous treatment of the Other as everything and nothing. Nationalists warn of the menace to their own way of life by the growing presence of aliens. The Other is seen as the knife in the throat of the nation. Nationalists are panicky and driven by friend–foe calculations, suffering from a judgment disorder that convinces them that the Other nation lives at its own expense. Nationalists are driven by the feeling that all nations are caught up in an animal struggle for survival, and that only the fittest survive. Every other speech of Jörg Haider of the FPÖ in Austria insinuates that 'East Europeans' are endangering the state, the constitution and democracy. Neo-Nazis in the new half of Germany shout 'Ausländer 'raus!', liken Poles to hungry pigs, attribute shortages of bicycles to the Vietnamese and the lack of food to the Jews, and accuse Turks of taking over German communities. French supporters of Jean-Marie Le Pen warn of the Arab 'invasion' of France. Lithuanian antisemites whisper old stories about Jews who once sacrificed Christian children and used their blood to make Passover bread, and recall the same blood-libellous tales of Jewish grain merchants and millers who put glass in their flour to make Gentile women bleed when they kneaded the dough. Croatian nationalists denounce Serbians as Četniks or as Bolshevik butchers who murder their victims and mutilate their bodies; Serbian nationalists reciprocate by denouncing Croats as Ustaše fascists who are hell-bent on eliminating the Serbian nation. Both curse Muslims as foreign invaders of a !and in which the latter have in fact lived for five centuries.

Yet nationalism is not only fearful of the Other. It is also arrogant, confidently portraying the Other as inferior rubbish, as a worthless zero. The Other is seen as unworthy of respect or recognition because its smelly breath, strange food, unhygienic habits, loud and off-beat music, and incomprehensible babbling language which places it outside and beneath Us. It follows that the Other has few if any entitlements, not even when it constitutes a majority or minority of the population resident in the vicinity of Our nation. Wherever a member of the nation is, there is the nation. It is true (as Lenin emphasized) that the nationalism of a conquering nation should be distinguished from the nationalism of those whom they conquer, and that conquering nationalism always seems uglier and more culpable. It is also true that nationalism can be more or less militant, and that its substantive themes can be highly variable, ranging from attachment to consumption and a treasured form of currency to boundary-altering forms of political separatism. Yet despite such variations, nationalists suffer from a single-minded arrogance. This leads them to taunt and spit at the Other, to label them as wogs, *Scheisse* and *tapis*, to discriminate against them in institutional settings, to prohibit the public use of minority languages ('linguicide'), or even, in the extreme case, to press for the expulsion of the Other for the purpose of creating a homogeneous territorial nation.

This murderous *reductio ad absurdum* of nationalism surfaced on the southern fringes of Europe during and after the First World War, with the mass extirpation of Armenians from Turkey in 1915 and, after the crushing defeat of the Greek army by the Turks in Anatolia in 1922, the expulsion by Greece of some 400,000 Turks and a reciprocal expulsion by the Turks of perhaps 1.5 million destitute and panic-stricken Greeks from the lands of Asia Minor, where they had lived with others since the time of Homer.[17] The herding and murdering of nations was repeated by Stalin and by Hitler, who insisted on the elimination of the Jews and others, and organized the transfer of South Tirolians and other German-speaking peoples living outside the *Vaterland* to Germany itself. The same bizarre and bloody process has lately reappeared in the armed defence of 'Serbian autonomous republics' and the military occupation by Serbia of Kosovo in former Yugoslavia. The Kosovo region in fact proved to be the testing ground of Serbian expansionism. Its nationalist spokesmen, tossed between the horns of arrogance and fear common to all nationalists, attacked Albanian Kosovars as dirty, backward Muslims who are not a genuine Yugoslav nation (*nacija*) but a mere unimportant nationality (*nacionalnost*) of non-Slavs. At the same time, they viewed Kosovars as fanatical conquerors, calling for 'the severing of the right hand of all those who carry the green flag of Islam' (Vuk Draskovic) in the historic cradle of the Serbian nation, where King Lazar and his army were slaughtered while defending Christendom and civilization against the crescent and scimitar of all-conquering Islam. This same view of Muslims as worthless invaders is currently tearing Bosnia-Herzegovina to shreds. European Muslims – the Jews of the late twentieth century – are shot at, herded at gunpoint from their burning homes, summarily executed in nearby houses or marched in columns to railway sidings past rotting corpses to concentration camps, where they are raped or castrated, and then made to wait, with bulging eyes and lanternous faces, for the arrival of their own deaths.

DEMOCRACY

Nationalism is evidently a serious and dirty business, in this case resulting in the forcible tearing apart of Yugoslavia and the destabilization of the whole Balkan region, with more than two and a half million refugees and many thousands killed or wounded. How can processes of this kind be explained?

Contrary to the most popular explanation, nationalism is not caused by the periodic re-emergence in the human breast of atavistic instincts of *Blut und Boden*. Such emphasis on the primordial roots of nationalism correctly pinpoints its deeply emotive dimensions, but, devoid of any historical understanding, it cannot account for why nationalism appears when and where it does. Furthermore, contemporary nationalism of the Serbian, French, English or Georgian variety is not primarily understandable in neo-Marxian terms as the political response of either a beleaguered or expansionist bourgeoisie (Austro-Marxism), or of classes exploited by capitalist imperialism (Tom Nairn), or by the reckless, creative destruction of the global capitalist economy (Slavoj Zizek). Class domination, deindustrialization, unemployment and the formation of a new underclass of anxious citizens are indeed contemporary consequences of economies structured by commodity production and exchange, but they do not spontaneously provoke the growth of nationalism. For that to happen, there must be at least some elements of a pre-existing shared sense of nationhood that is in turn capable of manipulation and public deployment by power groups taking advantage of the openness and *déracinement* cultivated by actually existing democratic mechanisms.

If nationalist tensions are not entirely blameable upon capitalism then neither are they ultimately traceable to the operations of 'real socialism'. The ruling Communist party bureaucracies of countries such as Romania, Hungary, Slovenia and Poland undoubtedly stimulated nationalist tendencies in their effort to legitimate their grip on power, but the conclusion that nationalism is a toxic product of communism is unwarranted. Nationalism (as the Magyar resistance to the Habsburg empire and many other examples suggest) pre-dated the era of twentieth-century communism in power and, besides, in Central and Eastern Europe nationalism has emerged much more forcefully in the phase of post-communism.

Since the 'velvet revolutions' of 1989–91, the nationalist card has been played not only by communist parties and organizations struggling to retain their power – Milosević in Serbia, Kravchuk in the Ukraine, and Iliescu in Romania are examples. It has been used as frequently by the anti-communist opponents of the *ancien régime* – Gamsakhurdia in Georgia, Tudjman in Croatia and Yeltsin in Russia – who in this respect share something of fundamental importance with their communist foes. Both groups have learned that in the early stages of democratization, when anti-communists lack money, and communists lack ideas and conviction, nationalism can warm hearts, change minds and win votes, encouraging citizens to embrace a shock-absorbing identity that washes away their sense of futility, encourages 'solidarity of the culpable' (Šiklova) and gives them the feeling of protection against the ongoing disequilibrium and disorientation produced by the first steps towards democracy.

The tightly coupled relationship between national identity, nationalism and democracy does not warrant either the solipsistic conclusion that national identity, the 'raw material' of nationalism, is a pathological, outdated, hopefully declining force that in the meantime is best cold-shouldered by observers and citizens alike; or the tragic deduction that democracy is somehow the root 'cause' of nationalism, and that therefore the grip of nationalism can be broken only by abandoning democracy. Monist interpretations of nationalism (as of any other phenomenon examined by the social sciences) are inadequate precisely because of their one-sidedness. That is why the novel thesis presented here aims not to replace existing accounts of nationalism but to *complicate* our understanding of a force of fundamental importance in the life and times of modern Europe.

Among the likely casualties of this new interpretation are Paine's thesis that the defence of national identity is a basic condition of democratic government, and the corresponding vision, championed by Woodrow Wilson, Mazzini and Paine himself, of a holy alliance of self-governing nations working in harmonious partnership for the common good of humanity. This vision was at the same time too simple and too dangerous. It was blind to the difference between national identity and nationalism, underestimated the anti-democratic potential of the struggle for national identity, failed to foresee the murderous *reductio ad absurdum* of nationalism; and for these three reasons alone it has today left behind a trail of confusion about the proper relationship between national identity and democratic institutions.

NATIONAL SELF-DETERMINATION?

This confusion cannot be undone by speculative arguments between those who conclude that 'nationalism is the ideology of the twenty-first century' (Conor Cruise O'Brien) and their opponents who rely on the equally broad-brushed conclusion that 'the Owl of Minerva is now hovering over nations and nationalism' (Hobsbawm). Such generalizations understate the uneven patterns of distribution of European nationalism, simplify its multiple causes, and short-circuit the normative and strategic problem of how to disarm nationalism. As I see it, there is an urgent need to stretch the limits of the contemporary sociological and democratic imagination, to think differently about the intertwined problems of nationalism, national identity and democracy, and to consider how the limits of democracy can be overcome in practice by inventing new democratic methods of preventing the growth of democracy's own poisonous fruits.

Solving the problem of nationalism by democratic means is possible, but not easy. The thesis presented here is that since democratic mechanisms facilitate the transformation of national identity into nationalism, democracy is best served by abandoning the doctrine of national self-determination and regarding a shared sense of national identity as a legitimate but *limited* form of life. This thesis contains a paradoxical corollary: national identity, an important support of democratic institutions, is best preserved by restricting its scope in favour of *non-national* identities that reduce the probability of its transformation into anti-democratic nationalism.

In the European context it is now possible to envisage – by means of this thesis – a cluster of four interdependent mechanisms which together can curb the force of nationalism and at the same time guarantee citizens' access to their respective national identities:

1. The first of these remedies is to decentre the institutions of the nation-state through the development of interlocking networks of democratically accountable subnational and supranational state institutions. Their combined effect, if rendered accountable to their citizens, would be to improve the effectiveness and legitimacy of state institutions, and, more pertinently, to complicate the lines of political power, thereby reducing the room for manoeuvre of single nation-states and frustrating the nationalist fantasy of securing nations through strong, sovereign states that are prepared in principle to launch war on their neighbours or to crush their domestic opponents in the name of national preservation or salvation.

In effect, this remedy involves renewing – but at the same time democratizing – the more complex patterns of political power typical of the late medieval and early modern periods. The modern process of European state-building entailed the eclipse of numerous units of power – free cities, principalities, provinces, estates, manors and deliberative assemblies – such that the five hundred or so political units that dotted the region in 1500 were reduced to around 25 units in 1900. There are now signs of a reversal of this process of building centralized state institutions. One symptom of this 'scattering' of political power is the renewed interest in local government as a flexible forum for conducting local politics and competently administering local policies, partly in response to the declining effectiveness of macroeconomic management and the retreat of the national welfare state in Western Europe.[18]

The same decentring of the nation-state 'downwards and sideways' is evident in the vigorous development of regional ideas and regional power in areas such as Catalonia, Wallonia, Emilia-Romagna, Andalucia, Scotland and the Basque region. Especially striking is the rapid growth and competitive success of industrial regions comprising interdependent networks of firms caught up in a process of double convergence (Sabel). Large firms increasingly attempt to decentralize into looser networks of operating units, subsidiaries and subcontractors producing more specialized products through more flexible production methods. Meanwhile, small firms attempt to build themselves into the wider forms of loan finance, marketing facilities, research and development, and other common services for which large firms were once renowned, and which are now provided increasingly at the regional level.[19]

Finally, the trend towards a *Europe des régions* has been supplemented by the accelerating growth of supranational political institutions such as the European Parliament, the Council of Europe, and the European Court of Justice. An earlier phase of experiments with intergovernmental negotiations and economic cooperation has been complemented by a process of treaty-making and a drive to political and legal union which, though still highly undemocratic and controversial, is likely to prove as consequential for the political shape of Europe as the Congress of Vienna in 1814, the Treaty of Versailles in 1919, or the Yalta Summit in 1945.

Member states of the European Union are required increasingly to accept the *acquis communautaire*, the body of treaties, laws and directives which have been agreed by its makers; there is a relative shift away from policymaking by consensus towards qualified majority voting; and a consequent quickening pace of Euro-legislation in all policy fields. In 1970, for example, the then European Community's Council of Ministers, on which each member government has a representative, adopted 345 regulations, decisions and directives (the three types of Community law); by 1987 that total had reached 623, and it has risen further since that time. From standards of central heating and housing to the purity of beer and wine, the cleanliness of beaches and the conditions of women's employment, the populations of the EU are increasingly touched and shaped by European political integration. This process arguably hastens the decline of nation-state sovereignty and facilitates the birth of a post-national Europe, in the sense that it adds to the pressure on nationalist movements, parties, governments and leaders to recognize the fact and legitimacy of countervailing political powers, even in such sensitive matters as 'national economic policy' and the resolution of so-called 'national conflicts'.

2. The formulation and application of internationally recognized legal guarantees of national identity is a vital adjunct of the breaking down of the sovereignty of the nation-state. Such formal guarantees were pioneered in the four Geneva Conventions commencing in 1929 and expressed forcefully in the Universal Declaration of the Rights of Man

ratified by the United Nations in December 1948: 'Everyone is entitled to the rights and freedoms set forth in this declaration, without distinction of any kind such as race, colour, sex, language, religion, political or other opinions, *national* or social *origin*, property, birth, or other status' (italics mine).

The Badinter proposals for resolving the Yugoslav crisis extend and refine this principle of guaranteeing citizens' entitlement to national identity by means of international supervision, thereby departing from the old Paineite maxim that all sovereignty appertains to the territorially bounded nation. The EC report coordinated by the former French Justice Minister and President of France's Constitutional Court, Robert Badinter, called for applications for EC recognition of the statehood of the various Yugoslav republics and shortly thereafter recommended the recognition of Slovenia, Croatia and Macedonia, subject to their governments' acceptance of formal guarantees of the civil and political freedoms of national minorities, the acceptance of international arms control agreements, and no forcible redrawing of existing nation-state boundaries.

The report, implemented only in part and plagued by war, has far-reaching implications for the subjects of nationhood, nationalism and democracy. It supposes that governments have a primary obligation to respect the wishes of their populations, but it does not fall back on the old premise that each nation requires a sovereign state covering the territory in which it lives. 'Where the sentiment of nationality exists in any force', wrote J.S. Mill, 'there is a *prima facie* case for uniting all the members of the nationality under the same government, and a government to themselves apart.' The Badinter report spots a murderous difficulty lurking in this early modern doctrine of national self-determination: if the political boundaries of the earth are to be fixed by the criterion of nationhood, then, since nations do not see eye to eye (why otherwise have state borders?) and do not live in discrete geographic entities, there will be no end to boundary disputes. Every border is seen as necessarily faulty and as capable of improvement through the annexation of some outlying territory in which one's own nation is living; and since this annexation must normally be imposed by the conqueror upon the conquered, the struggle for 'national autonomy' contains the seeds of 'territorial cleansing', pushing and shoving, refugees, statelessness, pogroms and war. The report correctly understands that in the European context civil wars sparked off by nationalist pressures, rather than war between homogeneous nation-states, have become the major threat to regional stability.

The Badinter report also reminds Europeans of the increasingly multinational character of their states. Of course, most European states have always been multinational, but recently that fact has been accentuated by large-scale migrations. The permanent entry into Western Europe of more than 15 million non-EC people during the past half-century has ensured that mononational states no longer exist, and that even the oldest and most culturally 'homogeneous' of civil societies in countries or regions such as Spain, England, Portugal, France and Germany are now vertical mosaics of nationalities which do not humbly accept their position as satellites of the currently dominant national identity. The report challenges the early modern assumption that national loyalties are exclusive, and that democracy is therefore only possible in a nationally homogenous state.

The report calls instead for a new compromise between nations *within* states. It sees that the peaceful and democratic functioning of European states and societies necessitates reliance upon supranational monitoring and enforcement mechanisms, and it urges recognition of the new principle that the various nations of any single state are entitled to their nationhood, and thus to live differently, as free equals. The Badinter report 'de-politicizes' and 'de-territorializes' national identity. It recaptures something of the eighteenth-century view, championed by thinkers like Burke and Herder, that nationality is best understood as a cultural entity; that is, as an identity belonging to civil society, not the state. It sees national identity as a *civil* entitlement of citizens, the squeezing or attempted abolition of which, even when ostensibly pursued by states in the name either of higher forms of human solidarity or of protecting the 'core national identity' (Isaiah Berlin), serves only to trigger off resentment, hatred and violence among national groupings.

3. Of equal importance as a guarantor of national identity and democracy against nationalism is a factor that has been barely discussed in the literature on the subject: the development of a pluralist mosaic of identities within civil society. This third antidote to nationalism is as effective as it is paradoxical. It presumes that the survival and flourishing of national identity is only possible within a self-organizing civil society, which, however, provides spaces for citizens to act upon *other* chosen or inherited identities, thus *limiting* the probable role of national identity in the overall operation of state and civil institutions, political parties,

communications media and other intermediary bodies. The paradox bears a striking parallel to the question of religious tolerance: the practice of a particular religion in a multi-religious society requires – if bigotry and bloodshed are to be avoided – the principle of freedom of religious worship, which in practice entails recognition of the legitimacy of *other* religions and, hence, the need for secularism which simultaneously guarantees the freedom *not* to be religious. The same maxim ought to be carried over into matters of national identity, for it is clear that to model either state institutions or civil society solely on the principle of national identity means privileging one aspect of citizens' lives, devaluing others, and contradicting the pluralism so vital for a democratic civil society, thus rendering those citizens' lives nation-centred and one-dimensional, and, thus, susceptible to the rise of nationalism.

The straitjacketing effect of nation-centred politics in Croatia has been well described by Slavenka Drakulić: 'Nationalism has been forced on people like an ill-fitting shirt. You may feel that the sleeves are too short and the collar too tight. You might not like the colour, and the cloth may itch. But you wear it because there is no other. No one is allowed *not* to be Croatian.'[20] The converse of this point is that an open, self-governing civil society protected by various tiers of state institutions requires the cultivation of a complex habitat of nested spaces in which citizens can protect themselves against the dangers of 'uprootedness' in a democracy by learning how to belong to a variety of organizations which enable them to put down roots, thereby preserving particular memories of the past, a measure of stability in the present, and particular expectations for the future. These spaces can further counteract nationalist pressures by helping citizens to overcome their own parochialism. Through their participation in the relatively local organizations of civil society, citizens find the most effective cure of their localism by learning about the wider world, coming to see that their sense of national identity – thinking and feeling themselves to be German, Irish or Turkish – is not essentially superior to that of other nations, and that nationality is only one possible identity among others.

4. Perhaps the most difficult to cultivate antidote to nationalism is the fostering of an *international* civil society in which citizens of various nationalities can intermingle, display at least a minimal sense of mutual understanding and respect, and generate a sense of solidarity, especially

in times of crisis (for example, during natural disasters, economic collapse or political upheaval).

During the second half of the eighteenth century, this friendship among citizens of various nations was called cosmopolitanism. Exposure to foreign contacts came in a variety of overlapping and sometimes contradictory ways: young men sent abroad to study; foreigners invited and welcomed as teachers; involvement in European wars which took 'nationals' elsewhere in Europe; increased travel among the 'respectable' classes and regular diplomatic relations with courts; expanding commerce; and the ever faster and wider circulation of foreign fashions in philosophy, letters, instruction, dress and social intercourse. A history of eighteenth-century cosmopolitanism has yet to be written, but it is clear that in the writings of Pietro Verri, Immanuel Kant, Thomas Paine and others the 'true cosmopolite' and the 'loyal patriot' were one and the same figure.[21] There was seen to be no contradiction between feeling oneself to be a citizen of the wider world (the Greek roots of *kosmopolitēs* are from *kosmos*, world, and *politēs*, citizen), and wanting to enlighten and to transform that little corner of the European world where one had been born or had been brought by destiny to live, work, love and die. The phase of early modern cosmopolitanism soon declined. Paine continued until his last breath to champion the cause of republican democracy around the world and Kant still looked at the history of the world *in weltbürgerlicher Absicht*, but these figures were among the last voices of a declining age. With the French revolution the era of cosmopolitanism declined and into its place stepped nationalism, nation-state building and nation-state rivalry. Some continued to work for 'internationalism', guided by the principle that 'in proportion as the antagonism between classes within the nation vanishes, the hostility of one nation to another will come to an end' (Marx and Engels). But slowly and surely the word 'patriot' became charged with all the hatred and love of modern nationalism, while the word 'cosmopolite' became the symbol of an ideal political unity that in practice could never be achieved.

A pressing theoretical and political question in today's Europe is whether a new form of the old cosmopolitanism is developing in tandem with the process of supranational political integration in the West and the attempted dismantling of totalitarian regimes in parts of Central and Eastern Europe. Is the growth of an international civil society in Europe possible or actual? Raymond Aron is among those who have answered firmly in the negative: 'Rights and duties, which in Europe, as elsewhere, are interdependent, can hardly be called multinational. In fact, they are quintessentially national. . . . Though the European Community tends to grant all the citizens of its member states the same economic and social rights, there are no such animals as 'European citizens'. There are only French, German or Italian citizens.'[22]

Aron's conclusion is based not only on the legal tautology that individuals can only become citizens because they belong to a sovereign state which is the sole guarantor of citizenship rights and duties. It also does not take account of the growth of multinational states and societies, and of the trend towards the definition of the rights of *European* citizenship, available to all who live within the European Union region. When the Maastricht Treaty of Union is finally implemented, this trend will be greatly strengthened. Citizens of any state resident in another member state will be entitled to vote and to stand for office at the levels of local government and the European parliament. Citizens will enjoy the rights to information across frontiers, to petition the European parliament, and to make use of a parliamentary ombudsman. And they will be entitled, when travelling abroad, to full diplomatic protection by any other EU member state.

These projected entitlements provide further evidence that Europe – at least the Europe of the European Union – is witnessing the slow, unplanned, blind and painful birth of a new species of political animal, the European citizen. This transnational citizenry is not yet constitutionally guaranteed. Its 'informal' or pre-legal status renders it less than fully visible, ensures its strength as a normative ideal, and makes it vulnerable to countervailing trends. The habitat of the new European citizen is an emerging international civil society of personal contacts, networks, conferences, political parties, social initiatives, trade unions, small businesses and large firms, friendships, and local and regional forums. Within this non-governmental habitat, individuals and groups of various nations and persuasions take advantage of new communications technologies – fax machines, answerphones, satellite broadcasting – which break down the apparently 'natural' barriers of geographic distance and state borders, increase the physical and cultural mobility of people, and even simulate the possibility of being simultaneously in two or more places. The new European citizens intermingle across frontiers for various purposes without making a cult of national origins, national identity and 'foreigners'. These citizens see and feel the importance of the *metaxu* (Simone Weil). They value nests, such as national identity, in which citizens are warmed and nourished, and gain confidence in themselves. Yet they also recognize otherness as a right and a duty for everybody. These new citizens maintain that in the contemporary world identity is more a matter of politics and choice than fate. They have an allergic reaction to nationalism and deep empathy for people suffering discrimination or enforced exile from their cherished nations or territories. They are humble about their national identity, interested in others, concerned for their well-being, and consequently unwilling to indulge the feelings of revenge and narcissistic satisfaction characteristic of nationalists. European citizens are late modern cosmopolitans.

No doubt the internationalization of civil society is destroyed by nationalism and genocidal war, as in south-central Europe, where for many people daily life is now a non-citizens' hell of expulsion, terror and bloodshed. These social exchanges among a plurality of citizens can also be squeezed or suffocated by the power of transnational corporations (such as Ford, Volkswagen and Sony) seeking to coordinate their national markets, to trim and discipline their workforces, and to dominate European social life through profit-driven matrix management and marketing. It is also true that xenophobes and other anti-democratic forces are taking advantage of the new European habitat. Nevertheless, the long-term growth of European-wide exchanges among citizens whose social and political views are predominantly pluralist and republican is among the most remarkable features of contemporary Europe. Within these exchanges, there are few traces of Marxian class-struggle politics and nineteenth-century dreams of abolishing state institutions, and nationalism is considered an anathema. Instead there is an underlying belief that not only Europe from the Atlantic to the Urals, but indeed the world beyond, should be a coat of many colours, a region marked by a precarious, non-violent yet permanently contested balance between governors and citizens.

Sometimes this new democratic republicanism erupts dramatically, as in the velvet revolutions of 1989–91. At other times it is expressed through vague references to citizenship rights and duties across frontiers (as in the Maastricht Treaty of Union). But most often the formation of a European civil society is an undramatic, nearly invisible process that seems unworthy of the attention of journalists, intellectuals and policymakers. It clearly requires detailed sociological investigation. For could it be that this new European citizenry, providing that it is not stillborn and that it is nurtured with adequate funding, and legal and political guarantees, will prove to be the best antidote yet invented to the perils of nationalism and the poisonous fruits of democracy?

NOTES

1. Helmut Beumann and W. Schroeder (eds), *Aspekte der Nationenbildung im Mittelalter* (Sigmaringen, 1978); Helmut Beumann, 'Zur Nationenbildung im Mittelalter', in Otto Dann (ed.), *Nationalismus in vorindustrieller Zeit* (Munich, 1986), pp. 21–33; and Bernard Guenée, *L'Occident aux xiv-ième à xv-ième siècles* (Paris, 1981), ch. 3.
2. *Encyclopédie*, 17 vols (Paris, 1751–65), vol. 11, p. 36.
3. The example of the English Parliament during the Tudor period is analysed by G.R. Elton, 'English national self-consciousness and the parliament in the sixteenth century', in Otto Dann (ed.), *Nationalismus in vorindustrieller Zeit*, pp. 73–82. The French case is considered in R. Bickart, *Les Parlements et la notion de souveraineté national* (Paris, 1932).
4. The case of the Netherlands is examined in Johan Huizinga, 'How Holland became a nation', in his *Verzamelde Werken*, 9 vols (Haarlem, 1948–53), vol. 2, pp. 266–83.
5. Thomas Paine, *Rights of Man. Part First* and *Rights of Man. Part Second*, in Philip S. Foner (ed.), *The Complete Writings of Thomas Paine* (New York, 1945), pp. 243–458.
6. *Rights of Man. Part First*, in Foner (ed.), *The Complete Writings of Thomas Paine*, p. 341.
7. K. Deutsch, *Nationalism and Its Alternatives* (New York, 1969), p. 19.
8. Klaus von Beyme, 'Social and economic conditions for ethnic strife in the Soviet Union', in Alastair McAuley (ed.), *Soviet Federalism, Nationalism and Economic Decentralisation* (Leicester and London, 1991), pp. 89–109; and Adam Michnik, 'Nationalism', *Social Research*, 58 (4), winter 1991, pp. 757–63.
9. The contours of national identity are well examined in Philip Schlesinger, 'On national identity: Some conceptions and misconceptions criticized', *Social Science Information*, 26 (2), 1987, pp. 219–64; Ernest Gellner, *Nations and Nationalism* (Oxford, 1983); and Benedict Anderson, *Imagined Communities: Reflections on the Origin and Spread of Nationalism*, revised edn (London and New York, 1991).
10. The spatial metaphor of boundaries is developed in Fredrik Barth, 'Ethnic groups and boundaries', in *Process and Form in Social Life: Selected Essays of Fredrik Barth* (London, 1981), pp. 198–227.
11. John Keane, *Democracy and Civil Society. On the Predicaments of European Socialism, the Prospects for Democracy and the Problem of Controlling Social and Political Power* (London and New York, 1988), and *The Media and Democracy* (Oxford, 1991).
12. Jan Jozef Lipski, 'Two fatherlands – two patriotisms', *Survey*, 26 (4), autumn 1982, pp. 159–75.
13. Jacques Godechot, *La Grande Nation*, 2nd edn (Paris, 1983); Eric Hobsbawm, *Nations and Nationalism since 1780* (Cambridge and New York, 1990); Hugh Seton-Watson, *Nations and States: An Enquiry into the Origins of Nations and the Politics of Nationalism* (London, 1977); and Benedict Anderson, *Imagined Communities*, revised edn, 1991.
14. Cited in Marianne Weber, *Max Weber: A Biography* (New York and London, 1975), p. 653.
15. Eric Hobsbawm, *Nations and Nationalism since 1780*.

16. John Keane, 'The modern democratic revolution: Reflections on Lyotard's *The Postmodern Condition*', in Andrew Benjamin (ed.), *Judging Lyotard* (London and New York, 1992), pp. 81–98.
17. See Charles B. Eddy, *Greece and the Greek Refugees* (London, 1931); and C.A. Macartney, 'Refugees', in *Encyclopedia of the Social Sciences* (London, 1931), vol. 13, pp. 200–5.
18. Richard Batley and Gerry Stoker (eds), *Local Government in Europe: Trends and Developments* (London, 1991).
19. See Charles Sabel, 'Flexible specialisation and the re-emergence of regional economies', in P. Hirst and J. Zeitlin (eds), *Reversing Industrial Decline? Industrial Structure and Policy in Britain and her Competitors* (Oxford, 1989), pp. 17–70.
20. Slavenka Drakulić, 'The smothering pull of nationhood', *Yugofax*, 31 October 1991, p. 3.
21. The Italian case is examined in Franco Venturi, *Italy and the Enlightenment: Studies in a Cosmopolitan Century* (New York, 1972). See also Thomas J. Schlereth, *The Cosmopolitan Ideal in Enlightenment Thought: Its Form and Function in the Ideas of Franklin, Hume and Voltaire, 1694–1790* (Notre Dame and London, 1977); Eugen Lemberg, *Geschichte des Nationalismus in Europa* (Stuttgart, 1950), pp. 123–7; Joseph Texte, *Jean-Jacques Rousseau and the Cosmopolitan Spirit in Literature: A Study of the Literary Relations between France and England during the Eighteenth Century* (London and New York, 1899).
22. Raymond Aron, 'Is multinational citizenship possible?', *Social Research*, winter 1974, pp. 652–3.

11

The Significance of Preconceptions: Europe of Civil Societies and Europe of Nationalities

Elżbieta Skotnicka-Illasiewicz and Włodzimierz Wesołowski

INTRODUCTION

In this text we wish to develop and explain the claim that there are two types of political parties in Poland: those opting for 'civil society' and those opting for a 'spiritual community' (Wesolowski, 1994a). To this end, the chapter focuses on Poland's merger into Europe as the recurrent theme in political debate in Poland. Politicians attempt to define the gains and losses, and promises and threats of Poland's integration into Europe. The way groups and individuals define themselves with respect to this question is an outright reflection of divisions in their political philosophies.

Political arguments which overtly refer to 'facts' are quite often informed by political philosophies rather than real social tendencies. The issue of integration into Europe evokes, in addition, resentments and emotions. Ideological preconceptions have, in effect, a high potential for becoming weapons in political battles. There is, however, a reverse direction of influence. Strengthening one or another real tendency may diminish or enhance the chances of utilizing preconceptions in political action. Because of the everlasting presence of nationalism in Polish politics – and its possible accentuation by the debate on 'entering Europe' – our research programme on the Polish political elite included the question of the present form of infusion of ideologically loaded arguments on Poland, Europe, and the relation between the two.[1]

Thus we may take it for granted that visions of tomorrow's Europe are consciously or subconsciously related to beliefs about the nature of society and country. Traditionally, the European 'West' has always been the principal reference point for Polish intellectual elites (Jedlicki, 1993). After half a century of coercive and oppressive 'Eastern' dominance, it was only natural that the Poles turned 'West' when they regained their full sovereignty in 1989.

The route of systemic transformations taken by the post-Solidarity government seemed only natural, both to the general public and to the political class, the post-communist political opposition notwithstanding (Skotnicka-Illasiewicz, 1992). The new goal was now to adopt West European economic principles and institutions. At the very onset of the systemic transformation in 1989, no mention was yet made of any integration with the European Twelve. For pragmatic reasons, this was a programme for the future. However, when the Berlin Wall collapsed, the need for a precise definition of the 'return to Europe' concept became more urgent.

At first, the mental barriers imposed by the recent continental split were strong. These barriers were apparent in the mentality of the political elites, both 'East' and 'West', and in the lay consciousness of the societies which these elites represented. There was no doubt, however, that the main goal of systemic transformation in Poland was to change the geopolitical situation of the country and to reinstall Poland among the economically developed West European democracies. The idea of integration with Europe as a concomitant to the 'great systemic change' at home began to sprout in the awareness of the modernizing elite. As this idea emerged, it took the form of prospective association with the European Community, followed by Poland's eventual membership in both the European Community and NATO. These goals were based on the conviction that this was the only road to economic prosperity and political security for Poland, and that only this solution would protect Polish people from being sucked once again into the hegemony of the Soviet Union (now Russia). People were well aware that, to achieve this goal, they would have to put up with much sacrifice and hardship, but to shy away from the challenge would lead to the economic and political marginalization of Poland once and for all.

To achieve this goal, certain conditions must be fulfilled and social costs are inevitable. Initially, these challenges were thought to be considerably lower than today's more realistic estimates have shown.

Nevertheless, four years after the inauguration of the process of integration, 70% of Poles still accept the idea of Poland merging with the European Community (now the European Union). Nowadays people are only more aware than they were to begin with of the distance which must be covered in order to reach this goal (CBOS, 1994).[2]

The attitudes towards integration reflected in the programmes of different political parties, and those of members of parliament, are much more polarized today than they were at the beginning, in 1989–91. This polarization is reflected in the evaluation of both the idea of integration itself and the procedures leading to integration.

VISIONS OF EUROPE, VISIONS OF POLAND

The political leaders of the first term of parliamentary office (1991–3) reveal very polarized attitudes. In the most general sense, this polarization has to do with the acceptance or rejection of 'merging with Europe' as the answer to systemic transformation and civilizational modernization in Poland. It must be assumed that, after 1989, when Poland became a sovereign democracy, the goal of all parliamentary deputies was to construct a prosperous state. This assumption by no means conflicts with another theoretical assumption: that this prosperity, and the ways of achieving it, may be conceptualized in many different ways.[3] We believe that these differences stem from different images of one's country and its developmental goals, and different ways of defining Poland's relationships with other countries. Politicians differ in their reform paradigms and their perceptions of the role of Europe (Skotnicka-Illasiewicz, 1995) and Poland's direct neighbours (Germany, in particular).

When one asks what the leaders of the parliamentary parties have to say, one can reconstruct two dominant tendencies in their perception of Europe. The first group perceives Europe as a configuration of civil societies with high cooperative potential; the second perceives it as a configuration of ethnic communities with high dominance potential. These two polarities are based on different economic, political and cultural assumptions, and different visions of the equilibrium/ disequilibrium process between the nation-states of Europe. The level of equilibrium which Poland can achieve defines its final situation in

Europe – that is, its economic, political and cultural location, based on partnership, dominance or submission.

A vision of cooperation of civil societies as states

The opinions of parliamentary deputies characteristic of this approach to the European issue first and foremost reflect the feeling that the integration route is obvious, because integration is good and necessary. According to this approach, the purpose of the ongoing transformation is to reach a Western-style democracy, with its concomitant principles of economic cooperation based on a free market and free competition. However, this general tendency is combined with the perception of contradictions and barriers. It is therefore important to understand what exactly this 'obviousness' implies.

The meanings attributed to this 'obviousness' are different for the Euro-enthusiasts and the Euro-rationalists. The former are the advocates of aggressive and accelerated integration, whereas the latter tend to prefer controlled integration drawn out in time. Both groups agree that the goal as such is generally expedient. The goal is eventual integration with Europe, and membership in the economic and military structures of the European Union and NATO respectively. However, their arguments in favour of integration differ: the Euro-enthusiasts are concerned mainly with taking advantage of the chance to flee, once and for all, from the supremacy of the eastern neighbour with all the political, economic and cultural consequences. For the Euro-rationalists, on the other hand, such integration is, first and foremost, the obvious implication of the logic of world affairs and, therefore, also of the logic of European culture. The vast potential for dominance, with its tendency to subordinate the weaker to the more powerful, previously so characteristic of this culture, is now giving way to a new order based on the voluntary cooperation of partners – though not free from competition, mostly economic. According to this approach, the 'East-or-West' alternative is real but it is definitely better to merge with the West. However, the most outstanding new feature of West European nations is that they no longer demonstrate dominating tendencies. They are forging a new quality in nation-state coexistence. This new belief embraces Germany, hitherto an 'eternal' enemy of Poland. The deputies of the Liberal Democratic Congress, the Democratic Union, and the representatives of the liberal wing of the post-communist socialist party (the SLD) are the most pronounced advocates of 'Europe' as a shared space of civic nations.

Resolute integration: The Euro-Enthusiasts

The 'resolute integration' attitude is reflected in those statements of the parliamentary deputies who propagate bravery, imagination and risk. These utterances or opinions are manifestations of involvement and activity, and they treat the initiated process of integration as a challenge – one which is risky, but which also carries the promise that Poland will finally 'catch up' with the rest of Europe.

> 'We must remember that a battle of interests is being waged in Europe, a world-wide and regional battle; and if you want to join in, you must know the rules of the game.' (3: SLD)[4]
>
> '[integration] . . . guarantees that the Polish economy will not move back to socialism . . . it guarantees that our economy will enter and integrate with the economic organism of Western Europe. . . . There is a chance of some virtues, killed by communism or uprooted even earlier, such as thriftiness, laboriousness, and responsibility, being spread and strengthened.' (26: UD, moved to PK)
>
> 'Integration is inevitable, there is no alternative. It is the natural course of events, both in Poland and in Europe.' (6: SLD)

The Euro-enthusiasts' approach is supported by the acceleration argument. In other words, integration is essential because time is short and the international situation, favourable for Poland today, may change tomorrow. The advocates of acceleration are aware of the public costs of economic conversion, especially for marginalized social groups. The most frequently mentioned casualties are farmers and the employees of technologically outdated industries. The Euro-enthusiasts who call for acceleration believe that to reject this challenge would mean losing the great opportunity that history has offered Poland and that the Poles themselves have opened up with their 1989 revolution. In this group of arguments the theme of consistency, not slowing down and sticking to the chosen path, runs through many utterances:

> 'You can't open up in five branches and close down in two other branches, for instance agriculture. It's either-or . . . Either you're going to shut yourself up in an economic ghetto, and therefore a political and cultural ghetto too, or you're going to open up and become part of Europe with all

the consequences, including the fact that your five-hectare farm on sand . . . must go bankrupt.' (10: PC, later independent)

Those deputies who opt for consistent acceleration sometimes mention the threat to the chosen path. One frequently mentioned threat is inefficient negotiation with Western partners. The apprehensions caused by the risks involved in acceleration are balanced by the belief that there is no alternative to merging with Europe and by the imperative need to build economic prosperity at home as quickly as possible. The Euro-enthusiasts also believe that Polish society, capable of heroic effort, can meet the challenge.

> 'If the politicians finally understand . . . that integration is essential . . . then our ability to mobilize ourselves and our vitality . . . which surpasses by far the vitality of the Czechs, Hungarians, Slovaks, and Germans together, will guarantee success. It would be a catastrophe, were the politicians to ignore this opportunity.' (14: UD)
> 'As a nation we learn fast, we are dynamic, intelligent, albeit neurotic.' (14: UD)

This faith in the 'transformative power' of the Polish nation is, at the same time, a manifestation of faith in the ability of individuals and groups to build a civic society, where relationships are based on negotiations – once they are free of the constraints of the command economy.

Many Euro-enthusiasts are often economists. Hence their argumentation is supported by economic analysis of the assumptions of the process of integration. This by no means dampens our impression that their argumentation is often tinted by the shivers of emotion accompanying 'adventure' and 'risk'. They interpret the inevitability of the chosen path and the lack of alternatives in terms of 'creative risk' or 'a hard game but a great one'. This approach is represented both by members of the governing coalition and the opposition. Significant differences in the evaluation of the process spring from different perceptions of the barriers on the road to success.

Parliamentary deputies representing the governing coalition (1991–3) more frequently mention objective internal and external circumstances as the most important barriers to the successful realization of the process of integration. They, more frequently than the others, mention the need to overcome barriers on both sides, including those which are rooted in human mentality. Their argumentation often includes comments on the 'significance of the international image of Poland'. Such comments can be interpreted as an unhesitating perception of 'Europe' as the central ideal model. However, the majority of arguments refer to the economic-civilizational disproportions between East and West, which no treaties can level and whose levelling will require an enormous amount of effort from all members of society. This type of barrier is well reflected in the statement by one of the leaders of the Liberal Democratic Congress:

> 'When we speak of our joining the organizational structures of the European Community we are referring to certain standards, according to which we shall treat them and they will treat us. But we shall only be able to reach this level of integration by marching at home.... What I mean is, the integration issue is the issue of public lavatories in Bialystok. This is how to integrate with Europe. Switzerland is not a member of the Community and no one has any complexes about that. ... Nobody bothers there if no one has signed the Accord with the European Community.' (17: KLD)

Controlled integration: The Euro-Rationalists

In the statements of the vast majority of deputies opting for the vision of Europe as a space for cooperating states, we find a theme which may be defined as 'controlled integration'. This theme is based on the belief, signalled earlier, that, in the current world situation, Poland and the Poles, like other countries in the region, are in a position of forced 'obviousness'. This 'obviousness' is forced, however, not by external coercion or foreign dominance, but by Poles' own perceptions, based on the fear of marginalization. West European integration, initiated by Schuman, de Gaspari and Adenauer, sprang from the fear of economic marginalization by the United States. Today, Eastern Europe is being forced into integration with Western Europe mainly because it is afraid of being marginalized in the world economy. Bridging the gap is seen as the principal goal, and this goal is determining the range of adjustment processes which should eventually lead to the integration of Poland with the European Union. Marginalization is understood in various ways, as we can see from politicians' statements:

> 'We cannot be marginalized because we are already on the margin. Integration is not an option, it is a necessity because we cannot move any further back on this margin.' (14: UD)

> 'If we do not develop this interplay of interests together, our openness may

marginalize us in Europe instead of strengthening our position as partner.'
(03: SLD)

In less emotional opinions, the fear of marginalization is justified by referring to the logic of the changing world. In some opinions, 'marginalization' also implies the danger of being drawn into the range of influence of the former Soviet Union or of remaining in no man's land, beyond the organizational structures of East and West alike. It is noteworthy that the danger of getting under 'Eastern' influence is emphatically accentuated by the deputies from the SLD parliamentary party: their biographies reveal that their long experience as members of the Communist party had exposed them to direct contact with the political and economic structures of 'Big Brother', and probably taught them a lesson. One of the SLD deputies explicitly defines his pro-integrative option as a specific manifestation of cognitive dissonance:

> 'The leftist option is, to some extent, schizophrenic: if you're on the Left you shouldn't be supporting integration with Europe. But then every country, every system must be integrated into some form of logic nowadays. In the past it was logical to be a member of Comecon, the Warsaw Pact, some sort of pro-Soviet organization. Be what it may, sovereign or not, good or bad – that's to be disputed. Every policy has its good sides and its bad sides. Today's policy has its good sides and its bad sides . . . but . . . once we have chosen to go capitalist, now that the Soviet Union and the Warsaw Pact are falling to pieces, we should seek some sort of stability, and today this stability is guaranteed by NATO and the EEC and we must hold on to this logic, take this path and not let ourselves be shoved onto the margin.' (05: SLD)

Among the Euro-rationalists who opt for integration, a considerable number believe that the process is proceeding too quickly and should definitely be slowed down. Their main justification is the fear that the nation has limited capacity to adjust, or that this capacity may be running out altogether. These deputies refer to the psychocultural limitations caused by civilizational backwardness and the weak economy in Poland.

> 'People have limited ability to accommodate to civilizational change. In my opinion, we've gone too far. We should slow down, respect the people.'(7: Sol)
> 'So as not to strain the cord of social endurance, people's ability to adapt . . . I personally would not force things where it's not necessary, because

we must complete the economic reform, but I wouldn't force things. . . . I would rather try to develop cooperation, youth exchanges, but I wouldn't wage wars over changes which can be postponed, which people may be afraid of, which may lead to fear of the integration which hasn't yet begun, which will only begin in a couple of years. I would really prefer to respect people here and take their state of mind into consideration.' (7: Sol)

A different set of arguments in favour of slowing down the process of integration points to the faulty strategy in negotiations with Western partners. The 'forced tempo strategy' must lead to the increase, not the decrease, in disproportions between Polish and Western economies, and this must delay, if not ruin altogether, the chances of relations based on partnership in the future. The advocates of this approach (many of them professional economists) claim that first we must tidy up the economy at home in order to make it competitive for our future partners. In their opinion, the current state of the economy being what it is, negotiations with Western partners must lead to asymmetric relationships.

> 'We couldn't make it if integration proceeded too fast, everything would go to pieces.' (12: PC)
>
> 'Our economy is weak and uncompetitive, and therefore it is threatened. If we were to be thrown into the deep waters of European competition, the economy might collapse completely. In my opinion we should shield ourselves a bit at first, build some fences, reinforce ourselves internally, reinforce at least some branches of industry . . . select certain national industries, strengthen them, give them a better chance, and then integrate.' (1: UP)
>
> 'Make the economy competitive, able to compete and then integrate, open up.' (11: PC)
>
> 'If we don't modify the structure of the Polish economy first, or – to be more precise – if we don't bring the large industrial plants up to a reasonable technological standard . . . the Polish economy will be nothing more than a satellite of the Federal Republic [of Germany]: if this condition is not fulfilled, we have no chance at all of matching [them].' (2: UP)

And finally, the third important argument in favour of slowing down the transformation (or at least not accelerating it) refers to a specific form of historical determinism. The deputies who use this argument claim that the integrative process has been going on for a long time – it began 'in Gierek's days' – and is an inevitable consequence of 'the logic of history'. This type of attitude can also be traced in the views of some deputies with 'Solidarity' roots:

> 'Even in the communist days Poland was approaching Europe. This was a sentence imposed upon us by superior Western civilization. Gierek was also approaching Europe but he tried to take shortcuts and he ignored the necessary regulators. But the Solidarity administrations intensified this process, made it more realistic by introducing proper regulators.' (9: Sol)

As opposed to the advocates of accelerated integration, the proponents of a slowdown of the integration process believe that both the speed and the strategy of integration should be modified. The politicians responsible for the negotiations – that is, representatives of the factions which came to power after 1989 – are accused of disrespect for plain facts. Both the advocates of integrative slowdown and the advocates of acceleration draw attention to the same objective barriers. The former, however, are convinced that there is an additional barrier: in their opinion the politicians responsible for the implementation of the process are incompetent and behave irrationally.

> 'We have agreed to tougher conditions of adjustment than those demanded of the Czechs or the Hungarians.' (1: UP)
> 'The parliamentary deputies don't know exactly what "association with the EC" means. We approve of a certain slogan but we don't know the details or the consequences.' (10: PC)
> 'It is impossible to foresee how society and politicians will react, and this is a stumbling-block. After all, I'm not one of those who shout out loud that the Euro-regions will deprive Poland of her independence, but you should have foreseen that certain names would evoke a negative public response: if the Carpathian Region were called "an area of border cooperation", for instance, instead of a "Euro-region", there would have been less opposition.' (10: Sol)[5]

The incompetence of the politicians responsible for the integration – that is, for the implementation of the concept of cooperating societies – is criticized, but this criticism does not mean total negation of this direction of reform as such, nor is it accompanied by the charge of bad intentions.

In our attempt to reconstruct the vision of Europe as a shared space of civil societies striving for cooperation, we have presented two mutations of this vision. In both cases the justification for the perception of Europe as a reference point for Polish aspirations is the same. Also similar are the definitions of Poland's retardation. They evoke images of a superior centre and an inferior periphery. However, the planned routes and speed of reform are different. In the first case, the use of the term 'acceleration' implies that Poland's distance to Europe can be rated on a graded scale and that fast progress along this scale is feasible. The distance can be greatly reduced by an adequate effort by the nation if it is properly motivated. In the second case, the prognosis is less optimistic. The diagnosis indicates a technological gap, and differences in the strength of economies in general and their competitiveness in particular. Rapid progress is not possible, and, if forced, may be ruinous. Balancing the two forces – of international competitiveness and international cooperation – is seen as a difficult task. Thus, caution is recommended.

A Europe of ethnic communities

Those deputies who opted for the vision of a Europe of civil societies with strong cooperative potential showed a preponderance of pragmatic and economic-civilizational argumentation. Such opinions were frequently voiced by those MPs who had educational backgrounds in economics. Whether or not they were enthusiasts of integration, their arguments were more rational and less emotional. Presumably, the perception of Europe presented previously goes hand in hand with the perception of society as having all the prerequisites enabling it to act as a 'cooperative' state prepared to enter a partnership. In other words this is a vision of civil society consisting of individuals, occupational groups and social strata, which compete and cooperate with each other. This competition follows the principles of market and meritocracy, and is regulated not by means of devastating struggles but by means of negotiations. The principal, if not supreme, goal of such negotiations is to achieve pragmatic cooperation.

A different conception of the organization of the European space and a different vision of the internal organization of society in Poland underlie the perception of Europe as a set of distinct ethnic communities. According to this conception, society is not a set of voluntarily cooperating individuals and groups – it is a community, naturally related by ties of origin, tradition, culture and shared psychological traits. Nations are communities of this type. The interests of individuals and groups must be subordinated to the protection of the continuity and uniqueness of the community. The defence of common national interests always has priority over individual and particular interests. The individual or group who does not respect these tenets is perceived as alien, an outsider, and hence is a potential threat to the community. When the relationship between Poland and Europe is perceived like this, cultural and religious identity, and political-military issues, not economic ones, come to the fore. Appeals to values predominate over appeals to economic pragmatism. Poland's position in a Europe thus structured is either perceived as a function of the 'superiority' (moral and spiritual) of the Poles or of the 'inferiority' imposed on them. The dominance potential of the community is measured in terms of its ability to impose and execute its supremacy or at least to defend itself against the dominance of others. The vision of Europe derived from this type of ideology must lead (more or less consciously) to the questioning of the concept of European integration. This ideology ignores the fact that the integrative model developed in Europe after the Second World War assumes the abjuration of dominance in international relations.

The threat to national identity and mores: Guardians of morals

The 'threat to national identity' argument carries special weight in Polish history and is tantamount to an accusation of 'national treason'. This argument, based on nineteenth-century tradition, where the vision of the 'stateless nation' played such an important role (Kurczewska, 1979; Walicki, 1994), is a reference to national-democratic or – in extreme cases – nationalist ideology. In the vision of Europe based on cultural criteria, Poland and the Poles are perceived as the 'last bastion' of European values and traditions, or as the 'area of expansion of European *evil*'. Both of these arguments are used to justify the cry for 'closure'. The first is used to support the call for 'closure in order to survive, and to retain and safeguard the dying European values' – that is, the vision of Poland as a peculiar museum but also as an axiological model.

> 'We must defend Poland against the influence of drug addiction and the departure from ethical principles. Only thanks to us has Europe finally noticed that there is not a single form of evil which cannot be traced back to Europe: antisemitism, the negation of the conservative outlook – this is defined as a threat to freedom – the whole abortion issue, which has eventually led to degeneration and to the problem of euthanasia.
>
> There is some bizarre cult of AIDS victims in Europe – they are treated as heroes, and anyone who rejects such an approach is accused of being an old-fashioned stick-in-the-mud. Now this is an attempt to reduce the

> human being to the level of bodily pleasures . . . [there is] contempt for unborn children, contempt for the family, the institution of marriage, although we find some positive things as well, such as respect for the elderly.' (18: ZChN)

The second type of argument is used as 'a defence against' the devastating effects of European demoralization on 'unprepared' Polish society.

> 'We may talk about the moral or customs-related aftermaths of merging with Europe but in my opinion, despite the obvious negative consequences, what is really wrong is that Polish society is not independent enough, not culturally sovereign and independent, and that is why it absorbs all the bad and shoddy things from Europe.' (26: PK)

The experience of threat may also manifest itself in ostentatious strength. If, for obvious reasons, the attributes of this strength – a strong economy, a strong political position – cannot be objectively tested, then one must refer to moral strength, measured by subjective feelings. In this case two strategies are used to reduce the threat. One strategy is to stress that 'Poland is in Europe', 'it never left Europe', *ergo* 'there is no need to return to Europe'. In other words, when geographic and cultural criteria (which are beyond discussion) are applied, Poland is on an equal par with other countries. But when Poland's position is measured on moral standards, it is found to be relatively better, morally stronger than a Europe which is relatively inferior and morally weaker.

> 'I always question this "Poland approaching Europe" stuff. Poland has no need to approach any Europe because Poland has been a part of Europe for a long time, for ever, from the very beginning of our existence. We may talk of Western Europe, by which we mean rich democracies which have managed to become rich at our cost. After all, who if not we "held back the enemy", "shed our last drop of blood"? If we had surrendered, then who knows where such as England would be now? I question the expression that Poland should return somewhere – it never left Europe. Rather, it was Western Europe which surrendered to the Soviet Union in Tehran and Yalta. At the most, we are returning to democracy and of that I fully approve.' (18: ZChN)

The above quotation refers to the vision of Europe-as-stronghold and Poland as *Antemurale Christianitatis*, protecting Europe from the Turkish invasion (generalized as the Asian threat) (Szczucki, 1989). The Poland–Europe relationship goes hand in hand with the creditor–debtor paradigm, based on the assumption that Poland and the Poles are 'relatively superior' creditors. The alleged attributes of its superiority are generosity, courage, sacrifice and co-responsibility for the common European fate – not lost in feeble feelings of insecurity. This statement also reflects disapproval of West Europeans. The author accuses them of cunning (they gained at our cost) and lack of courage (who knows where they would be now?).

In other words, the arguments in favour of 'closure' are twofold. The first group of arguments refers to the Poles' weak resistance – that is, their inferiority: they are going through an identity crisis and therefore readily absorb any novelties coming from Europe, a Europe from which they were walled off until recently, a Europe which may not be 'better' but which is certainly 'more attractive'. The second group of arguments refers to the 'inferiority' of the patterns conveyed by 'perverse Europe' and therefore to the 'superiority' of Poland and the Poles.

These arguments, indicative of threatened moral superiority, are often vicarious or reinforcing. As mentioned before, threatened identity is an extremely capacious term in Polish tradition and is therefore used to bolster both economic and political arguments.

The fear of degradation: Protectors of economic and political sovereignty

Another attitude that accompanies the anti-integrative stand may be defined as 'the fear of integration'. This point of view is manifest – depending on the ideology of the party that the deputy represents – either in the vision of Poland-as-debtor-of-Europe or in the vision of Poland-as-petitioner. Both these feelings are rooted in the feeling of threat, particularly threat to recently regained independence.

The first few years of 'open frontiers' and obvious confrontation have produced the fear that Poland will be unable to retain its identity and uniqueness – an autotelic value – in its relationships with more powerful partners. This type of attitude is rooted in the doubt as to whether Poland can match the standards necessary for partnership, and also in Poles' lack of faith in their own society, perceived by them as incapable of cooperative partnership.

Protectors characteristically propagate an attitude of controlled semi-openness. They do not openly reject the process of integration but they doubt whether it can be successful. Their statements and opinions are tinted with intense anxiety, distrust and defensiveness, rather than faith in cooperation. In their opinion, while developing the conditions for integration, one must be cunning, shrewd, crafty as a peasant, but one must never openly state one's true terms of negotiation.

The fear of Europe manifests itself in three different dimensions: economic, cultural and political. Argumentation in favour of controlled semi-openness is accompanied first and foremost by economic justifications. According to this approach, the economically 'weaker' party in any transaction or contract is always in an inferior position:

> 'We are not yet ready for the compulsory opening-up which is to take place in four years from now. This is openness by treaty. Western firms will probably wipe out most of our firms because these [firms] won't be competitive enough.' (3: SLD)
>
> 'This cannot be hurried. Due to forty years' isolation, Polish society has an encoded aversion to its neighbours, to integration. It feels insecure and is negatively disposed towards any form of opening up.' (29: PSL)

There is also another line of argumentation: Poland and the Poles will make a poor business of the whole thing because they are too trustful and too naive, compared with their Western partners. The MPs who use this type of argument explain that Poland is incapable of defending itself – not only against competitive goods from the West but also against disloyalty and even blatant dishonesty on the part of the Western partners.

> 'We're being flooded with Western goods and our own products are not selling well, [while at the same time] our Western partners are very unwilling to import goods from Poland, and they seek (dishonestly) pretexts for not doing so, like the recent foot-and-mouth disease pretext.' (11: PC)

The economic arguments in favour of considerable modification or even withdrawal from the process of integration with Europe are especially pronounced as regards agriculture (*Dwa lata* . . ., 1994). Many of the MPs interviewed – often unrelated to the peasant electorate – indicate the negative consequences of this process by referring to agriculture:

> 'If we throw our primitive agriculture into the deep European waters without reinforcing it beforehand, it will lose neck and crop.' (11: PC)
>
> 'If we are to integrate on the economic-agricultural plane as well, we must ask ourselves what will happen to our farmers, our produce. Are we to produce first and then lie at somebody's mercy and be slaves to others' prices? We must defend our own interests first. We must know how to

defend them (maybe not directly). We cannot let the Polish economy and Polish agriculture go to ruin. We cannot open up and then be left with nothing ourselves.' (28: PSL)

The last sentence in this quotation is the key to the whole attitude. Integration is treated here as a horse market, a game between two opponents, one cunning and one sly – not a political partnership.

When taken to the extreme, the critique of the 'immersing in Europe' formula takes the form of total negation of any integration with the European Union, since this would allegedly lead to the loss of sovereignty. In our sample, such opinions were voiced by one MP from ZChN and all the representatives of the KPN parliamentary party. In a nutshell, this opinion is expressed in the following quotation:

'To say that . . . we want to "join up with Europe", whereas "Europe doesn't want to accept its poor kinsmen" is to spread a bunch of illusions. I am pronouncedly against Poland's merging with Europe understood as a centralized, or even federal, state organism. In Europe, Mrs Thatcher, like myself, is against integration. It was she who said that Eastern Europe doesn't want this solution because it has already experienced similar solutions in the past.' (18: ZChN)

This train of thought underscores opposite opinions to those which have formed the foundation for Polish geopolitics since 1989. This vision of 'Europe' is based first and foremost on political criteria – criteria which are determined by geopolitical status. In this vision, geopolitical status is seen as an asymmetrical relationship between 'strong' and 'weak' countries. Current Polish foreign policy is totally rejected in the follow-up to the previous quotation. The author compares Polish integration into the European Community with its previous subordination to Comecon. No alternative is suggested. This alternative appears, however, in the statements of the KPN deputies, particularly in the opinion of one of the leaders of this party:

'Poland is too small, too weak, to deserve to be treated like a partner. Therefore, in my opinion, Poland must develop some alternatives to integration with the European Community. Closer cooperation with the Far East might be an alternative or reconstruction of relationships from communist times – with Arab countries. Or else we might try to establish relationships with anti-EEC countries such as Australia or the USA. The conception of integration with the EEC, with no alternative solutions, poses a threat to Poland. If, on the other hand, we have some alternatives, then both Poland and the EEC may profit by it. Then we may be able to negotiate better contacts, partnership agreements. Another alternative is to try to establish interest groups based on a Polish–Ukrainian axis. Slovakia, the Balkan countries and the Baltic republics may then join in. We must have counterbalance on the one hand, and power on the other hand.' (23: KPN)

According to another KPN representative, we should aim at such a power system in which 'the EEC will beg us to join in' (24: KPN). The KPN option, manifest in the statements of our respondents, is much more radical than the options voiced by the ZChN deputies (with the one exception quoted earlier). The ZChN representatives are not totally opposed to economic integration. The leader of this party says that:

> 'Economic self-sufficiency is an obsolete category. . . . and in my opinion, as Poland's economic status improves, economic bonds will be feasible.' (19: ZChN)

However, like the remaining MPs representing this point of view, he is afraid of the infiltration of destructive mores from the West and in this respect he is an advocate of 'closure'. The KPN deputies think otherwise: they do not dramatize the negative influence of 'opening up' on Polish morals and identity, but they are definitely against opening up economically and, particularly, politically. They are convinced that Poland will be forced into the position of 'petitioner' in the political and economic spheres.

CONCLUSION

Among the approaches to Polish integration with Europe – accepting or rejecting – we can distinguish several variations. We have presented those tendencies and interpretations which seem to be particularly prototypical but we have by no means reviewed the whole spectrum of evaluations and attitudes. When we look more thoroughly at many individuals, we find that the general and sharp types of approaches presented previously become more fuzzy.

We can distinguish two dominant tendencies in the analysed material. One tendency is to perceive the integrative process as a 'zero-sum game', where only one party can 'win'. According to this reasoning, only the 'more powerful party' can win – that is, the united European Union. This type of thinking is expressed by a relatively large group of deputies who have several doubts about integration. A few use this type of argumentation to reject the idea of integration altogether.

The second tendency – definitely the most frequent – consists in the perception of integration as modernization. According to this option, integration is a complex process, but is essentially positive. Naturally, it is not free of difficulties and threats, but it will unquestionably lead to profit eventually.

Despite the hardships and adversities which accompany the process of systemic transformation, caused by the need to adjust to the standards set by the European Union, the people of Poland still definitely support the integration process (CBOS, 1994). The fear of 'lagging behind' or 'being ousted from' an integrated Europe is so great that it stimulates activity and effort. The greater part of the Polish political class also opts for integration (*Dwa lata* . . ., 1994). The critics of integration presented here are rather in a minority.

Polish nationalism is quite different from the re-emerging Russian one. Its roots are defensive, not aggressive (Stefanowicz, 1993). In the past, Poland was a country that fought for over a century (1795–1918) to regain state independence and to retain its national identity. The defensive approach, and the distrust of wealthy and powerful nations can be explained by reference to historical experience. This does not mean to say, however, that we do not treat the existence of a specific form of nationalism on the Polish political scene as a serious matter. Ethnic-national closure, national-moral 'purity' and Polish state 'separateness' from Europe are not the proper instruments to achieve modernity, democracy and economic development. Moreover, there is always the danger of instrumentalizing this type of thinking in the event of extreme crisis. Throughout post-communist Europe, the hotbed of such crisis (be it economic or political) is still kindling 'beneath the surface' of increasingly stable conditions of life.

NOTES

1. Our discussion is based on material obtained by means of in-depth interviews with 28 parliamentary deputies to the parliament of the Republic of Poland (term of office 1991–3). According to a 'mini' opinion poll among parliamentary journalists, the respondents were defined as 'outstanding parliamentarians'. The journalists' list tallied with the list of party leaders and most active politicians: Wojciech Arkuszewski, Jadwiga Berak, Marek Borowski, Ryszard Bugaj, Wiesław Chrzanowski, Jerzy Eysymont, Bronisław Geremek, Andrzej Hardy, Jerzy

Jaskiernia, Jarosław Kaczyński, Krzysztof Kamiński, Kryzysztof Król, Jerzy Kulas, Barbara Labuda, Mirosław Lewandowski, Teresa Liszcz, Aleksander Łuczak, Stafan Niesiołowski, Józef Oleksy, Stafan Pastuszewski, Alojzy Pietrzyk, Jan Rulewski, Edward Rzepka, Grażyna Staniszewska, Wlodzimierz Sumara, Donald Tusk, Michał Ujazdowski, and Wiesława Ziółkowska. Interviews were conducted in the period June to August 1993.
2. The largest support for 'integration into Europe' is expressed by entrepreneurs, managers and students (approximately 80% of each of these categories), small farmers (50%) and pensioners (68%).
3. The pragmatic effect of these discrepancies with regard to the implementation of the different conceptions predominant in the post-Solidarity governments is a separate problem.
4. The letters and numbers in parentheses after each quoted opinion indicate the political parties to which deputies are affiliated (the numbers refer to the list of interviews). The abbreviations stand for the following parties:

   KLD – Kongres Liberalno-Demokratyczny [Liberal Democratic Congress]
   KPN – Konfederacja Polski Niepodległej [Confederation for Independent Poland]
   PC – Porozumienie Centrum [Central Alliance]
   PSL – Polskie Stronnictwo Ludowe [Polish Peasant Party]
   PChD – Partia Chrześcijańsko-Demokratyczna [Christian Democratic Party]
   PK – Partia Konserwatywna [Conservative Party]
   PL – Porozumienie Ludowe [Peasants' Alliance]
   Sol – Solidarność [Solidarity trade union]
   SLD – Sojusz Lewicy Demokratycznej [Democratic Left Alliance]
   UD – Unia Demokratyczna [Democratic Union]
   UP – Unia Pracy [Labour Union]
   UPR – Unia Polityki Realnej [Real-politik Union]
   ZChN – Zjednoczenie Chrześcijańsko-Narodowe [Christian National Union]

5. This is a reference to the Carpathian Euro-region, which is to encompass Polish, Slovakian and Ukrainian border territory.

REFERENCES

Dwa lata umowy stowarzyszeniowej Polska–Wspólnoty Europejskie 1994 [The Association of Poland with the European Community Agreement, two years after]. Materials for parliamentary deputies, second term of office of parliament, 14 December 1993 (Warsaw: BSE-Biuro Studiów i Analiz Kancelarii Sejmu, February).

CBOS 1994 *Polacy o unii europejskiej* [Poles on European Union]. Research report (September).

Jedlicki, J. 1993 *Źle urodzeni czyli o doświadczeniu historycznym (Scripta i postscripta)* [The Humbly Born: Historical Experience (Text and Postscript)] (London: Aneks; Warsaw: Polityka).

Kurczewska, J. 1979 *Naród w socjologii i ideologii polskiej* [The Nation in Polish Sociology and Ideology] (Warsaw: Panswowe Wydawnictwo Naukowe).

Skotnicka-Illasiewicz, E. 1992 'Kompleks polski' [The Polish Complex], in J. Niżnik (ed.), *Postrzeganie Europy* [Perceiving Europe] (Warsaw: TWzKRz).

Skotnicka-Illasiewicz, E. 1995 'Wisje "Europy" w programach partii politycznych' [Visions of 'Europe' in Political Party Programmes], in *Bariery europskiej tożsamości* [The barriers against European identity].

Federal trust for Education and Research 1991 *Europe's Future: Four Scenarios* (London: Salomon Bros. International).

Stefanowicz, J. 1993 *Rzeczpospolitej pole ezpieczeństwa* [The Range of Security of the Polish Republic] (Warsaw: Adam Marszalek and ISP PAN).

Szczucki, L. 1989 in J. Kloczkowski (ed.), *Uniwersalizm i swojskość kultury polskiej* [Universal and Vernacular Nature of Polish Culture] (Lublin: RW KUL).

Walicki, A. 1994 *Poland between East and West: The Controversies over Self-definition and Modernization in Partitioned Poland*. The August Zaleski Lectures, Harvard University, 18–22 April.

Wesolowski, W. 1993 'Some problems of political representation in contemporary Poland'. Paper presented at the conference 'Emergence of New Party Systems and Transitions to Democracy', Centre for Mediterranean Studies, University of Bristol, 17–19 September.

Wesolowski, W. 1994a 'The nature of social ties and democracy: Poland after Solidarity', in John A. Hall (ed.), *Civil Society: Theory, History, Comparison* (Cambridge: Polity Press).

Wesolowski, W. 1994b 'Social bonds in post-communist societies', in M. Alestalo, E. Allard, A. Rychard and W. Wesolowski (eds), *Transformation of Europe: Social Conditions and Consequences* (Warsaw: IFIS Publishers).

12

Conclusion

Sukumar Periwal

'Yet *another* volume on nationalism?' a tired reader sighs, browsing through a bookshop or library. 'Why?'

In recent years 'nationalism' has become an eponymous word, a word one cannot escape, a word like 'modern' or 'politics' or 'identity', a word one encounters so many times every day, whether in the morning newspaper or in the evening news on television, a word which has become so much part of our daily vocabulary that it passes submerged into the diffused mental structures that allow us to comprehend the world in which we live. Everyone has some intuition about what 'nationalism' is. And yet, as Ernest Gellner and others have powerfully pointed out, nationalism is by no means a self-evident notion.

This book seeks to clarify the meaning of the word 'nationalism' as it is used in daily discourse. The authors who have contributed to this volume are important participants in a debate which is central to contemporary social science, a debate in which sociologists, political scientists and anthropologists bring their varying paradigms and perspectives to bear on the issue of nationalism. In their contributions to this book, these authors address questions concerning nationalism from widely differing points of view. These perspectives vary radically in their degree of abstraction, their concern for typological arrangement, and in their emphasis on factual historical, ethnographical and political examples. And yet all the contributors to this book share the basic premises that 'nationalism' is not a self-evident phenomenon or notion, and that the attempt to understand nationalism is important because nationalism is a crucial and inescapable component of politics and identity in the modern world.

'Politics', 'identity', 'modernity': these words point to two aspects of the debate on nationalism. First, far from being a unitary concept with sharp, clearly defined boundaries, the very notion 'nationalism' is inextricably intertwined in an intricate web with other complex concepts. (Furthermore, as several of the essays in this book remind us, 'nationalism' itself is analytically divisible into other concepts: secession, irredentism, self-determination, to name just three.) Secondly, the use of the words 'politics', 'identity' and 'modernity' in this context points to an understanding of nationalism which is shared by the contributors to this book, an understanding that nationalism is all about the construction and contestation of concepts of identity in the social conditions specific to modernity; that it is, in this sense, essentially political.

This understanding contrasts sharply with the common intuition that nationalism is somehow 'natural'. Insofar as most people think about nationalism at all, they seem to assume rather vaguely that since people live in groups, speak different languages, cook in diverse ways, and above all else, *look* different, then such divisions of the world must always have been the case, 'nations' must always have existed, and states are synonymous with 'nations'. We have the United *Nations*, relations between states are called inter*national* relations, inter*national* peacekeepers try to defuse tensions in various trouble-spots around the world, elections are monitored by inter*national* observers . . . Such a list could go on indefinitely, but the point, of course, is that the prevalent worldview assumes the equation of 'state' and 'nation', an assumption which is itself essentially nationalist. Professor Gellner, after all, has defined nationalism as exactly this sense that 'the political and the national unit should be congruent'.

This assumption that the state and the nation are synonymous entities is so deeply entrenched in the late-twentieth-century worldview precisely because of the success of nationalist ideology. Furthermore, the assumption that 'state' and 'nation' are synonymous causes us to feel uneasy when the political unit and the national unit are not congruent. They *should* be. Nothing provokes greater outrage than 'imperialism', when groups who claim the privileged status of 'nation' are denied the 'right' to 'self-determination', whether in the form of enforced belonging to an 'alien' state or in the form of a more powerful state bullying a weaker one.

Nationalism is so much part of the way we perceive the world that we cannot help but sit up, so to speak, when we read that 'nationalism has no right whatever, rationally speaking, to exist'. This quote from Professor Gellner's introduction to this book is provocative precisely because it so bluntly contradicts one of the most basic tenets of the dominant worldview, an assumption which, as I have tried to explain, is essentially nationalistic. We might not think of ourselves as nationalists, indeed, we might well think of ourselves as being positively *inter*-nationalists, but the point is that nationalism and internationalism are two sides of the same coin and that the very ubiquity of the words debases the value of the conceptual currency.

Nationalism may not have a rational right to exist; however, the fact is that it *does* exist. As Professor Gellner remarks, it is this discrepancy which gives rise to theories of nationalism. His introduction to this volume places the other contributions within the broader context of the history of ideas, of the peculiar combination of the Kantian and Platonic moral philosophies which romantic nationalism represents. Professor Gellner has written extensively elsewhere on the social reality represented by nationalism, how nationalism is a phenomenon specific to the transition from agrarian society to industrial society, and on why it is a persistent feature in modern industrial societies. In his introduction to this volume, however, he uses an even broader brush than is his wont and on a canvas which he usually eschews, namely the field of the history of ideas. The picture of nationalism which results is fascinating and intellectually breathtaking.

However, as Professor Gellner also points out in his introduction, 'the theoretical understanding of nationalism is an open and contentious field in which there is little that is firmly established'. Although he has elsewhere claimed in a somewhat tongue-in-cheek fashion that his own theory of nationalism is of Euclidean cogency, he recognizes that the theory does not always fit all cases, such as, for instance, China. John Hall takes up the daunting challenge of putting Professor Gellner in his place, literally: in Professor Hall's contribution to this volume, Gellner represents only one of several different ideal types of nationalism, 'the characteristic logic and social underpinning of each of which are high-lighted by a name, an exemplar and, somewhat loosely, a characteristic theorist'.

Thus, Professor Hall associates Gellner with a type of theory of nationalism which Hall calls 'the logic of industry'. A second type of theory of nationalism might be called 'the logic of the asocial society'. This theory, which Professor Hall associates with Michael Mann, explains the emergence of nationalism in Britain and France before industrialization by stressing the emergence in the eighteenth century of a new kind of politics in which the enlarging state found itself at loggerheads with an emerging civil society over issues of political representation and identity. A third type of nationalism, which Professor Hall calls 'revolution from above', stresses the role of reformist elites who undertook the task of popular mobilization to help their states survive in turbulent political conditions. A fourth type of nationalism is, as Professor Hall writes, a 'curious compound of desire and fear blessed by opportunity'. The emergence of new states in Latin America, for instance, shows how socially conservative colonial elites might try, without popular mobilization, to enhance their own position at the expense of a declining imperial power which they resent but also fear. The fifth type of nationalism is 'risorgimento nationalism' or 'nationalism from below'. Professor Hall associates this type with the work of Miroslav Hroch, who has described the three-stage process by which the collection of folklore gives way to an emerging ideology of nationalism which in turn leads to popular mobilization. Professor Hall names his last ideal type of nationalism 'integral nationalism': the illiberal belief that demands of blood take precedence over all other obligations, that ethnicity is prior to citizenship.

Professor Hall points to two possible criticisms of his typology: first, that the number of ideal types could be expanded (possibly *ad infinitum*, since particular cases inevitably escape ideal-typical constraints); and, secondly, that, in fact, a general theory is needed precisely to overcome this proliferation of ideal types and to generate an explanatory, rather than merely descriptive, framework. This tension between, on the one hand, the desire to *explain* the phenomenon of nationalism, and, on the other hand, the desire to note the ways in which the historical facts escape any general explanation, is a theme which resonates through many of the contributions to this volume. For example, as a professional anthropologist, Professor Chris Hann is sceptical of the possibility of a general theory which would explain all ethnographical cases; Professor Miroslav Hroch demonstrates similar scrupulosity in his eagerness to note historical exceptions to his largely empirically derived theoretical understanding of the process through which nationalism is generated.

In his valuable assessment of the current condition of nationalism theory, John Armstrong points to this tension between the desire for a comprehensive theory with explanatory value and the desire for historical and ethnographic accuracy. As Professor Armstrong writes, 'the *principal* source of disagreement among scholars searching for a general theory is the *way* in which material and ideal factors interact'. Professor Armstrong thinks that it is possible to find a general theory of nationalism and that such a theory requires a developmental approach, an 'examination of national identity and nationalism as historical processes'. He believes that a consensus is indeed emerging among scholars that such an approach is most appropriate; however, he also identifies several areas of lingering disagreement: opinions vary about the precise dating of the emergence of nations and nationalist feeling, the significance of ethno-religious feeling, the insistence of some on the importance of language as 'the prime indicator of nationalist cleavage'. Despite these differences, however, Professor Armstrong points out that very substantial agreement is emerging among scholars that nationalism cannot be treated as a primordial phenomenon. This admission is quite remarkable, coming as it does from one whose own distinguished writings have often been cited as 'primordialist' (as, for instance, by John Hall in his essay in this volume) by those who belong to the 'modernist' camp. Indeed, it seems to be the case that the opposition between 'primordialists' and 'modernists' is largely a device which scholars have constructed for their own rhetorical purposes: in actual fact, the two most prominent exemplars of the position known as 'primordialism' (Professor Armstrong and Anthony D. Smith) have disavowed 'primordialism' in their writings. Primordialism is not to be found in academe, but rather among the general public; and the mass belief that their nation has existed from time immemorial can be, and has been, very useful for politicians.

It is this emphasis on the political aspect of nationalism which Michael Mann stresses in his typically erudite and elegant contribution. Professor Mann here develops at some length the argument attributed to him by John Hall, that nations and nationalism have developed in response to the development of the modern state. Professor Mann shows that the nascent state and the local ethnic community merged together into the nation-state in three phases between the eighteenth and twentieth centuries. First, the enormous growth of militarization in the eighteenth century led to an unprecedented increase in the role played by the state in the everyday life of ordinary people, causing turbulent political protest. In the second 'industrial' phase, states changed in two ways: first, in the increasing acceptance of the principle of popular sovereignty, and, secondly, in the rapid expansion of non-military state functions. In the third 'modernist' phase, after the peace settlement of Versailles, the weakness of state structures led to the rise of an 'aggressive, statist and class-biased form of nationalism'. Professor Mann argues that it is the failure to institutionalize democracy which leads to exclusionary nationalism, but that the complete suppression of regionalist tendencies by authoritarian means also may result in aggressive nationalist movements. As Professor Mann concludes, 'the solution is, therefore, to achieve democracy – especially federal, inter-regional democracy. Unfortunately, this is easier said than done.'

Professor Mann's historical-sociological approach towards understanding nationalism is very similar to that of Miroslav Hroch. Both authors share a concern to understand the past in order to see better what can be done in the future. Professor Hroch's extensive research into the formation of nationalist movements leads him to conclusions similar to those of Professor Mann: that it would be wrong to condemn wholesale the drive for autonomy and communal belonging. As Professor Hroch writes:

> We ought indeed to criticize and to refuse nationalism as a way of thinking, and force as a method of struggle for power and for 'national interests', but we have to accept the fact that current national movements, based upon conflicts and tensions similar to the 'classical' ones, regard the right for self-determination as the only just solution of their problems.

Professor Hroch skilfully charts the dynamics which propel nationalist movements in certain typical directions. He identifies a certain snowball effect in his famous three-phase theory: scholarly research into the linguistic, cultural and historical attributes of the ethnic group gives rise to a second phase of patriots who seek to educate or 'awaken' their compatriots, leading to a final phase of mass political mobilization. Besides the political dimension identified by Professor Mann, Professor Hroch adds two further dimensions which condition the character of the national movement: the social structure of the ethnic group, and its historical experience of previously having or not having a state. Professor Hroch distinguishes three kinds of political demands: the substitution of cultural demands for political demands, especially under an oppressive regime; the demand for participation in political structures; and, ultimately, where participation only resulted in institutionalized minority status, the radical demand for autonomy within their 'own' territory. The variety and complexity of political demands illustrates, for Professor Hroch, that 'all theories of "nationalism" which define national goals as the struggle for independence, do not correspond to empirical facts. As products of ignorance and unacceptable simplification, they cannot be treated seriously.'

Professor Hroch is here echoing a point made earlier by Professors Hall and Armstrong: that the attempt to create any definitive theory of nationalism must 'correspond to empirical facts'. As I noted earlier, this academic scrupulosity represents one pole of the fundamental tension between, on the one hand, the desire to explain phenomena associated with the notion of nationalism, and, on the other hand, the wish to avoid sweeping, general claims which brush away 'facts' that do not fit with the theory. It might well be argued that *any* theory which is based on deduction simply cannot, by definition, cover all the facts. One might then choose to simply avoid the very attempt to theorize about complex social phenomena. Historians and anthropologists seem more likely to take such a position than their colleagues in sociology or political science.

Nicholas Stargardt's polished contribution to this volume represents just such an attempt to present one particular debate on nationalism in its intellectual-historical context, rather than to extrapolate broader, possibly fallacious, conclusions. Dr Stargardt's fascinating discussion of the Austrian Social Democrats' national programme allows the reader to draw his/her own conclusions about the relevance in contemporary Central Europe of a theoretical debate which was distinguished by its 'tenacity and rigorous consistency'. Dr Stargardt's discussion of the politics of nationalism in the *fin-de-siècle* Habsburg Empire is especially interesting to read in the light of Professor Hroch's preceding discussion of the same set of issues. Such figures as Otto Bauer, Karl Renner, Victor Adler and Thomas Masaryk were engaged in an intense debate on whether national interests should be defined in cultural-linguistic terms, or in terms of territorial belonging or socio-economic advancement. The federalist programme of the Austrian Social Democrats was indeed complex; however, its value lay in precisely this sensitivity to the complexity of ethnic divisions in the Austro-Hungarian population. As Dr Stargardt points out, many of the problems which have subsequently plagued Central Europe may have arisen from the fact that 'it was apparent only to a handful of humanist-minded intellectuals how great the social and political costs would be of fulfilling nineteenth-century liberal programmes and carving out homogeneous nation-states'.

Dr Stargardt's chapter is largely concerned with a programme put forward by a group of 'humanist-minded intellectuals', a programme which represents an interesting alternative to the relatively simple-minded notion of a world composed of homogeneous nation-states. Neither the 'federal nationalists' (exemplified by Thomas Masaryk and Edvard Beneš) nor the 'federal centralizers' (such figures as Carl Renner and Otto Bauer) wanted to get rid of the structures of the multinational Austro-Hungarian Empire. And yet, by a profound irony of history, both 'groups would find themselves at the end of the First World War at the head of states whose foundation they had opposed in the prewar period', Masaryk as the first president of Czechoslovakia and Renner as the first Chancellor of German Austria, with Beneš and Bauer as their respective foreign ministers. The academic literature on nationalism has paid much attention to the role of intellectuals in the establishment of national movements and the 'invention' of nations; however, as Dr Stargardt's chapter illuminatingly suggests, intellectuals are often swept by history in directions which they would not necessarily prefer.

Chris Hann's contribution to this book takes up the question of the role of intellectuals in the contemporary context. While broadly agreeing with Gellner that nationalist intellectuals are not 'awakeners' of dormant nations but rather 'inventors' of new entities, Professor Hann believes that the professionalization of academic life has made intellectuals far more self-conscious of the consequences of their work. This context of heightened sensitivity means that we must ask hard questions about the ethical responsibility of contemporary intellectuals in their propagation of the ideology of nationalism. As Professor Hann pointedly asks:

> What are we to say about the role of intellectuals in contemporary contexts where they cannot possibly be presented as the unwitting agents of modernizing processes, grounded in economic transformation, where it is plain that the goal of intellectual creativity is fundamentally at odds with the rational organization of economic life, not to mention inter-state relations and geopolitics? What difference does it make if the intellectual cannot present himself as one of 'the people', but is promoting their cause from the outside, with his legitimacy entirely grounded in his scholarship?

Professor Hann discusses two examples of such intellectuals and their relation to the national causes that they champion: Paul Robert Magocsi who has espoused the notion of a distinctive 'Carpatho-Rusyn' identity, and Wolfgang Feurstein who has supported the cause of the Lazi people in Anatolia. While recognizing the quality of their scholarly work, Professor Hann is uncomfortable with the premises which guide the work of these intellectuals and with the ethics and pragmatic consequences of such work. The world is full of complex borderlands, zones of ambiguity in which cultures shade into one another. Yet the ideology of nationalism requires sharp boundaries between cultures, and Professor Hann believes that the intellectuals he discusses cling to this notion of the sharp boundary and to the essentialist notion that the 'true' identity of a people has been 'violated' by the imposition of a 'foreign' identity. On the other hand, Professor Hann considers these intellectuals to be liberal humanists rather than proto-fascists. He is also uncomfortable with the new conventional wisdom among academics that all collective identities are situational constructions which must be critically exposed. As he wisely points out, taken to its postmodern extreme, 'the critical deconstruction of ethnic and national loyalties is liable to blind anthropologists to an understanding of the force of these identities, and of the many ways in which they enrich the lives of group members'. As a result, Professor Hann takes an intermediate position which seeks to understand fully the commitments to groups and boundaries which we all have. In terms of pragmatic political strategies, Professor Hann's position leads to an acknowledgment that it is important to recognize ethnic collectivities and to try to guarantee their rights, despite realizing that this consolidates basically fictional entities. 'This strategy is warranted because anything else would ignore the reality of other powerful fictions already well entrenched.'

Professor Hann's position on the ethical responsibility of intellectuals in the contemporary context of a world in which nationalism is the dominant ideology (even in the minds of those who abhor nationalism) is especially important on the level of what might, awkwardly, be called meta-theory. What are our responsibilities, as readers and writers of texts on nationalism? As John Hall jokingly pointed out in his contribution to this volume, in the 1980s, Alexander Yakovlev changed his mind on the nationalities question in the Soviet Union 'because reading Gellner made him convinced that nationalism had to be recognized in order to reach capitalist development. This is perhaps less empirical support for Gellner's theory than direct creation of the evidence!' And, as Professor Hall mentions, it is perhaps no coincidence that many of the 'nation-builders' of post-imperial states in Africa and Asia were students at the Sorbonne and the London School of Economics. Intellectual work does have its consequences and it might well be argued that even the production of *this* text contributes to the enhancement of the discourse of nationalism, insofar as it perpetuates and diffuses the concept, albeit in generally critical terms. As advertising executives know, any publicity, even negative publicity, is good publicity, since it enhances 'name recognition'.

But why, in the first place, do we think of nationalism in critical, even negative, terms? Furthermore, what justification do we have for the employment of these normative criteria in our scholarly, supposedly dispassionate, discourse? It is, perhaps, not advisable to entirely disassociate normativity from the social sciences, nor is it always possible. Certainly, many of the contributors to this volume are deeply influenced by their liberal worldview, perhaps none so much as Hudson Meadwell, whose fundamental premise in his theory of why there has been no successful case of secession in the developed 'West' is that 'liberalism constitutes the best possible political regime'. Professor Meadwell's stimulating and provocative account of the Québécois movement for independence sets out to answer the paradox that while there has so far been no case in which a secessionist movement in the West has succeeded, one such case (Quebec) is at least potentially poised to achieve a peaceful transition to independence. Professor Meadwell argues that it is the distinctive political-institutional structure of Canada, the combination of consociation and federalism, which has brought about the possible secession of Quebec. In general terms, though, Professor Meadwell claims that 'local nationalism loses its primordial base, and corporate groups are the exception rather than the norm, within liberal capitalism'.

Professor Meadwell believes that institutional plurality is actually capable of having a positively stimulating effect on nationalist movements, even in the historically unpropitious circumstances of the 'developed West'. In his contribution to this book, Hans van Amersfoort also discusses the relation between the plurality of political institutions and its effects on ethnic conflicts within a multi-ethnic state. In general, Professor van Amersfoort believes that institutional plurality is at least part of the solution to ethnic conflicts, though it is far from being the universal panacea for all such problems that ardent proponents of consociationalism would claim. As Professor van Amersfoort writes:

> It seems that only in the context of relatively long periods of gradual political and economic development does institutional plurality contribute to the solution of ethnic antagonisms in the state population. However, the prerequisites for making institutional plurality successful seem to be rare in the present-day world and can hardly be consciously created.

In turbulent times when societies are undergoing dramatic systemic transformations and feel themselves to be in a crisis situation, institutional plurality may even exacerbate ethnic conflicts, by allowing the immediate unmediated articulation of ethnic demands.

Professors Meadwell and van Amersfoort raise an important problem: institutional political arrangements which enable groups to articulate their aspirations are often capable of leading to increased tensions between groups and, perhaps, even to the breakdown of the state. In his important and far-reaching contribution to this volume, John Keane tackles the problematic relation between democracy and nationalism head-on. As he writes:

> There is an urgent need to stretch the limits of the contemporary sociological and democratic imagination, to think differently about the intertwined problems of nationalism, national identity and democracy, and to consider how the limits of democracy can be overcome in practice by inventing new democratic methods of preventing the growth of democracy's own poisonous fruits.

Professor Keane suggests that the democratic cause is best served by abandoning the notion of national self-determination and by regarding belonging to a nation as a legitimate but limited right. In the European context, Professor Keane proposes four mechanisms which might reduce the power of nationalism while preserving the popular sense of national identity: to displace the primacy of the nation-state by establishing networks of democratically accountable subnational and supranational institutions; to clearly define and apply international legal guarantees of national identity; to develop a plural multiplicity of identities within civil society; and to foster a genuinely international civil society in which people of diverse nationalities can intermingle. Concluding on a cautiously optimistic note, Professor Keane believes that Europe (at least, Western Europe) 'is witnessing the slow, unplanned, blind and painful birth of a new species of political animal, the European citizen'. These European citizens, through their trans-state affiliations, and personal and business relations, manifest an aversion to exclusionary nationalism: as such, they are 'late modern cosmopolitans', and the gradual enlargement of this group of people and the provision of financial and legal support for such a concept might well 'prove to be the best antidote yet invented to the perils of nationalism and the poisonous fruits of democracy'.

Professor Keane's measured optimism about the possibility of overcoming exclusionary nationalism in Europe through the nurturing of a genuinely European citizenry is a notion which is likely to elicit sighs among most 'non-Europeans' (by which I mean citizens of states that do not belong to the European Union, including the countries of Central and Eastern Europe). Any non-European who has tried to get a tourist visa, let alone a work or residence permit, for countries in the European Union, is all too painfully aware of the walls which 'Europe' has built about itself. 'European' citizens may travel freely within their rich ghetto and feel as cosmopolitan as they please: however, this 'cosmopolitanism' has very clearly demarcated limits. Indeed, the process by which Western Europe consolidates itself may well give rise to reactive sentiments among those who feel excluded from this club of rich states. One might, perhaps, apply to the contemporary European context Professor Gellner's powerful insight that nationalism arises precisely among those who are not allowed to assimilate. (As Professor Hall, in my view correctly, writes in his essay, 'the notion of blocked mobility, properly understood in the sense of humiliation . . . is precisely at the heart of Gellner's real and best attempt to produce a general theory of nationalism'.)

Examples of such nationalist reactions are to be found in abundance in the penultimate chapter of this book, a thoughtful and entertaining survey of the attitudes held by Polish parliamentarians towards the process of European integration. Elżbieta Skotnicka-Illasiewicz and Wlodzimierz Wesolowski discern a polarization among these important political actors, a divide between those, on the one hand, who believe that rapid, even 'accelerated', integration into 'Europe' is vital for Poland's future, and those who oppose moves towards integration (or at least the rapidity of this process) on the grounds that this would lead to the disappearance of the distinctiveness and vitality of Polish national identity. As Dr Skotnicka-Illasiewicz and Professor Wesolowski write, the statements and opinions of those who argue for a 'closed' Poland 'are tinted with intense anxiety, distrust, and defensiveness, rather than faith in cooperation'.

None of the contributors to this book claims to have any easy answers to the problem of nationalism. While agreeing that nationalism *is* a problem, several argue for a proper understanding and even appreciation of why national or ethnic identity is a value which so many people cherish and for which many are still willing to die. The spectrum of views expressed here is wide. And all of the distinguished academics who have contributed to this book would agree that there is a need for an even greater range of thought on nationalism. As Professor Gellner writes, the 'current situation has stimulated the debate: we need both ideas and information'.

Index

Abkhazian–Georgian conflict 37
Adler, Victor 87, 88, 89, 93, 234
Africa 10, 163, 237; *see also* Arabs
aggressive nationalism 6, 44, 53, 54–5, 59–62, 233; *see also* integral nationalism
Alba, Victor 35–6
Albanian national movement 74
Algeria 10
Amersfoort, Hans van 177–9, 237–8
anarchism 56, 59
Anatolia *see* Lazi people
Andalucia 198
Anderson, Benedict 4, 11, 30n34, 32n65, 36, 46
anthropology, and ethno-national identity 124–5, 236
antisemitism *see* Jews
Arabs 10, 172, 193
Armenia 36, 37, 120, 194
Aron, Raymond 23, 203–4
Ascherson, Neal 119–20, 124–5
Asia 185, 237
assimilation 122, 165, 172, 239
Austria 45, 50, 51, 63n6, 193; *see also* Habsburg Empire
Austrian Empire 46, 48–9, 52, 70, 71, 74; Kremsier reform proposals 17–18, 89, 91
Austrian Netherlands 49, 52
Austro-Hungary 18, 72, 73, 75, 108, 184; Social Democrats' national programme 83–105, 234–5
authoritarianism 56, 58–62, 177
autonomy 72–4, 78, 81, 82, 85, 174, 175
Azeri–Armenian warfare 37

Badeni, Count Kasimir Felix 85–6

Badinter proposals for Yugoslavia 200–1
Balkans 52, 73, 74, 174, 195
Baltic states 63n6, 70, 75
Basques 25, 41, 56, 58, 61, 69, 168, 172, 198
Bauer, Otto 89, 92, 93, 95–6, 97–100, 104n56, 105nn62,77, 234, 235
Belarus, Belorussians 38, 69, 78, 82
Belgium 62, 140, 151, 169, 173, 177, 184
Beneš, Edvard 91, 92, 95, 100, 235
Berger, Peter 40
Berlin Wall, collapse of 185, 209
Bernstein, Eduard 89
Bohemia 70, 85, 86, 88, 99
Bojko ethnographic group 109, 113
Bolivar, Simon 15
Bosnia-Herzegovina 195
Bourassa, Robert 153–4, 155, 156–7
Brest-Litovsk, treaties of 84, 100
Breton, Raymond 167
Bretons 172
Breuilly, John 14, 20
Britain 22, 23, 45, 46, 48, 51, 52, 55; Act of Union (1707) 142; emergence of nationalism in 12–14, 159n8, 231; *see also* England; English nationalism
British nationalism 13
Buchanan, Allen 130, 133
Bulgaria, Bulgarians 57, 69, 73, 76, 78, 184
Burke, Edmund 201

Canada 62, 167, 173; Quebec 25, 41, 129–61, 173, 237
capitalism 6, 12, 21, 45–6, 47, 51, 52, 53–4, 97, 195–6, 236; Renner's 'personality principle' 94–5; and secession 130, 149, 150, 158

Index

Carpatho-Rusyn identity 107–16, 123, 124, 236
Catalonia, Catalans 25, 35, 41, 56, 58, 69, 130, 142–3, 144, 168, 198
Central Asia 185
Central Europe 4–5, 6, 39, 67–85, 196; *see also individual countries*
China 230
Cisleithanian-Austria 71, 88, 89, 91, 95
citizenship 46, 166, 167–8, 171, 179, 183, 186–9; European 204–6
civil rights 67, 73–4, 184
civil society 7, 12–13, 22, 26, 47, 156, 159n17, 183, 186, 187, 192, 201–2, 231, 238; European, as antidote to dangers of nationalism 202–6, 238; Polish political parties and Europe as configuration of 208–26
civil war 27, 177, 200–1
class 22, 40, 45, 46, 48, 51–2, 55, 56, 58, 59, 183, 195, 205; Austrian Social Democratic programme 94–5
Clausewitz, Karl von 14–15
closure, Polish arguments in favour of national 219–21, 225
collective identity 40, 229, 236; non-national 198; *see also* cultural identity; ethnic identity; national identity
Colley, Linda 13
colonialism 164; *see also* imperialism
communication 3, 10–11, 52, 107, 165, 204
communism 7, 24, 170, 180, 185, 196
community/society 1, 5, 99, 105n71
conferences on nationalism 35
Connor, Walker 165
consociation 25; and federalism in Canada 133, 134, 135–41, 143, 144, 148–50, 157, 237; and institutional plurality 177–9, 238
cosmopolitanism 4, 125, 203, 205, 239
Croatia, Croats 28, 60, 63n6, 69, 72, 74, 75, 78, 82, 100, 193, 196, 200, 202
cultural identity 186, 219; Lemko 111–12, 114–15, 123
cultural nationalism 51, 70, 71, 73–4, 77–8, 79, 83–101 *passim*, 234; transition from, to political nationalism 16–17, 23, 66–8, 79–80

culture 2, 3, 10, 44, 45, 46, 106, 163, 165, 168–9, 171–2, 201; Lazi 116–17, 118, 122–3, 126
Czech national identity, nationalism 5, 17, 18, 52, 69, 71, 72, 77, 78, 85, 86, 87, 90, 91–2, 100, 103n41
Czech Republic 37, 133
Czechoslovakia 6, 84, 109, 110, 185, 235

Dabrowski, Henryk 188
Danes *see* Denmark
Darwinism 6, 18, 20
decentralization 142, 198–9, 238
decolonization 9, 23–4, 173; *see also* post-colonial states
democracy 44, 48, 53, 60–1, 62–3, 71, 73–5, 182–207, 233, 238–9; consociational *see* consociation; methods of combating dangers of nationalism 197–206; programme of Austrian Social Democrats 83–105
Denmark, Danes 56, 66, 67
Deutsch, Karl 165, 185
diaspora groups 36, 110, 113, 118, 122, 123
Diderot, Denis 183
Drakulić, Slavenka 202
Duplessis, Maurice 148
Dutch empire 23; *see also* Netherlands

Eastern Europe 5, 6, 20, 60, 67–85, 107, 170, 180, 196, 214; *see also individual countries*
economic development 8–9; Polish parties' arguments about integration into Europe 209, 212–25
economic factors 40–1, 44, 45–6, 47, 49, 51–2, 77; and Austrian Social Democrats 94–5, 234; and secession and federalization 24–5, 41, 130–1, 132, 149, 157–8, 174; *see also* class; industrial society
Emilia-Romagna 198
Engels, Friedrich 104n59, 203
England 13, 41, 66, 201; *see also* Britain
English nationalism, national identity 13–14, 34–5, 37, 38, 63n2, 206n3; *see also under* Britain

Estonia, Estonians 59, 69, 77, 78, 84, 100
ethnic cleansing 20, 61, 62
ethnic communities, Polish view of Europe as configuration of 210, 218–25
ethnic conflicts, violence 62; and consociation/federation 61, 83–5, 138, 145; and institutional plurality 162–80, 237–8
ethnic groups 35–6, 49, 162–5; intellectuals and 106–26, 235–6; and national movements 65–82, 150, 233–4
ethnic identity 46, 48, 53, 240; ethno-religious 36–7, 232
ethnicity, importance in integral nationalism 18, 50–60, 231
Europe, Polish political parties and integration into 208–26, 239–40
European citizenship as antidote to dangers of nationalism 182–207, 238–9
European Union 141, 199, 204, 209, 210, 211, 223, 224
exclusionary nationalism 53, 56, 59, 62, 168–9, 194, 239

fascism 58, 59, 63n4
federalism 23, 25, 26, 49, 53, 61–3, 169, 174, 175, 177; of Austrian Social Democrats 83–105, 234–5; and consociation in Canada 133, 134, 135–41, 143, 144, 148–50, 152, 157, 237
Feuerstein, Wolfgang 118–23, 124, 125, 236
Finland, Finns 63n3, 69, 70, 72, 73, 77
First World War 56–7, 75, 78, 92, 100, 109, 194
Fischof, Albert 89
Flanders, Flemish 69, 168, 172
Forsyth, Murray 137
France 23–4, 42n2, 45, 46, 48, 66, 145, 165, 168, 169, 172, 201; nationalism 12–14, 19, 35, 38, 42n2, 50–1, 55, 56, 189–90, 193, 203, 206n3, 231; *see also* Basques
French Revolution 13, 16, 50, 53, 189–90, 191, 203
functionalism 11, 21, 32n63

Galicia, Galicians 72, 76, 108, 109
Gellner, Ernest 10–12, 17, 20, 21, 22, 30nn34,38, 32n63, 49, 51, 52, 106, 107, 108, 125, 165, 228, 229, 230, 235, 236–7, 239, 240
Gemeinschaft/Gesellschaft 1, 5, 99, 105n71
Geneva Conventions 199
genocide 168, 194, 205
Georgia, Georgians 26, 37, 84, 196; and Lazi 116, 117, 121–2, 123
German nationalism 18–20, 40, 55, 56, 57, 60, 86, 87, 88, 95–6, 193, 194; *see also* Nazism
Germany, Germans 15, 17, 22, 46, 50, 51, 54, 66, 75, 124, 180, 184, 189, 201, 210, 211
Great Britain *see* Britain
Greece, Greeks 59, 60, 68, 69, 74, 75, 76, 77, 78, 80, 184, 194; classical Athens 145
Greenfeld, Liah 34–5, 36–7, 40, 63n2
Grimm brothers 39

Habsburg Empire 6, 17–18, 23, 49, 51, 56, 67, 68, 72, 76, 95, 109, 170, 234–5; *see also* Austria
Haider, Jörg 193
Hartmann, Ludo Moritz 88, 96
Hechter, Michael 164
Hemşinli people 120
Herder, J. G. von 5, 6, 17, 97, 125, 201
Hilferding, Rudolf 95
Hintze, Otto 12
Hirschman, Albert 18
historical sociology 135, 136
Hitler, Adolf 20, 87, 194; *see also* Nazism
Hobsbawm, Eric 19, 36, 191, 197
Holland *see* Netherlands
Hollweg, Bethmann 19
Hroch, Miroslav 16–17, 42n2, 51, 52, 231, 233–4
Hucul ethnographic group 109
Humboldt, Alexander von 15
Hume, David 13
Hungary 18, 37, 49, 52, 57, 58, 63n6, 70, 71, 72, 80, 84, 180, 186, 189, 196; and Carpatho-Rusyn identity 108, 110, 111, 112, 115; *see also* Magyars

identity *see* collective identity
illiberal societies, secession from 144–7
illiberality of integral nationalism 18
immigration 168, 170–3
imperialism 55, 229; *see also* colonialism
independence, struggle for 67, 72–6 *passim*, 81, 95; Quebec 129–61, 237
industrial phase of state development 46, 53–4, 233
industrial society as cause of nationalism 3, 10–11, 21, 47, 51, 52, 107, 134, 230
industrialization 41
institutional plurality 162–81, 191–2, 237–8
integral nationalism 18–20, 21, 56; *see also* aggressive nationalism
intellectuals, role in nationalism 101, 106–26, 235–7
inter-governmental agreements 61
international civil society 202–6
international intervention 27–8, 199–201, 238
international political economy, and secession 130–1
international relations 219; consociation analogous to 136
internationalism 19–20, 21, 24, 96–7, 203, 230; authoritarian right and 56, 59
Ireland, Irish 16, 52, 68, 130, 131, 144–6, 164; *see also* Northern Ireland
irredentism 20, 83, 168, 229
Israel 5, 36
Italy 20, 25, 46, 50, 52, 55, 57, 60, 66, 184, 189, 198

Jakovlev, Alexander 11–12, 236
Japan 14, 15, 60
Jews 5, 36, 56, 59, 60, 172, 180, 193, 194

Kant, Kantianism 1, 2, 3, 4, 5, 12, 98, 203, 230
Kautsky, Karl 88–9, 97, 99, 104nn56,59
Kazakhs 84
Kenyatta, Jomo 11
Kirgizia 84
Kohn, Hans 63n2, 76

Kościuszko, Tadeusz 188
Kurds 119, 121, 122

language 17, 38–9, 48–9, 50, 52, 61, 66, 68, 168, 169, 186, 194, 232; Austria-Hungary 85–6, 88, 89, 97–8; and Lemko/Lazuri collective identity 111, 115, 116–17, 119, 120, 123, 126; in Quebec nationalism 146, 150
Latin America 9, 15, 231
Latvia, Latvians 69, 77, 78, 84, 100
Lazi people 116–23, 124–5, 126, 236
Lebanon 177
Lemko ethnographic group 109, 110, 111–16, 123, 124, 125, 126
Lenin, Leninism 7, 65, 85, 97, 194
Lévesque, Rene 153
liberalism: related to nationalism 1–2, 3, 5, 6, 16, 22–3, 27–8; and secession 25, 41, 129–61, 237
Lijphart, Arend 42n2, 167, 177, 178, 179
Linz, J. 25
literacy 45, 46, 47, 50, 52
Lithuania, Lithuanians 69, 72, 73, 77, 78, 193
local self-government, participation of national movements 70–2
Lueger, Karl 93
Lunt, Horace 38
Luxembourg 184
Luxemburg, Rosa 95
Lynch, John 15

Maastricht Treaty of Union 204, 205
Macedonia, Macedonians 38, 74, 82, 200
Magocsi, Paul Robert 110–16, 118, 123, 125, 236
Magyars 17, 51, 63n3, 68, 69, 72–80 *passim*, 84, 196; *see also* Hungary
Mann, Michael 13, 231, 232–3
Mann, Thomas 187
Marx, Marxism 2, 3, 6, 38, 41, 51, 104n56, 195, 203, 205; Austrian 85–101, 195
Masaryk, Thomas G. 5, 6, 7, 23, 87, 91, 92, 100, 103n43, 105n62, 109, 234, 235
Maurras, Charles 19, 20

Mazzini, Giuseppe 16, 197
Meadwell, Hudson 24, 237, 238
Meciar, Vladimir 26
Michnik, Adam 189
Mickiewicz, Adam 189
migration 61, 84, 164, 201; *see also* immigration
Mikesell, Marvin 165
militarization 12, 13, 14, 45, 46, 47–9, 50–1, 54, 55–6, 100, 134, 165, 232
Mill, John Stuart 16, 200
minority rights 28, 61, 92, 100, 126, 200–1
modernist phase of nation/state formation 46, 57–62
modernity 2–3, 10, 11, 22, 44–5, 46, 229, 232
Moldavia 84
Moore, Barrington 14
Moravia 86, 88
Moynihan, Daniel Patrick 11
municipal self-government, participation of national movements 70–2
Murphy, Alexander B. 165

Nairn, Tom 24, 25, 195
nation(s) 11, 44, 46–63, 165, 182–5, 229, 232; Austrian Social Democrats' views 90–1, 93, 97–100; Polish political parties and 208–26
nation-state 22, 46, 61, 66, 79, 83, 134, 166, 167–8, 184–5, 203, 211, 232; decentralization 198–9, 238
national identity 35–6, 40, 42, 46, 99, 134, 182–3, 232, 240; and citizenship 186–9, 205; and democracy 195–7; Polish political parties and threat to 219–21; preservation of 182, 197–206, 238–9
national movements 49, 52, 65–82, 233–4; role of intellectuals 106–26, 235–6
national stereotypes/images 14, 50–1, 123, 126, 193–4
nationalism(s): defined 9–11, 44, 65–6, 191–5; and democracy 195–7; moral philosophy of 1–7; nature and importance of 228–40; origins and rise of 35, 133, 134, 189–95; political theory of 44–63, 232–3; typology 8–33, 230–1
nationalism theory 8, 21, 34–43, 231–2
nationalist leaders 11, 26, 79–80, 81, 106
nationalities 163, 172, 173–4, 175, 177, 180, 185–6
'nationalities' question in Austria 83–105
NATO 209, 211, 215
Nazism 19, 59, 60, 63n6, 193
Netherlands 23, 45, 66, 140, 159n17, 168, 169, 173, 175, 178, 179, 183
Nietzsche, Friedrich Wilhelm 6
Nigeria 10
Nolte, Ernst 18
Northern Ireland 25, 37, 62, 178
Norwegians 68, 69, 73, 77, 78, 79

Occitan 38, 168
Ossetians 37
Ottoman Empire 46, 48, 51, 67, 68, 74, 76, 81, 116, 117, 170

Paine, Thomas 183–4, 188, 189, 197, 200, 203
Pakistan 160n27
Palacky, Frantisek 17
Palacky, Jan 89, 91
Parizeau, Jacques 25, 161n40
Pavić, Milorad 192
peasant, in national constructs 5, 39–40, 52
Pernerstorfer, Engelbert 87
Piedmont 46
Pieradzka, Krystyna 113
Plamenatz, John 20
Platonic moral philosophy 1, 2, 4, 230
pluralism, plurality 125, 135, 138, 205; of identity in civil society 201–2; institutional 162–81, 191–2, 237–8
Pocock, J.G.A. 37
Poland 59, 61, 95, 108–16 *passim*, 123, 124, 126; attitude of parliamentarians to European integration 208–26, 239–40
Poles 56, 60, 193

Polish nationalism 4, 52, 68–80 *passim*, 85, 91, 99, 100, 108, 123, 126, 184, 185, 188–9, 196, 208, 219–25
political regime, importance of 22–3, 68, 69, 76–7, 79, 80; Quebec 129–61
political theory of nationalism 44–63, 232–3
political violence, ethnic factors in 177–9
Portugal 56, 57, 60, 66, 190, 201
post-colonial states 11, 24, 25, 27, 107, 237
post-communist world 25–7
postmodernism 125, 236
primordialism 4, 11, 35–6, 165, 195, 229, 232
Prussia 14–15, 18, 45, 46, 50, 51, 67

Quebec 25, 41, 129–61, 173, 237

Rabushka, Alwin 166, 167, 176–7, 178, 179
race, and nation 55
racism 55, 56, 59, 60
regionalism 49, 175; European 198–9
Reinfuss, Roman 112, 113
religion: and authoritarian right 58, 59; institutional plurality and tolerance 169, 175, 178, 179; Lemko/Lazi 114, 117, 124; related to national identity 36–7, 45, 49, 51, 61, 193, 194–5, 219; role of Catholic church in secession movements 146, 147, 148
Renan, Ernest 97, 192
Renner, Karl 90–1, 92, 93, 94, 95–7, 100, 234, 235
republicanism 145, 146, 184, 205
risorgimento nationalism 16–18, 20, 21, 65–82, 231, 233–4
Rokkan, Stein 165
Romania, Romanians 57, 58, 63n6, 73, 74, 84, 115, 180, 184, 196
Romantic movement, German 50
romantic nationalism 2, 3–7, 39, 230
roots 4–5, 110, 202
Russia, Russians 26–7, 48, 51, 60, 67–76 *passim*, 96, 101, 109, 117, 186, 190, 196, 209, 225

St Germain Peace Conference 84, 92, 95
Schönerer, Georg von 87
Scotland 25, 41, 68, 130, 141–2, 164, 186, 198
secession 41, 72–6, 77, 78, 81, 82, 166, 168, 229; from liberal regimes 25, 41, 129–61, 237
Second World War 60, 179
self-determination 65–82, 85, 182, 184–5, 229; limited value of 197, 238
separation *see* secession
Serbia, Serbs 60, 68, 69, 72–8 *passim*, 184, 193, 194–5, 196
Seton-Watson, Hugh 36
Shepsle, Kenneth A. 166, 167, 176–7, 178, 179
Slavs 17, 18, 59, 94, 96, 100, 108–10
Slovakia, Slovaks 52, 63n6, 69, 75, 77, 78, 82, 84, 110, 111, 112, 115, 126n2, 133
Slovenia, Slovenes 41, 69, 71, 74, 76, 77, 78, 82, 100, 185, 186, 196, 200
Smith, Adam 13, 25
Smith, Anthony D. 10, 27, 165, 232
Snyder, Jack 134
social mobility, blocked 17, 21, 52, 239
socialism 56, 59, 98, 196; Austrian 83–105, 234–5; *see also* communism; Marxism
South Tirol 174, 194
Soviet Union 12, 25–7, 34, 57, 60, 61, 62, 83, 84–5, 95, 160n27, 174, 180, 236; crisis and collapse 7, 9, 84, 133, 168, 185–6
Spain 25, 26, 51, 55–62 *passim*, 66, 151, 198, 201; and Latin America 15; *see also* Basques; Catalonia
Stalin, Joseph 84, 85, 92, 194
Staniszkis, Jadwiga 11
state 27–8, 183; Canadian 129–61; multi-ethnic, and institutional plurality 162–81, 237–8; multinational 18, 83–105, 204; related to nation, nationalism 12, 14, 22, 44–63, 78, 79, 185, 187, 229, 231, 232–3; Western unitary 133–4, 135–6
state–society relations *see* consociation
Stepan, A. 25

subcultural segmentation 135–41, 144
Sweden 66
Switzerland 18, 49, 51, 62, 174, 178

territory, and nation/state 22, 52, 61, 62, 72, 173–4, 183, 186, 234
Third World 11, 24, 27, 39, 107
Tilly, Charles 12
Tönnies, Ferdinand 99, 105n71
Toussaint l'Ouverture 16
trade, nationalism by 24–5
Transcaucasia 37, 185
transnational *see* international
transnational corporations 205
Trieste 57
Trudeau, Pierre 152, 153
Turkey, Turks 116–23, 124–5, 126, 193, 194, 236
Turkmenistan 84
Tyrol 51, 174, 194

Ukraine, Ukrainians 26, 37, 38, 60, 63n6, 69–78 *passim*, 82, 83, 108–16 *passim*, 123, 124, 126, 196
United Nations 173, 199–200
United States 10, 13, 23–4, 34–5, 41, 49, 53, 138, 159n12, 166, 167, 175, 177, 183, 188; secession of South 130, 131, 144, 145–6

universalism 1–6, 13, 18
USSR *see* Soviet Union
Uzbekistan 84

Verri, Pietro 203
Versailles, treaty of 9, 18, 19, 20, 84, 100, 199

Wallonia 198
Watkins, Susan Cotts 10, 54
Webb, Sidney 20
Weber, Eugen 10
Weber, Max 8, 19, 20, 22, 32n63, 38, 83, 88, 93, 96, 99, 100, 104n56, 190
Welsh 69
Wenskus, Reinhard 36, 38
Wilkes, John 13–14
Wilson, Woodrow 9, 65, 100, 197
Wusten, Herman van der 177–9

xenophobia 168, 171, 180, 205

Yugoslavia 25–6, 28, 34, 37, 39, 61, 62, 115, 177, 180, 194–5, 200

Zionism 5, 36